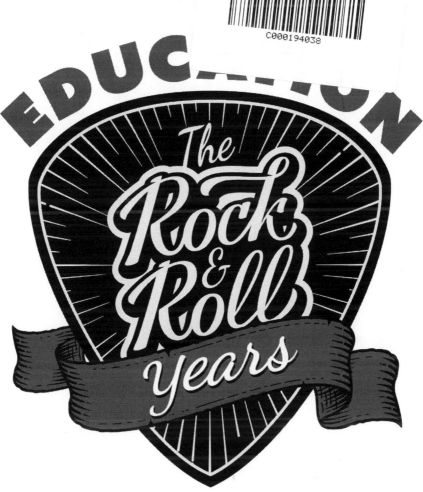

A Northern perspective on a lifetime of learning, teaching and leading

LES WALTON

First published in 2021 by Critical Publishing Ltd

British Library Cataloguing in Publication Data
A CIP record for this book is available from the British Library

ISBN: 978-1-914171-32-1

This book is also available in the following e-book formats:
EPUB ISBN: 978-1-914171-33-8
Adobe e-book ISBN: 978-1-914171-34-5

The right of Les Walton to be identified as the Author of this work has been asserted by him in accordance with the Copyright, Design and Patents Act 1988.

Cover and text design by Out of House Limited
Project management by Newgen Publishing UK
Printed and bound in Great Britain by 4edge, Essex

Critical Publishing
3 Connaught Road
St Albans
AL3 5RX

www.criticalpublishing.com

PAPER FROM
RESPONSIBLE
SOURCES

ACKNOWLEDGEMENTS

My gratitude goes to Neale Saul, my great friend and artist, who drew the cartoons and to Kevin McDermid, who edited my work and destroyed my self-esteem and self-belief in my ability to do joined-up writing. Also, thanks to Bruce Gillham, who helped me to organise my brain, and Ian Reid, who has supported this project through thick and thin.

Particular appreciation goes to my colleagues within the Association of Education Advisers, who put up with me professionally and are then prepared to meet again in God's Departure Lounge every Friday night, where clear and concise education ideas are formulated and then forgotten the next morning.

My heartfelt thanks to my wife, Diane, and my children and grandchildren, who have given me so much morale-boosting love.

I would also like to celebrate the dedication and resilience of colleagues with whom I have had the honour of working over the years. Many of them unselfishly devote their lives to addressing the needs of children and communities within the North East of England and across the UK.

To present and former colleagues within:

1. Blaydon East Secondary Modern School
2. Blaydon Comprehensive School
3. Norham High School
4. North Tyneside Metropolitan Council
5. Bradford District Council
6. Tyne Met College
7. Young People's Learning Agency
8. Education Funding Agency
9. Schools North East
10. North East Chambers of Commerce
11. Coping with Cancer North East
12. The Northern Education Trust
13. Northern Education Associates
14. The Association of Education Advisers

Note: many of the people and organisations included in the text are anonymised.

The following photographs are reproduced by kind permission of Alamy:

Rab Butler (p 21); Ellen Wilkinson (p 23); Archie Andrews (p 42); Sir Cyril Burt (p 46); Maurice Chevalier (p 74); Bill Haley and the Comets (p 78); Kahlil Gibran (p 114); National Union of School Students (p 117); Fritz Perls (p 123); Margaret Thatcher (p 142); James Callaghan (p 146); Mary Warnock (p 151); Kenneth Baker (p 175); John Major (p 183); John Patten (p 204); David Blunkett (p 246); Lord Adonis (p 268); Michael Gove (p 276); Downhills (p 280); Estelle Morris (p 285).

The photograph in the 'About the author' section is copyright Russell Sach © 2021

ENDORSEMENTS

'Education: The Rock and Roll Years' is visionary, practical, rebellious, idiosyncratic and beautifully idiomatic. Its strength is combining personal experience with key principles. This is an excellent piece of writing.

Professor Andy Hargreaves
Boston College and University of Ottawa

I loved this book: it's honest, unpretentious and informative, just like its author. Anyone working with young people today should read, pause and consider the difference that could have been made to the life chances of several generations had the ideas, lessons and experience contained within these pages been absorbed into our nation's educational bloodstream.

Lord David Puttnam
British film producer and educator

Les Walton is a remarkable man and in this book his personality comes shining through. We are treated to stories about Elsie and why she didn't go to school and Jack the Caretaker, who ruled the school like a rod of iron. But there are also stories about the big personalities who walked the corridors of power and the shifts in education policy over many decades. We read about dealing with the aftermath of riots, moving accounts of brushes with death and a careful analysis of systems thinking. Not only is the book full of compelling and humorous stories, but it also has a poignancy and a depth of insight that only someone with Les's unique career in education can capture. I loved it.

Steve Munby
former CEO, National College for School Leadership

I have known Les for many years and his knowledge and belief in the power of education have underpinned our relationship throughout this time. His strong sense of moral purpose comes across every time I hear him speak, as well as in this well-crafted and comprehensive overview of an educational era that many of us have lived and breathed. The way that Les weaves anecdote and example of how real people responded to real challenges is what makes this book so fascinating. I loved it!

Sir David Carter
former Schools Commissioner for England

Insightful, entertaining and wise. This is a highly recommended read for anyone inspired by those, such as Les Walton, who have truly made a difference in education.

Dame Alison Peacock
Chief Executive of the Chartered College of Teaching

Les is one of the most effective public servants I have ever worked with. He is a man of deep principle, fully committed to improving the educational opportunities of young people everywhere. He combines a formidable intellect with a very down-to-earth style, which makes him immensely popular.

Sir David Bell
Vice-Chancellor, University of Sunderland,
and former Permanent Secretary and Chief HMI

Les Walton has achieved great things at the most senior levels of education. The thing that marks him out is, no matter how senior his post, he has never forgotten that the purpose of education is to give opportunities, excite minds and change things. His reflections, which show how education and learning have done all these things in his life, make good reading and remind everyone why education is one of the most important things if a society is to thrive.

Baroness Morris of Yardley
former Secretary of State for Education

Les Walton is one of the most experienced, knowledgeable people in education. His perspective and ability to listen have characterised everything he has achieved and this book is testimony to it all. His understanding of the need to work with and build coalitions for change has been palpable. Les is always someone whose passion for education shines through – he has always combined an unerring capacity to judge situations with the ability to then make real world change happen.

Dominic Herrington
Schools Commissioner for England

If education is rock and roll, Les Walton would be in the Hall of Fame for his enduring contribution over so many years. This beautiful book chronicles an extraordinary leadership journey from Les's working-class provenance on Tyneside to becoming a national leader of education in the true sense of the phrase. It is utterly authentic and we see in print the man we know and love. As a polymath, Les has drawn on a wide range of sources that transcend the somewhat utilitarian vogue in education publishing. We read of Kahlil Gibran's wisdom alongside Bill Hayley and the Comets. Mary Warnock is juxtaposed with the Beach Boys. All of this makes for a riotous and disarmingly honest capture of all things about education in England since the '44 Act. You can dip into any chapter and find distilled wisdom. Thoroughly recommended. This truly is 'Talkin' 'bout my generation'.

Professor Colin Diamond CBE
University of Birmingham

Les has led an astonishing life in education – from the head of Norham High School, which serves the deprived Meadow Well estate in North Shields, to a college principal, director of education in North Tyneside and Chair of the YPLA. This gives him a unique perspective on the English education system over half a century. This book is funny, clever and compelling. The personal stories of leadership are often heart-rending and also entirely relevant to our current social and political circumstances. For example, the riot which surrounded his school and the decisions that the leadership team took the day after to create a sanctuary for children. Part-anecdote and part-analysis, this book charts an extraordinary professional journey.

Leora Cruddas
CEO, Confederation of School Trusts

Les has a unique perspective on the education system and a passion to shape it so that it delivers the best for every single child and young person. He is also a brilliant Chair, with a deep understanding of the dynamics of good governance and how to inspire board members to draw on their different experiences, listen to each other's perspective and through that to focus on their shared ambition to support the next generation, who have all the potential to change the world.

Peter Lauener
former Chief Executive of the Young People's Learning Agency
and the Education and Skills Funding Agency

Les is a giant in the education arena. He has continually strived to make the world of education and schools accessible to all. For many years he has been a powerful advocate for the voice of children and schools, particularly those who face social and economic hardships. 'Education: the Rock and Roll Years' is a great way for those of us in the world of business and commerce to gain a better insight into the world of education.

James Ramsbotham CBE
CEO of the North East Chambers of Commerce

When I first met Les Walton, his clarity of purpose and talk of the need for integrity instantly made a deep impression on me. Les had been parachuted into the middle of an acrimonious education revolution taking place in my city. But he managed to cut through the conflict through sheer force of personality and clear thinking. He was one of the most impressive people I had ever met.

William Stewart
Editor, Times Educational Supplement News

'Education: The Rock and Roll Years' is a uniquely humorous and personal in-depth understanding and insight of the political and social influences on education since the birth of our modern education system.

Carl Ward
Executive Chair, Foundation for Education Development

The history of the changing shape of the education system in England and the North East needs to be told, and I can think of no one better placed to do it than Les Walton. Not only has he been at the forefront of every education innovation of any worth, but he is funny too. He can tell a story with wisdom and humour.

Gill Alexander
Chair of Newcastle Diocesan Board and Former CEO Hartlepool MBC

Les Walton has done more than any other single person to promote high educational standards and high professional collaborative standards in schools and among educators in his beloved home region, the North East of England.

David Pearmain
Founding Chair of Schools North East

I have worked with many impressive leaders in education, who, through their distinguished careers, have made a big impact. Les fits that bill, but he is one of the most interesting, because he is one of the few who have worked across all of education. That has given him a fascinating perspective which this book eloquently sets out.

David Hughes
CEO, Association of Colleges

Les Walton is one of the leading thinkers and practitioners in developing corporate governance. He has a remarkable record across education, spanning every sector and every level. His stories of governance at school, FE College, multi-academy trusts, regional and national level are fascinating: he makes governance entertaining, which is rare.

Emma Knights
CEO, National Governance Association

The resilience and fortitude Les showed, in coming to terms with the second diagnosis of cancer during his period in national office, was awe-inspiring.

David Igoe
former CEO of the 6th Form Colleges' Association

DEDICATION

This book is dedicated to my wife and my whole family who have given me so much love and support over many years. It is also dedicated to all children, particularly in the North East, who always deserve better.

ABOUT THE AUTHOR

Les Walton has a unique record of being a successful leader and innovator within most education sectors.

As headteacher, his school was identified by HMI as *'one of the most successful urban schools in the country'.* In his time as Director of Education, the Council achieved Beacon Status for 'tackling school failure'. All its schools were deemed successful by Ofsted. Les led the merger of two FE colleges, the process of which was described as *'exemplary'* by the DfE. The success rates moved from bottom to top quartile during the merger period.

Les was first invited to Number 10 to advise Prime Minister John Major. During Tony Blair's time in office, he was involved in numerous New Labour Government education initiatives. Later, Les was appointed by Secretary of State, Ed Balls, to lead and establish the Young People's Learning Agency. Secretary of State, Michael Gove, then asked Les to support the establishment of the Education Funding Agency and chair the Advisory Group. Both Boards have been widely recognised as setting high standards for governance and effectiveness.

Les has also instigated and founded a number of influential and successful education organisations, including Schools North East, the Northern Education Trust and the Association of Education Advisers. He has been recognised for his work through being awarded the Order of British Empire in 1996 and Commander of the British Empire in 2013.

Les continues to radically influence the education system. He has a track record of education innovation. His work reflects his unwavering commitment to improving some of the country's most challenging schools.

This is a personal retrospective on a life of experience. Les has often described himself as the 'Forrest Gump of Education', as he seems to have been present at all the major education developments since the Second World War.

The stance taken avoids personal negativity, though it comes from a negative view of school and its impact on the lives of children. It is also full of hope that the challenging human potential at the top of Maslow's hierarchy, self-actualisation, can realistically be achieved.

It is an optimistic, humorous, self-mocking account, which is designed to emphasise the seriousness of the issues addressed by sleight of hand. The matters are cunningly illuminated through the reflections of a simple Geordie lad. There are messages here for all those engaged in the process of lifelong learning.

PROLOGUE

This book is for anyone who cares about children, why they learn, how they learn and what they learn.

Let me say from the start that I am in love with the sight, the shape and the sounds of education.

I am also in love with jazz, blues and particularly rock and roll. I was born at the birth of the modern education system and grew up in a period when rock and roll stormed onto the scene. Rock and roll influenced daily life, fashion, attitudes and language in a way few other social developments have equalled.

It is not surprising that people of my generation have had a certain iconoclastic and challenging approach to the received *wisdom* of those in power.

Looking back over my three-quarters of a century in education, it has certainly been rocking and rolling, a series of ups and downs. What has helped me to survive and occasionally thrive? The answer is, of course, learning! Continuously learning. Learning as if my life depended on it, which for the human race, is an essential truth.

Sadly, we have forgotten more than we have learned in our continual quest to improve the education of the children we love. We need to reflect on current educational thinking by reflecting on our experiences of education. I'll cover it all: the curriculum, the discipline, academies – even school meals.

The greatest resource anyone has is themselves. It is by going into our own personal history and standing back from the present that we can see more clearly the world in which we exist. We will never see the full picture if our noses are pressed against the canvas.

Each of us should dig deep into our own backgrounds and ask straightforward questions. What is our view of how children should learn? Where do our beliefs and values come from? To what extent are our values and beliefs learned from our experiences of childhood and our own education? Why do we think a particular approach to leadership is the right one? What has led to our present views on how children should be educated? Do we understand the context in which we work and why it is the way it is?

I hope I will stimulate anyone who has a real interest in education to reflect on their own lives. Remember, the past is where we learn to lead – the future is how we apply this learning.

Throughout my life, education has been fought over by political parties, advocacy groups, pressure groups, lobby groups, campaign groups, interest groups, parent organisations, teacher organisations, employer organisations; I could go on. It continually changes, while staying the same. It tries new ideas, repeats old ones and introduces old ideas as though they have been just invented.

I have always tried to remain apolitical in my professional life. Unfortunately, the problem with education is that every time we say anything worth saying, it is positioned within a political perspective. You may decide I am a wishy-washy liberal or a socialist conservative! Actually, I write unashamedly from my own northern Geordie point of view.

Les Walton, 2021

CONTENTS

PART TWO. TEACHING: CARING, CAPABLE, CHILD-CENTRED

PART ONE

Learning:
how not to learn or repetition, regurgitation and repression

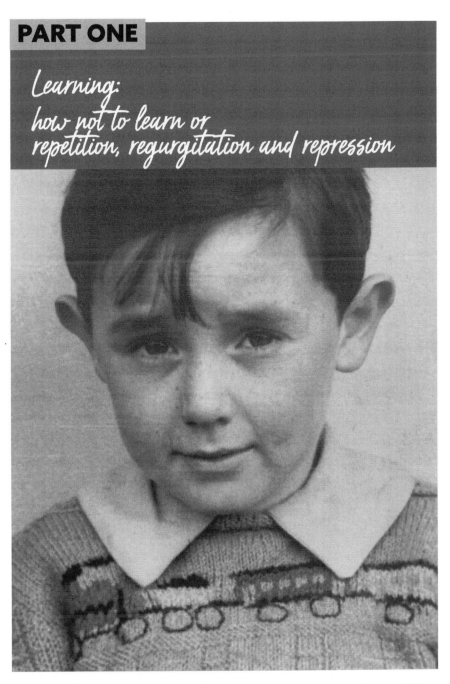

I write from the point of view of a child or a young person. I am trying to tell the truth as an adult voice sometimes cannot.

CHAPTER 1

THE IMPORTANCE OF HUMOUR

I have tried to inject a sense of fun into this story of our modern education system since 1945. This will automatically throw me out of the group that considers education as no laughing matter. Humour can allow us to reflect on serious matters in a positive way. It is also subversive. It is for my reader to decide whether the humour is still alive and well in our schools and colleges. As Andrew Carnegie said, *'there is little success where there is little laughter'*. I will also try to remember what I have learned. My first learning point is, therefore,

Enjoy life, have fun and nurture your sense of humour.

Take this book of funny stories. Whenever the staff start causing bother, crack a joke.

When we entered the twenty-first century, like most of us, I looked back reflectively over the previous decades. In doing so, I found that there were widening divisions opening up between schools, local authorities and the Department for Education (DfE).

Peter Woods, in his book *The Divided School*, which I first read in 1979, described a number of marked and interpenetrating divisions *within* schools: between teachers and pupils, parents and teachers, parents and children and between pupils themselves. He suggested that schools effectively contained a number of 'invisible doors', which had the capacity to change people as they went through them, moving from one context to another.

I seemed to be going through similar invisible doors, as I moved from a school to a local authority and then to the DfE. When these groups, all working in their own unique spaces, came into contact, the atmosphere was often tense and edgy.

One of my survival techniques, continuously employed from my time as a pupil in school, then as a young teacher, then as a headteacher and eventually as a director of education, was the use of humour. Humour is, of course, not merely a means to get by on a day-to-day basis, it can do so much more. For example, humour can provide:

● **a balm of stress relief;**

● **a unifying experience for divided teams;**

● **a means for motivating colleagues;**

● **a motor for generating ideas; and**

● **an effective diffuser of tension and frustration.**

More dangerously, Machiavellian humour can also be used to destroy people.

Peter Woods described the centrality of humour within his book, through which I was suitably inspired to develop a 'humour index'. This provided a measured continuum of different types of humour, ranging from the most destructive to the most productive, via sarcasm, cynicism, jokiness, defusing and so on through to creative.

I shall always remember a rather pompous superhead, who was giving a talk on how to provide outstanding leadership. About 40 of us were sitting listening to his tales about how he motivated staff, who saw him as some sort of Moses figure. It was he who would save them from themselves and lead them to the promised land of Ofsted Grade 1.

He then asked us to stand up if we had ever behaved stupidly in front of our colleagues. Only one headteacher stood up. No one else stirred a muscle.

When he was asked why he had responded, he answered that he:

hated to see a superhead standing up by himself.

On my continuum, I suspect that this humorous comment would not be positioned at the *creative* end of my classification system!

In 2002, when I returned from Bradford to work again in the North East, I had got used to waking up every morning to the Bradford local radio. The morning phone-ins

were all about the key issues of the day – things like the traffic problems, the latest on local council actions and the like.

Newcastle morning radio was *very* different. One morning, as I was driving down the Coast Road from Newcastle to North Shields, our local DJ was on the phone to a woman who was clearly talking to another person at the same time. When quizzed on who was in the room with her, she said it was her chiropodist, who was cutting her toenails. Then came a voice from the background, shouting:

Sorry for disturbing your programme but I had a particularly tough big toe to deal with.

I suddenly realised how much I missed the North East. Why would I ever want to work anywhere else in the world? I think it is often through this sort of humour and throw-away comments that we can truly engage with and understand other people.

If inspectors do ever analyse the humour within a school – using the Walton Humour Index, perhaps – they would soon spot whether or not it was improving. We can all remember the teacher who was sarcastic and 'put down' individual students with con-siderable cruelty. We all also remember with affection those brilliant school leaders, who used gentle humour to defuse anger, whether it was in their interactions with students or members of the school staff.

There is something about Geordie humour that is both sentimental and gentle while, at the same time, being totally subversive. Remember the genius of Bobby Thompson and his sage advice?

Always wear yer shoes a week before you put them on, they'll be more comfortable.

I would describe the best Geordie comedians as sentimental surrealists. I remember Bobby Hooper reminding us of the time when we used to 'bool' old car tyres with a stick:

Ah remember when ah booled me tyre to Whitley Bay. When ah got there, ah lost me stick and had te waalk all the way back.

As I continued my journey in education, I often wondered whether the jokey, defusing, creative humour I'd so often heard in the staff room and at headteachers' meetings was increasingly being replaced by a more cynical atmosphere. Fewer and fewer headteachers spent any time laughing at themselves.

The role has now become subject to scrutiny that is so critical and negative that the self-deprecating headteacher is fast disappearing. It is now dangerous to joke about yourself, because it may be taken down and used in evidence against you.

These old quiz question chestnuts:

Why do headteachers not look out of the window in the morning?

Because they need something to do in the afternoon.

Why is a headteacher's brain worth one thousand pounds?

Because it's scarcely been used.

are unlikely to surface during a spot inspection!

It's a fact many former students consider that the best part of their school life was not about the great learning experiences, the knowledge sharing and other such scholarly pursuits, but about all the fun they had.

I also strongly believe that individual lessons taught with humour are very powerful in making points that are easily lost. This is true even in the mundane field of learning the importance of punctuation!

Compare the following:

A woman without her man is nothing.

A woman: without her, man is nothing.

Clearly, you can't beat a colon, by which I mean, of course, the colon as a punctuation mark, not the bodily organ.

While I was Director of Education we would often receive a number of prestigious visitors. For example, I was once asked to show Jack Straw, who was then Shadow Home Secretary, around a local housing estate.

After touring for a while we stopped the car and he asked a local resident:

Have you lived here all your life?

Quick as a flash the answer came back:

Not yet, bonnie lad.

When Prince Charles visited another Tyneside estate, he asked:

How do you feel about being on this estate?

To which the local resident riposted:

Probably as bad as you feel now.

Jack Straw touring the Meadow Well Estate.

One of the most memorable meetings was when Prime Minister Tony Blair visited our region. When being introduced to a mayoress, he asked her husband about the chain around *his* neck and why it had the word 'Consort' engraved on it. Affecting to think that the question was about where it was manufactured, the answer came back:

Probably made at Consort (Consett) Iron Works.

I also remember observing the lesson of a science teacher who had a reputation for delivering completely humourless but allegedly effective lessons. A boy within the class had been arguing that it was perfectly reasonable to watch the match on the telly and do his homework at the same time. The atmosphere in the room immediately became tense, as it appeared the boy was challenging the teacher:

You cannot have your cake and eat it, said the teacher.

So what's the point of a cake? responded the boy.

After what seemed an eternity, the teacher burst out laughing. The atmosphere changed immediately and the tension dissipated. No one lost. The teacher's humanity had won.

It is important that our education leaders do laugh at themselves. Self-effacing leaders must show that they are just as vulnerable and error-prone as the rest of us. Hubris avoidance should be obligatory.

Ronald Reagan was a great self-effacer. In his bid for the 1980 Presidency of the USA, he quipped about his age:

Thomas Jefferson once said, 'One should not worry about chronological age, compared to the ability to perform a task.' Ever since Thomas Jefferson told me that, I've stopped worrying about my age.

Of course, you may describe what I have said as 'Deja Poo', easily defined as the feeling a teacher gets at a staff meeting when she's heard all this stuff before.

CHAPTER 2

THOUGHTS FROM THE WOMB

I arrive as one of the chosen many; a member of probably the most intelligent species on the planet. The education system and family I am born into are designed to help me succeed but within limits.

Never underestimate the enormous potential that children have.

Have you anything for someone who has more neural connections than all the trees in the Amazon?

My story starts inside my mother's womb. For many people, it may start a little later in life. For me, this is exactly the right place to begin. I am about to enter a world in which the immortal, gloomy phrases:

These students are not learning

or

This lot don't want to learn

will be used over and over again in talking about *us* in the education system.

I know many of you will not believe this, but what follows are my thoughts during the three months *before* I was born completely 'learn ready'. As Bruce Springsteen would *nearly* say 30 years after this pregnant moment:

Cause people like me, baby, we are born to learn.

The main thing on my mind in the womb is how I will learn to talk. I understand that I will be expected to learn the language of the country in which I am born. What will happen if I need to talk Chinese? These are silly thoughts but, remember, I am only a foetus.

As a clever foetus, I am also worried about what my parents and school will teach me. I know school will instruct me in the three R's, reading, writing and arithmetic. I also know I will be speaking with a Geordie accent within two years. I understand that my aspirations, expectations and hopes for the future will mainly come from Dad, Mam and school. The worrying bit is that I keep hearing Dad say:

As long as he doesn't go doon the pit and has clean hands.

That's aall that matters.

Even in the womb, I am beginning to think that being clever is not enough. I know I will need to learn how to learn. This may sound a bit negative, but I also have grounds for optimism. I am part of the human race, probably the most intelligent species on the planet. My brain is the most complex organ in the entire universe. The magnitude of my brain is 'mind-blowing'. I am told I have more neurons – acting like telephone wires in the brain – than all the trees in all the forests of both North and South America combined. I have more synapses – potential neural connections – than all the leaves in all the forests across the world!

Over millions of years of evolution, natural selection has favoured me. The fact that I and all the others being born now will, probably, be around for up to a century means that our predecessors have developed brains well able to adapt to interact flexibly with the immediate environment. In other words, with the ability to learn and able to change. That's what I and all my ancestors have been doing all along – *learning*.

I know my brain has inherited a myriad of useful adaptive systems – different forms of intelligence. I have a predilection for seeing things in different ways, including a set of preferred learning styles, inherited preferences, an ability to deal with wholes and parts simultaneously and a capacity for working collaboratively as well as independently. All these predispositions will combine in a particular and distinctive way in my brain. This instrument, my *brain*, is what makes me distinctively human and the process has not changed in its essential form in 30,000 years. More than this, it seems that 100,000 years ago the Waltons, and the rest, started to talk, and we have not stopped rabbiting on ever since! And as a result of this process, our brains grew and our skulls increased in size.

At this point, remember, I still have three months to go before I will be born. Understandably, I am anxious. Every other mammal delivers its young with its brain virtually fully developed. In my case, if I had to wait until my brain was fully ready before my birth, my mam would have to carry me for 27 months, and I would never make it down the birth canal! This is probably my biggest worry. In due course, my mam will deliver me, with some difficulty, at nine months with a brain which is only 40 per cent developed. Indeed, from that point on, my brain will not stop developing until I am 25 years old.

The good news is that I needn't panic at all. Miraculously my brain will come equipped with a whole series of intellectual predispositions to learn incredibly rapidly from my environment. Even in these earliest moments, my brain is extremely malleable and sensitive to external influences and I am rapidly able to distinguish my father's voice from my uncle's.

When I arrive, I will be ready for more stimulation and intellectual challenge. At *minus* three months I know that learning will be a consequence of thinking. Even babies know that simple and profound truth! So, the education system that I am about to enter should stimulate my thinking – not simply *instruct* me. The right stimulation at the right time was always critical to the survival of my ancestors. I desperately need my thinking stimulated now and after I am born. I know that my beautiful brain, the most complex in the universe, will not develop if I neglect it. I need to be taught how to learn! Remember, if I don't use it I may lose it and my brain will eliminate connections that are seldom or never used.

Sadly, the education system and family I am being born into will not fully recognise the need to stimulate me intellectually before and after birth. All my predispositions to learn with my miraculous brain will be limited by *what you adults think I am capable of*. As a result, even though my genetic structure is encoded to respond to any one of the 3000 and more languages currently spoken on this planet, by my teenage years, I will struggle to pass my French O-level examination. The truth is that the big window of opportunity for acquiring a language is wide open during the first ten years of my life. Why, then, will the education system invest most in my foreign language education after the age of 10, when many of my predispositions for learning a language have shut down? Similarly, when I need small group interaction as an infant, they will put me into big groups. Then, when as a sixth former I need to develop independence and operate in large and complex networks, why do they put me into small groups? Remember, I am a human baby and to frustrate my predisposition to learn is to destroy much of what it means for me to be human. Millions of babies agree with me. Do you?

So I bet you are all wondering how I will do. Will the education system I am about to enter keep me in my place or take me where no Walton has gone before – into the middle class?

CHAPTER 3

BORN IN THE UK

I am born just at the point when a world war ends and a new education age begins.
I start talking and never stop for the next three-quarters of a century. My favourite
topic of conversation is education. Perhaps, if I stop talking, I will do the world a
favour. I don't, of course!

Make mistakes, admit them, learn from them and move on.

You mean this Walton is going to work above ground?

was born on 8 June 1945. Just three days earlier, on 5 June, the Allied Control Council, the military occupation governing body for Germany, formally took power. So, my birth was smack bang between the suicide of Adolf Hitler on 30 April and 9 August, when a United States B-29 bomber, the *Bockscar*, dropped an atomic bomb, codenamed *Fat Man,* on Nagasaki in Japan. A fraction earlier the 1944 Education Act had come into force on 1 April 1945.

Victory in Europe, the dawn of the nuclear age and the 1944 Education Act were all to have a great impact on my life. However, it is principally the 1944 Act that has kept me awake at night for the next three-quarters of a century. For me, the legacy of the 1944 Act provided a fertile battleground for the educational arguments that have pursued me throughout my life.

More than 70 years later, in 'God's Departure Lounge' at my local pub, we continue to discuss school structures, the school curriculum and testing and our *near-life* experiences.

Basically, we are a bunch of old *gadgees*. The definition of a gadgee is either 'a senior citizen of the Geordie genre' or, someone who wanders around the streets after the pubs are closed, wondering whether they are going out or going home. The old gadgees I sit with talk either about football or education. We talk regularly about Newcastle United and repeat on a regular basis the holy mantra:

This is the last time I am going to buy a season ticket.

When we talk about education, I hear colleagues say things like:

- *UKIP's preferred model, the grammar school, was set up by the Labour Party.*

- *We have never managed to spread technical education in the UK.*

- *We used to love teaching more than testing.*

- *Our curriculum design is still based on the idea that there are academic and practical children.*

- *Primary children should specialise as well as focus on the basics.*

- *The South East's reaction to education change is always very different from the North East.*

- *Academies are comprehensive schools.*

Of course, my grumpy old friends say such things to create discussion – no, honestly. The scary thing is that all our arguments seem to have their genesis in an Education Act introduced over 70 years ago.

After the war, the incoming Labour Party Education Ministers, Ellen Wilkinson and following her death, George Tomlinson, together with the civil servants, were all adamant about establishing a *tripartite* system. This involved recommending that 70–75 per cent of places 'should be of the modern type', with the remaining 25–30 per cent being allocated to grammar and grammar technical places. Although the possibility of other systems did gradually emerge, by 1951 only 0.7 per cent of state secondary school pupils were being taught in comprehensive schools.

NEVER

...and all because the Geordies called him 'an old gadgee'; never was so much talked by so few about so little.

As it turned out, the system was actually *bipartite*. The grammar schools took, on average, the top 20 per cent of all children and secondary modern schools took most of the rest. The selection for grammar schools was made largely on the basis of the 'eleven-plus' examination, consisting of tests of intelligence and attainment in English and arithmetic. From the start, in the eyes of the public, children would either pass or fail at this time.

The grammar technical schools in the middle of the century were intended to have an intake of 10–15 per cent of all pupils. In fact, they never catered for much more than about 3 per cent. In addition, their intake was predominantly boys. With this in mind, it will be interesting in due course to observe the development of University Technology Colleges in the twenty-first century and how many young people will actually be attending them.

In the late 1940s, there were even arguments over whether there should be any examinations for 15 and 16 year-olds at all. In May 1946, *Circular 103: Examinations in Secondary Schools* advocated abolishing the external examination at 15 or 16, noting that as grammar school pupils were expected to stay in school until 17 or 18, any earlier examination would be unnecessary. It was also announced that there would be regulations to *prevent* schools – other than grammar schools – entering any pupils for external examinations under the age of 17. Even the grammar schools doing this would require special permission from the Ministry of Education.

This approach, actively preventing the majority of children from taking public examinations, continued right up to my first year of teaching in 1966. This was when the examinations for secondary modern schools were introduced, and in my first year as a teacher, I had the pleasure of listening to my headteacher and his deputy having heated arguments about the merits of having, or not having, examinations for our children.

In 1945 we began to see the beginning of the strange belief:

If it moves, we test it.

Later on, when I entered junior school as a pupil, I could be forgiven for believing that the teacher mantra was:

If it moves, hit it.

It was very clear in the 1940s that there should be a distinction between designing a curriculum for the more and the less able. In the secondary moderns, it was left up to teachers to design their own curriculum, while the grammar schools dealt with a much more prescriptive academic curriculum. As my first headteacher frequently told me:

There is one curriculum for the hewers of wood and one for the drawers of water.

During this period new primary schools continued with the class teaching approaches used in the former elementary schools, with their emphasis on basic literacy and numeracy. In some ways, it appears that not much has changed since the nineteenth century.

In the 1940s, there was a big difference between the North East and the south of England. The north of England had a much lower proportion of grammar school places than in the South East. Many decades later we were to see this difference re-emerging in the distribution pattern of academies and grant-maintained schools in the 1990s. In the early twenty-first century, the vast majority of academies can still be described as comprehensive schools. Indeed, until Theresa May became Prime Minister in 2016, there were no new attempts to re-introduce selective grammar schools.

I can hear what you are muttering to yourself:

Call yourself an educationalist? Your continual arguments suggest you and your gadgee friends have learned nothing in 70 years.

But remember what Confucius said:

Real knowledge is to know the extent of one's own ignorance.

So there! But at least I know I didn't know I didn't know.

Throughout my life in education, I have been driven by two key ambitions in order to improve the lives of children:

Know more today about the world than I knew yesterday;

and

Know more about yesterday so that I can understand today.

The system of education introduced after 1945 has remained in the consciousness of the education community continuously up to the present. Admittedly, reflecting on the birth of our modern education system is vital to understanding it. The important question is to ask whether reflection of this sort will help future citizens and can teachers eventually improve the education system which we all inhabit? Hopefully, the answer is 'yes'. On the other hand, educationalists have frequently seemed rather slow to learn from the mistakes of the past.

CHAPTER 4

BEING A GEORDIE

I am raised in the 'Land of the Three Rivers'; a very proud Geordie, born within the sound of the Newcastle upon Tyne Bigg Market underground toilets flushing.

Celebrate the regional differences, as well as the common interests that unite and educate our children.

Ye must be the Angel of the North.

I t is well known that there are three tribes living in the North East of England.

- The *Smoggies* from Teesside.
- The *Mackems* from Sunderland.
- The *Geordies* from Tyneside, Northern Durham and Northumberland.

One result of this has been that there is a political tribalism in the North East leading to an inability to agree to a north-eastern strategy for education. The thought of our political tribes uniting for the sake of our children is an unrealised hope. Education within the North East is now increasingly described and summarily evaluated by national politicians and education leaders as 'failing'.

In 1958 Nigerian author Chinua Achebe published *Things Fall Apart*. Written from the point of view of the Igbo tribe facing British colonialism in the 1890s, it attacks the misconception that African culture has always been savage and primitive. Indeed, as it had no kings or chiefs, African culture was increasingly vulnerable to invasion by western civilisation. The parallel is striking and the lack of regard for north-eastern culture, the region's limited cohesive political leadership and a centralised government keen on imposing national solutions may explain why 'things may fall apart' in the North East.

I have always celebrated my Geordie roots. These roots have provided a basis for growth as well as holding me down. We need to consider how we celebrate our regional strength while recognising our weaknesses and welcoming the opportunities that come from outside our region. Thus, my own north-eastern heritage has been a powerful force, which has both supported me *and* held me back throughout my life in education. Unfortunately, today my heritage has been side-lined and rarely features in the school curriculum, losing out to national and global concerns.

Why then, if a distinct heritage – so evidently celebrated in Wales, Scotland and Northern Ireland – is considered a vital part of the school curriculum elsewhere, is our English regional heritage so ignored?

I'm a Geordie. I was born in the North East of England to 'working-class' parents who had 'working-class parents'. But the reality is that my childhood influences and experiences were complex and cannot be summed up by the simple phrase 'working class'. For a start, my grandparents were as different as chalk and cheese.

My father, Charles Walton, was a fitter at Derwent Haugh Coke Works. The coking plant on the River Derwent was built in 1928, on the site of the Ambrose Crowley Iron Works, which for a time was the largest ironworks in Europe. Over the years the plant took coal from Chopwell Colliery and in the National Coal Board days from Marley Hill Colliery via the nearby Clockburn Drift, as well as from opencast mines. The coke produced was either sent directly to customers by rail or shipped from a staithe on the River Tyne.

My mother, Hilda Thompson, eventually became a wages clerk at Vickers-Armstrong at the Elswick and Scotswood works on the banks of the Tyne. By 1935, Vickers-Armstrong was already the third-largest manufacturing employer in Britain, behind Unilever and ICI.

My father's and mother's families could not have contrasted more. This is a great comfort, as I have always disliked the idea that the working class was some kind of homogenous group.

My father's father and mother were called Geordie and Bella Walton. If you ever come across Andy Capp and Florrie, his wife, you will know exactly what Geordie and Bella looked like. Geordie started work at the age of 12 as a latrine cleaner in the pit. He was small and wiry and always wore his cap indoors. He sat by the fire with his hat on:

... because I didn't want to get it wet wearing it outside.

He usually wore a three-piece suit with a watch and chain and a white silk scarf around his neck. He smoked a clay pipe. Bella had a backside like a kitchen cabinet. She dressed in a fur coat, when she went shopping, though underneath she always wore her 'pinny'. They owned their own house in Consett. In the field next to the house 'blind' pit ponies would run around.

Jimmy and Annie Thompson, my mother's parents, could not have been more different. Annie was a committed Methodist and Jimmy, a quarryman by trade, was an atheist and socialist. Jimmy was an incredibly cultured man. He loved music. His tastes ranged from classical opera to Dusty Springfield. They lived in a council house in Stanhope.

Annie was a marked contrast to Bella. She kept a really tidy house and would regularly go to the Wesleyan Chapel. Bella, on the other hand, lived in and owned a chaotic house. So, in spring I would often witness little chickens being incubated in the coal oven and then see them running around the room. Bella's furniture was always covered with a fine layer of red dust from Consett iron works. Annie's house was always immaculate. For lunch, Bella would make me condensed milk sandwiches, while Annie would always serve up ham and pease pudding.

However, there were also many similarities, too. Both Jimmy and Geordie smoked pipes, though Geordie used throwaway clay pipes, while Jimmy had clamped between his teeth the largest wooden pipe you would ever see. Jimmy always filled his pipe with *Warhorse* tobacco while Geordie smoked *Auld Twist*. They both drank tea from saucers, after pouring it from the hot cup. They both dipped Jacob's cream crackers in the tea and spat into the coal fire after lighting up.

Geordie and Jimmy also loved going to 'The Club'. On Sunday lunchtimes Geordie would bring jugs of beer back from the club, so he could carry on drinking in the afternoon. What he *didn't* know was Bella would secretly pour half of it down the sink and then top the jug up with water.

They both loved their allotments. Jimmy would spend his whole weekend on his allotment, which backed onto the Durham moors. An abiding memory of Geordie was sitting on a chair throughout the night in his allotment holding an umbrella over his beloved leeks. He did this to stop them from splitting just before the annual leek show. Geordie was a champion leek grower and a lot of the furniture in his house had been won in the competitions.

So, my memories of my father and mother are intertwined with my memories of their parents. My father was an outgoing man. He owned motorbikes. My mother, on the other hand, was more quiet and gentle. When I described this couple of contrasting backgrounds and personalities to a good friend of mine, he reminded me that it was my father who married the quiet church-going lady, while my mother married the adventurer.

Our neighbourhood was called *The Villas*. All my friends and I had nicknames. Mine was 'Chuck'. Chuck is related to Charlie, my father's name. I became Chuck because of the song:

Charlie, Charlie, Chuck, Chuck, Chuck, went to bed with two old ducks.

One just died, the other cried.

Old friends still continue to call me Chuck. To me, such memories are important, because they remind me that the many long, deep and close relationships are such an important part of the north-eastern environment and family life.

As a teacher in my first secondary school, I am delighted to say I had the opportunity to celebrate and share my own and the children's regional heritage. At the time *The Land of the Three Rivers* by Helen Gertrude Bowling was a core part of our curriculum.

As the twentieth century approached its end, I would become a part of an education system that is increasingly focused on a national curriculum and the national concerns that should be addressed by schools. Counter-intuitively, what strikes me most forcibly, when I remember my family background, is the power and importance of the industrial base in the North East, while I was growing up. So, the question is whether, with an increasingly centralised education system, we will lose our regional identity and with it our heritage – and will such a loss really matter?

I guess not everyone feels a connection with their regional cultural heritage like I do. I feel a strong bond with my fellow Geordies. I am proud to show visitors from elsewhere our castles, our mountains and our beautiful coastline. I take pride in our regional history, its music and dance. Because I have a better understanding of previous generations and the history of where they come from, I have been gifted with a powerful sense of belonging in an increasingly fragmented world. If Wales

The two-up two-down house where I was born.

insists on extending the Welsh language, and Northern Ireland and Scotland continue to encourage *the Gaelic*, then surely it is the least we should demand that there is, somewhere, a regional curriculum clearly embedded within the national curriculum.

It is so important that our young people understand their history and culture and are proud of their heritage. It is also important that we in the North East encourage new thinking and invite new opportunities. It is this balance that we need to get right.
To put it another way:

I'm a Geordie Internationalist.

CHAPTER 5

RED ELLEN

Around the time of my entry into the world, 'Red Ellen' Wilkinson, a fiery redhead and former communist, who favours the grammar school system, is appointed as our first female Education Secretary of State.

Learn from, but do not simply replicate, the experiences of our own childhood.

But Dad, the Secretary of State says today's average is no longer average.

Rab Butler, the creator of our modern education system, attended several preparatory schools, refused to go to Harrow, failed to win a scholarship to Eton and ended up in Marlborough College. He studied at Pembroke College Cambridge. Privileged, yes, but nevertheless he was a man with a clear vision for the post-war future.

I would love to have met Rab Butler and to have asked him if his own education and background influenced his desire to radically overhaul the English education system after the Second World War.

R A Butler: described by some as the 'best Prime Minister we never had'.

There isn't much doubt that those who have had the greatest influence on our education system have themselves had the narrowest of schooling experience. Of the 55 prime ministers to date, 20 were educated at Eton College, seven at Harrow School and six at Westminster School. Nine prime ministers to date have been educated at non-fee-paying schools. These include all five prime ministers to hold office between 1964 and 1977 – Wilson, Heath, Callaghan, Thatcher and Major.

Our five most recent prime ministers are a mixed bunch. Tony Blair attended Fettes College, Gordon Brown: Kirkcaldy High School, David Cameron: Eton College, Theresa May: Holton Park Girls' Grammar and Boris Johnson: Eton College. Equally striking is the fact that, apart from Gordon Brown, they were all students at Oxford.

Looking more recently we find that of the last six Secretaries of State for Education:

- Ed Balls attended Nottingham High School, an independent fee-paying day school. He then studied at Oxford and Harvard;

- Michael Gove was educated in a state school in Aberdeen and then won a scholarship to the independent Robert Gordon's College. He then went to Oxford;

- Nicky Morgan went to Surbiton High School, an independent day school. She then went to Oxford;

- Justine Greening attended Oakwood Comprehensive School. Then, after sixth form college, she went to Southampton University;

● Damien Hinds was a pupil at St. Ambrose College, a Voluntary Aided Roman Catholic Grammar. He studied at Oxford; and

● Gavin Williamson, the Secretary of State at the time of writing, was a pupil at Raincliffe Comprehensive School. He then studied at Bristol University.

The stand-out secretaries of state are Justine Greening and Gavin Williamson. They have been the only secretaries of state to attend a comprehensive school. Ironically, Justine Greening is the only secretary of state in recent years to promote the return of grammar schools.

The desire to replicate the past usually does not hold with most professions. So, surgeons, architects and generals would rarely wish for the return to cancer treatment without hormone therapy, buildings constructed using asbestos or operating in battle with Second World War tanks. Indeed, the education profession and education itself are concerned with a peculiar business, in which we often seem to go round in circles. Does the education business really not make much progress over time?

The first female Minister of Education, Ellen Wilkinson, was a major supporter of the selective system. Ellen had gone to university from a working-class home. She was born in Manchester on 8 October 1891, to a mother who was a cotton worker. She was the third of four children, but against the odds she won scholarships to Stretford Road Secondary School and then went to Manchester University.

Very much like Theresa May, she developed strong loyalties to selective secondary education, which she considered had helped her to gain access to higher education.

However, there were differences. Ellen's red hair and diminutive size earned her the nicknames 'Red Ellen' and the 'Fiery Particle'.

In this way, she was clearly very unlike Theresa May! Another difference was that, unlike Margaret Thatcher and Theresa May, both well-known grammar school pupils, Ellen was also a former member of the Communist Party.

At first, in 1912, she joined the Independent Labour Party. But in 1920 she became one of the original members of the Communist Party of Great Britain and in the following year, she visited Moscow as a British Communist representative. In 1923 she was elected as a Communist to Manchester City Council. Although she retained her Communist Party membership, it was as the official Labour candidate that she successfully contested the seat in Ashton-under-Lyne in the same year.

For a number of years after the conclusion of the First World War, Wilkinson was a member of the executive of the Plebs League. The League was the founder of the *Plebs Magazine*.

In 1924, having severed her connection with the Communist Party, she was elected to Parliament as the Labour member for Middlesbrough East. Later, in 1931, she lost this seat when she was a fiercely hostile critic of Ramsay MacDonald. However, she returned to Parliament in 1935 as a member for Jarrow. Three years later she published the book *The Town That Was Murdered*, in which she set forth in detail the history of Palmer's Shipyard. From this, after the closure of Palmer's, she drew from Jarrow's bitter experience by presenting a penetrating indictment of capitalism and a reasoned plea for a planned socialist economy. Famously, in 1936 she headed the march of the Jarrow unemployed to London.

Ellen Wilkinson leading the Jarrow march.

When Churchill became head of the war-time Coalition Government, Wilkinson was appointed Parliamentary Secretary to the Minister of Pensions and later in the same year became one of the two Parliamentary Secretaries to Herbert Morrison at the Ministry of Home Security. Emboldened by experience, it was apparently at her own urgent request that, after the war in 1945, she was appointed Minister of Education.

There is a story that, as the first woman to be appointed as a minister, she left Jarrow for London by the night train immediately after she knew she had been re-elected to Parliament. She saw in this appointment a unique opportunity to strike a resounding blow for the 'underprivileged' children of England and Wales.

As Minister of Education Ellen's main task was to implement the provisions of the 1944 Education Act. Rab Butler, who served as Education Minister from 1941 to 1945, oversaw the new act through Parliament. Understandably, it became known as the 'Butler Act'. Remarkably, the innovations proposed by the Act were supported by all major parties, achieving a consensus view on education rarely seen since.

Ellen then raised the question of the school leaving age. She estimated that the first stage of the Raising of School Leaving Age Scheme (ROSLA) would require the creation of over 200,000 new school places. Her plans to then increase the school-leaving age to 16 had to be abandoned when the government decided that the measure would be too expensive.

On 6 February 1947 the death of Miss Wilkinson, a 'champion of the working class', was announced. She died at St. Mary's Hospital, Paddington, aged 55. The cause was described as heart failure following an attack of bronchitis. For some months she had been unwell, affected by asthma. Another view expressed in some quarters was that, depressed by her failure to bring in all the reforms she believed were necessary, she took an overdose of barbiturates. In April, one month after her death, the school leaving age was raised to 15, despite Treasury requests for a delay. The *Times Educational Supplement* of February 1947 described her courage and cheerfulness, recalling a 'heroic and loveable character' with a quick temper and first-rate moral and physical courage.

George Tomlinson, MP for Farnsworth, succeeded Ellen Wilkinson as Minister of Education. He was educated at Rishton Wesleyan Day School in Lancashire and, at the age of 12, went to work as a half-timer in a weaving shed. This experience would then shape his view of education. George was able to expand access to secondary education, which he never had. It is an undeniable fact that Secretaries of State decide, in the end, what will impact children.

A couple of years ago a long-standing friend and close colleague of mine, Brian Oglethorpe, sadly died. Brian was a former headteacher of Oxclose Comprehensive School and Principal Education Adviser at Sunderland Local Education Authority. He once recounted to me his own time in an eleven-plus preparatory class in Canning Street School, Newcastle, in 1947. He remembered pupils:

being flogged with considerable frequency and well-practised technique with a leather strap on the hands for even minor misdemeanours, like blots on exercise books or repeated spelling mistakes.

jumping through the intelligence testing hoops and being on the top row of desks in the back of the class – desks being arranged from the back strictly according to ability.

Luckily for Brian, 1947–48 was also the year when selection took place with the destinations being the grammar or technical school, or simply a quick climb up the stairs to the Senior School in Canning Street. After a series of tests administered by the headmaster of Canning Street, Brian was told he had a place at Rutherford Grammar School – many of his friends were destined for the top floor at Canning Street. At this stage, a young Brian Oglethorpe would not have realised that his experience and upward trajectory were the results of the experience of a red-haired former communist with a fiery temper.

CHAPTER 6

PROGGY MAT MEMORIES

I have memories of outside toilets, tin baths and sitting on the 'proggy mat' in front of the 'nutty slack' spitting fire and hand-knitted woollen swimming trunks, which descend down my legs when 'plodging' in the sea. These memories will have a profound impact on my view of education in the next three-quarters of a century.

Our own recollections of school and childhood are possibly the biggest influences on how we see the world of education.

Nostalgia was far better in the good old days.

Memories are not realities. Politicians, civil servants, school leaders, all have memories of their own education. The danger is that they may believe too firmly in them and then their memories start to exert a powerful influence over their education plans.

I must admit that I'm just as bad. I have persuasive memories of my childhood, too. I do believe that 95 per cent of my memories are *probably, possibly, perhaps* true. But every time I journey into the past, my thoughts are complicated and may become 'false memories'. This is similar to the 'fake news' that we encounter nowadays. The only difference is that our false memories are not deliberately made up.

One of my favourite TV sketches is 'The Four Yorkshiremen'. It is about men drinking Chateau de Chasselas wine and reminiscing about their childhood – it's all about drinking cold tea, without milk, sugar or even tea; living in one room or in cardboard boxes or on the ground covered by a tarpaulin.

The punchline is delivered cold:

Try telling the young people of today that and they won't believe ya.

So, here I go about my early childhood.

I was named Leslie Howard Walton, supposedly after the famous film actor Leslie Howard, who played Ashley Wilkes in *Gone with the Wind*. Perhaps my name provides a clue to the ambitions of my parents? Not for them a Dave or a Kevin. Perhaps I have missed a trick over the years. Should I have introduced myself as Leslie Howard-Walton? In my alternative universe, the *Howard* would be pronounced *Hi-ard*. In this imaginary future I would be issuing invitations saying:

The Hiard-Waltons invite you to our hice spotty

instead of

Howay over to wor hoose party.

At birth, as I had the propensity to speak thousands of languages, speaking *posh* would have been no problem. I could have been the Jacob Rees-Mogg of Geordie Land. Though I must admit, unlike Jacob, my father wasn't a Lord, nor was my sister called Annunziata.

As you have already guessed, I wasn't a classmate of Jacob's at Eton either.

When my friends were being called home by their mothers, shouting, '*Billy, Derek, Jimmy*', Hilda Walton would follow up with '*Leslie Howard – time for tea*'. Johnny Cash was to describe this situation in his song, *A boy named Sue*. Unlike Sue, I was never a good fighter.

We played the usual football in the street as well as marbles and 'chucks'. Chucks were blocks of chalk, which you would throw in the air and try to catch on the back of your hand. Another favourite was 'Japanese and Americans' – why this was not 'Germans and British' I will never know! Without being arrogant, I was one of the best 'soldiers' in the group. After being shot I would grip my chest and proceed to fall down in slow motion, writhing on the ground and eventually expiring in agony after about ten minutes. I could stretch these agonising histrionics out for at least half an hour!

I was brought up in the midst of a massive work ethic. This was certainly a trait of both my mother's and father's families. Both my grandparents worked extremely hard down the pits or in the quarries. My mother, in turn, saw her role as staying at home and bringing up the kids. She worked hard constantly, was never guilty of standing still and even used to 'dust dust'.

My father saw his role as the breadwinner. As a consequence, I didn't see much of my father, as he did a lot of shift work and overtime. Often he would be in bed when I went to school and still at work when I returned.

My mother came from a family of committed Methodists and insisted that my sister and I both attended church and, of course, Sunday school every week. Education and hard work were seen clearly as providing *the* way out of poverty.

My father, my mother, my sister and I lived in a house with one living room downstairs, a scullery and an outside toilet. The floor was covered with oilcloth, a cheap floor covering, with the relative luxury of 'hooky' or 'proggy' mats on the top. These mats were made from rags cut into strips and then pushed or pulled through a hessian backing. Legend had it that, if you unguardedly took your jacket off in my grandmother's house, it was incorporated into the mat within minutes.

Our coal house, in the back yard, was filled with free coal from the National Coal Board. After helping to shovel the coal into the coal house, we bathed once a week in front of a coal fire in a metal bath tub. My dad and I would sit freezing in the scullery, waiting for my mam and sister to bathe. The rule was girls first, and the dirtiest last. I remember how cold my back was, compared to the parts heated by the fire.

The coal house and outside netty.

All my clothes, with the exception of my short trousers and shoes, were home knitted or stitched. This included knitted swimming trunks which, when wet, would immediately slide in a humiliating way down my legs!

One memorable Christmas present I received was a cowboy fort. It was made by my father from a Jaffa orange box and painted with creosote. Looking carefully, the words Jaffa could still be read on the side of the box. Naturally, I called it Fort Jaffa. The fort was inhabited by lead cowboys and Indians. I remember my father also made me a cowboy outfit with a real leather waistcoat.

My parents always sacrificed to give me one *bought* Christmas present. Memorable presents of this sort included a Wolves football shirt – because I liked the colour – an American jeep pedal car and a 'caser' leather football. The latter, when kicked, could dislocate an ankle in one go.

Looking back on all this, I now understand that the first years of my life were dominated by post-war austerity and rationing. And things could easily get worse. For example, due to continual rain in 1946, Britain's crops were ruined and bread rationing started again. Then the extreme winter frost of 1947 led to potato rationing. Confectionery and sugar rationing would not end until I was eight, and meat when I was nine. Ironically, my diet would probably be considered the 'bee's knees' today.

I had two access points to the outside world. One was the Arthur Mee's *Children's Encyclopaedia*. It had sections on great lives, bible stories and included things to make and do, as well as science subjects such as geology and astronomy.

The other important access to the world outside was the radio. As a 2 year-old, I would be glued to *Listen with Mother*, which ran right up to 1982. I remember snuggling up with my mam and waiting for the xylophone introduction and the question:

Are you sitting comfortably? Then I'll begin.

This phrase was later to be used in the lyrics of a Moody Blues song, '*Are you sitting comfortably?*'

I have often said that education leaders, particularly politicians, like to hark back to their own childhood and education and then attempt to 'revive' an education model based on these recollections. Frequently I've heard the call for 'strengthening the family', reinforcing strong values within children, promoting healthy lifestyles and the importance of high aspirations for parents and young people. Are my memories, and those of education reformers, as romanticised as those of the *Likely Lads* in the TV programme? We can be very selective about the virtues of the good old days. Some argue that poverty is relative to time and place. I wonder, how will people in 50 years' time write about their experiences of home and childhood?

In the end, we have a choice. You can ignore and walk away from your memories or face them head-on and get the best out of them. The memories I have recalled are warm and friendly. But there are others that we try to push deep down beneath the surface. We could let them emerge, dig them up and allow them to tear us apart. I will be coming to those memories at some later point.

Perhaps the main message from all this is that we should not base education policy on our own personal recollections of the past. Basing education on research might be a better way. For most of my career, education research was a place infrequently visited by most educational leaders about to launch another child-changing initiative. Hopefully, this is improving.

CHAPTER 7

CHALK AND TAWSE IN THE INFANT SCHOOL

In infant school I am strapped with a leather tawse, write on slates and get checked by Nitty Nora, the bug explorer.

History is written by the victors and education policy by the successful; the voices of those who have been disillusioned by education are rarely listened to.

I think I can pack in junior school. I've learned everything I need to know.

Most of my memories of my first experience of school are vague. But there is one that I cannot erase from my mind – the experience of being strapped with a leather tawse at the age of five. At that time the Book of Proverbs was often quoted as a reason for hitting children.

He that spareth the rod hateth his son: but he that loveth him correcteth him betimes. Withold not correction from a child: for if thou strike him with the rod, he shall not die. Thou shalt beat him with the rod, and deliver his soul from hell.

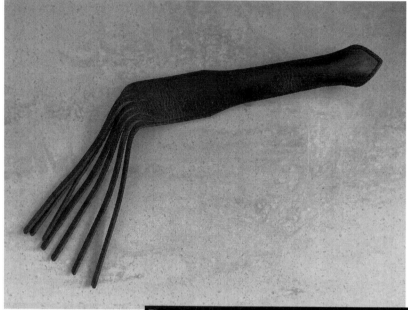
The actual tawse that was issued in schools at the time.

So, perhaps my rather negative memory of school is an unfair judgement on my early years' education; I was hit out of love and saved from hell at the same time. Even better news – it didn't kill me.

I started school at the age of four in September 1949. My infant school was for children between the ages of four and seven. It was on the same site as the junior school, but they were separate schools, with different headteachers.

When education became compulsory in England from 1877, infant schools were incorporated into the state school system. The late 1960s and 1970s saw hundreds of infant schools in Britain abolished and replaced by five-to-eight or five-to-nine first schools. However, the wheel turned, and some of these were then abolished in favour of a return to infant schools.

Indeed, by the early 1980s most schools had followed suit.

The first infant schools were established by Samuel Wilderspin and in Scotland, they were set up by Robert Owen at New Lanark. These experiments in turn influenced developments in continental Europe and North America.

My mother walked me to school for the first few days. The walk was about half a mile from where we lived, along a winding path through woods. After this, I walked to school and back with other children, including my older sister. It never occurred to anyone that it might be dangerous. There was safety in numbers and very little traffic.

My old junior school.

Classes were large, usually with 30–40 children in each and resources were minimal. It was not until nearly half a century later with the introduction of the *School Standards and Framework Act* in 1998 that classes in infant schools in England and Wales would be limited to no more than 30 children per teacher.

All the classrooms were simple, rather large, dull rooms. The furniture was no different from that which my mother used in her school in the early 1900s; a wooden high desk and chair for the teacher, a wooden-framed blackboard on an easel and two-seater desks for us children. Indeed, the teacher's desk was exactly the same, even in the 1960s. I once enquired as a young teacher why the teachers' desks were so much higher than those of the children. The answer, perhaps tongue in cheek, was that things were like this:

so that the nits could not jump from their heads into your hair.

At this early time, the 'nit nurse' would indeed make regular visits to check for head lice or *Pediculus Humanus,* as I like to call them! We would all line up to be examined in turn, our hair being combed carefully with a nit comb to see if there was any infestation. The nit nurse probably visited our school a couple of times a year, checking our heads with a fine-toothed comb. If lice were discovered, parents were instructed to treat their children's hair with a special lotion.

These inspections were carried out in full view of the rest of the class. If nits were found, you were subject to quite a lot of name-calling in the playground. Possibly because of the high visibility of the inspections, nit nurses were phased out in the 1990s and parents were encouraged to carry out checks at home.

As late as April 2011, the *Daily Mail* would run a headline '*RETURN OF THE NIT NURSE*'. It was suggested that many parents were too busy to check their children's heads and head lice were again spreading rapidly in primary schools. The article claimed that:

the inspections were a source of shame and embarrassment for generations of schoolchildren.

The *Mail* dramatically also reported that:

hundreds of parents have signed a petition calling for the nurses to be reinstated and claiming that head lice are now a nationwide health issue.

Obviously, 2011 was a year when a lot of nit-picking was going on. The *Wigan Courier* posted fond memories and requests for the return of '*Nitty Nora, the Bug Explorer*'.

In the classroom, things were learnt by rote and the times tables were tested once a week. The idea was that we would memorise information if we repeated it often enough. The alphabet was also something we learned by rote. Even today I can repeat exactly the same sing-song melody we all used to help us remember our tables and the alphabet in infant school. The girls, mainly, also sang and engaged in clapping games including 'Little Rubber Dolly'. It wasn't until Shirley Ellis's 'Clapping Song' came along in 1965 that I learned a whole new style and the classic lyrics:

Three six nine, the goose drank wine. The monkey chewed tobacco on the street car line.

While some people argue that rote learning is an outdated technique, it is still widely used today. On balance, though, it is increasingly being abandoned for newer techniques, such as critical thinking and associative learning.

Back in my infant class I always hoped I'd not be asked a question. I have always been anxious about mathematics, probably as a result of the way in which we were taught. Of course, I would not dare to question how we were taught. No one questioned authority in those days, but that doesn't mean to say that we weren't resentful at times.

Where's six year-old Wally?

I cannot recall ever using paint, glue, coloured card or crayons. I vaguely remember using chalk on slates, which we then cleaned off with a cloth. I hated the squeak of that slate pencil; it set my teeth on edge. We spent a lot of time copying letters from the blackboard. We weren't allowed pencils and proper exercise books until we could read and write. When we eventually arrived at the junior school, we were given desks with inkwells and wide-nibbed pens and began to learn 'joined-up' writing.

My happiest memories were of the music lessons. The Schools Broadcasting Council for the United Kingdom had been set up in 1947 and the wireless played a great part in my education. *Music and Movement* was one such programme. We would stretch, jump and crouch to the commands from the radio. I distinctly remember *being a tree* and waving my arms, when the radio announced that it was windy. We also sang folk songs from around the British Isles such as 'Loch Lomond', 'Oh no, John' and 'What shall we do with a drunken sailor?'. There were no other instruments for us, other than our voices.

Many years later the *Two Ronnies* would do their version of 'Drunken Sailor':

Hoorah! And up she rises. She's got legs of different sizes. One's very small and the other wins prizes.

I wish I had known that version when I was six.

Morning playtimes were milk times. The caretaker would wash the milk beakers, but they always stank of sour milk. When we eventually got it delivered in small third-pint bottles with foil tops, we would drink directly from them using drinking straws. In winter the milk would freeze and the bottle tops would stand proud above the bottles on a column of frozen milk.

Mysteriously, the dinner hour lasted an hour and a half. We ate our pease pudding, cabbage and stew. This was often followed by tapioca pudding or, as we called it, 'frog spawn' or 'fish eyes and glue'. Years later, in the 1960s, I taught in a small primary school. Every dinner time, those who stayed for school dinners were assembled in a crocodile and chaperoned by the teachers to a central kitchen about 15 minutes away.

We had no lines drawn on the playground or any climbing apparatus but we played with balls and ropes. In any case, we had plenty of war games we could act out. Games like 'being aircraft and dropping bombs', or 'shooting with a machine gun' were accompanied by more constructive plays, such as 'nurses and doctors' and 'operating on the wounded'. Yes, the impact of the War was still there.

We all have different memories of our early years of education. I must admit mine don't seem that great. Other friends of mine remember their infant school with much greater fondness.

There is one thing I am sure about. Sometime soon, as well as calling for the return of the nit nurse, there will be a demand for a return to the good old days in infant schools when children were 'seen and not heard'. Let's hope this will never happen. Let us also hope no one will be championing the return of tapioca.

CHAPTER 8

JESUS WANTS ME FOR A SUNBEAM

My Sunday school teaches me empathy, kindness and consideration and my primary school focuses on dull rote learning and stern discipline, occasionally combined with abusive and violent repression. I also decide to become a teacher.

Education is more than what we learn in school.

No, you can't do missionary work in Disneyland.

The Methodist Church was a central part of my early life. Later in my teenage years, when tragedy struck my family, apart from my mother and close family, it was the Church that cared for me. I attended Sunday morning and evening services, afternoon Sunday school and the Youth Fellowship on Sunday evenings.

Today many people may consider the idea of going every Sunday to a Sunday school a bit odd, perhaps even quaint. However, I have fond memories of Sunday school as an oasis of support, storytelling, singing, kindness and friendship. I have happy memories of some of the best moments of my childhood. It's a world that I recall with huge affection.

Sunday school also had a crucial influence on my personal development. It taught me to look beyond Tyneside to 'far-off lands'. I remember vividly singing *Jesus Wants Me for a Sunbeam* in Sunday school.

> *Jesus wants me for a sunbeam,*
> *To shine for him every day;*
> *In every way try to please him,*
> *At home, at school, at play.*

Like most very young children I subjected my parents to regular interrogations on many important questions. Things like:

> *Where did I come from?*
> *How big is God?*
> *What happens to naughty dogs after they die?*
> *What's a sunbeam and how will I become one?*

Years later, Max Schafer posed the question:

What if all of the sun's output of visible light was bundled into a laser-like beam that had a diameter of around 1 metre once it reaches Earth?

The answer was it would be like a hydrogen bomb going off, only much more violent. I am sure that was *not* what Jesus had in mind for me!

A big aspect of my early childhood at Sunday school was taking part in a charitable scheme called 'Sunny Smiles'. At Sunday school, we were given a little booklet featuring detachable photos of 'unfortunate' toddlers, pictures of children from Africa and children's homes in England. We were asked to tout them around to friends and family in return for a contribution. The buyer was then given the photo of the toddler. I remember being shocked by a neighbour who warned me that '*it was hard to sell the photos of the really ugly babies*'.

I remember my own secret strategy was to sell the ugly ones first and usually to my own family.

Two Sunday school events have left a lasting impression on me:

The Sunday School Anniversary – was the most terrifying, and

My Birthday Celebration – was the most disappointing.

Each year I had to learn my *piece* for the Anniversary. One year we were dressed as flowers and I recited '*I am a tulip*' to my doting parents. I used to be terrified that I would forget my words. However, it was at these classes that I learned the confidence to stand up in public and speak. This did not have a lasting effect and 20 years later I could still be physically sick before talking in a school assembly.

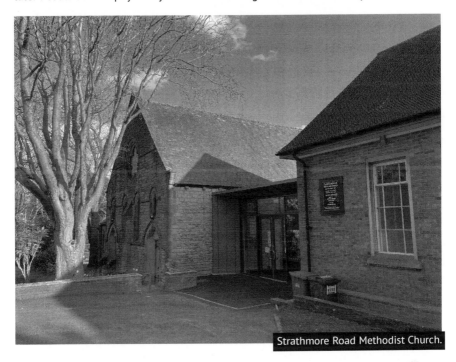
Strathmore Road Methodist Church.

The other event was a weekly celebration of birthdays.

- **There were no presents.**

- **The 'cake' consisted of a wooden ring with holes, in which candles were placed.**

Every Easter a brand new spring outfit was bought for me by my grandmother, Bella Walton, to wear at the Sunday school Anniversary, the most memorable of these outfits is a Harris tweed matching jacket and shorts. Bella used to take me to Burton's the Tailors in Consett. She would agree to buy the outfit and then haggle with the salesman. Bella never accepted there were fixed prices for things and, in the end, would always be able to negotiate a reduction.

The first Sunday school was probably the one that opened in 1751, in Nottingham. However, the pioneer of Sunday schools is commonly acknowledged to be Robert Raikes, editor of the *Gloucester Journal*. Raikes had seen the need to prevent children in the slums from descending into crime. In 1781, Raikes saw at first hand the plight of children living in the Gloucester slums. In the home of a friend, he opened the first school on a Sunday. This was the only day these boys and girls, living in slums and working in factories, could attend. Using the Bible as their textbook, he taught them to read and write. Within four years over 250,000 children were attending schools on Sunday throughout England.

In 1784, many new schools were opened, including the interdenominational Stockport Sunday School, which was constructed as a school for 5000 scholars and became the largest Sunday school in the world.

By 1831, it was reported that attendance at Sunday schools had grown to 1.2 million, approximately 25 per cent of the target population. They provided basic literacy education alongside religious instruction. Robert Raikes' schools are often thought of as the first schools of the English state system.

The Sunday school movement has had a deep radical effect on British society. In the early days, it was seen as dangerous and subversive to give the tools of literacy to the lower orders. Well into the twentieth century, Sunday school students parading at Whitsun would turn out in their thousands, bringing city centres to a standstill.

The Sunday school that I attended could certainly not be portrayed as radical or subversive. The values that were promoted could best be described as British Christian values.

At the time, maps of the world still depicted the dominance of Britain over the world. We were repeatedly told stories of British, more exactly Scottish, missionaries such as David Livingston and Mary Slessor, who worked in Africa, spreading the word of Jesus. These missionaries and their stories had a profound effect on me. Given this background, you can imagine my excitement when it was announced that the missionary's missionary, Gladys Aylward, who worked in China, would be visiting our village in the late 1950s.

In 1932, Gladys was born to a working-class family in North London. She spent her life savings on a train passage to Yangcheng.

The film of Gladys Aylward's life, *The Inn of the Sixth Happiness*, was made in 1958, starring Ingrid Bergman and was based on the book *The Small Woman* by Alan Burgess. Ingrid Bergman was a strikingly tall blonde Swedish actress. We were, therefore, all quite surprised when a small dark-haired Gladys turned up, speaking with a North London accent!

At Sunday school we all sang lustily '*Remember all the children, that live in far-off lands*'. We were secure in the belief that our job was to make all those children free and bring them joyfully to our beliefs and way of life!

While my beliefs may have changed since my childhood, values are more constant. I consider myself fortunate to have attended a school in which values for life: learning to love people, learning to live with diversity and learning to challenge inequalities within the world were at the heart of the curriculum.

It was around this time that I decided I wanted to become a teacher, preferably within the Methodist Church. I was never to deviate from this objective.

CHAPTER 9

CUP FINALS AND GOOD CONDUCT

My primary school teaches me not to talk to my neighbours in class, my Sunday school teaches me to love my neighbours and my football club teaches me to boo, abuse and hate my enemies.

Schools may promote values, norms and behaviours that are very different from the communities they serve.

HOWAY MAN

SAUL

Newcastle supporter listening to the last time we played in Europe.

So, my education continued through the difficult period of early childhood. Up to this point I had received instruction from my family, my school and the Church. A fourth group of education providers, still influential today, were to be football, radio and TV. Newcastle United, or *the Magpies*, *Educating Archie* and *Billy Bunter* were to be my new teachers.

I was probably a member of the first generation in human history where education was not strictly limited and defined by family or Church. Here begins another new challenge for future school leaders to grapple with. How much should they separate classroom education from what goes on in the outside world?

I was inducted into the worship of Newcastle United around the same time as I started Sunday school. To some extent they were similar. Football has for decades been described as a religion on Tyneside. For example, football involved singing, of a sort, and quite often quiet prayers were being whispered.

But there were also differences. Here on the terraces I was taught to hate my enemies – the despicable Mackems. The most distant 'far-off land' the Magpies travelled to, as a member of the English Football League First Division, was Portsmouth. The 70,000 who stood to watch the match at St James' Park were mostly men, usually wearing jackets and ties. 'Naughty' words were occasionally uttered.

In 1951 the atmosphere was electric. Newcastle United had beaten Wolverhampton Wanderers to get to the Final at Wembley. The icing on the cake was that the defeated Wolves had previously beaten the enemy, Sunderland, before facing Newcastle in the semi-final.

I listened to the Cup Final match on the wooden-veneered Murphy radio with my father and uncle.

This was a full two years before we were able to watch the first televised FA Cup Final on my uncle's new Bush Bakelite 12-inch screen TV. I remember that, in order to make the picture bigger, a magnifying pane of glass was strapped to the front of the TV. Outside, proudly fixed to the chimney stack, was the first H-shaped aerial in the village.

Anyway, back to the Cup Final. My mother and my aunty stayed in the back scullery as my father, my uncle and I settled down to listen in the front room. As the first-half progressed, with no goals, the language in the room became slightly richer. At half-time, because of the bad language emitting from my dad and my uncle, my mother gave me the 'red card' and banned me from going back in for the second half.

As a result of this sending off, I missed Jackie Milburn scoring the two winning goals, starting a tradition of Newcastle fans never managing to see Newcastle winning the FA Cup. That experience taught me that swearing at football matches is bad. I also learned that adults, even my mam, can be very unfair. In this case, the separation between children and adults was very clear.

However, separation from adults was particularly unusual at St James' Park. I remember that, in order for me to get a better view of the match, my father would sometimes pass me down to the front over the heads of all the men standing jam-packed together. Anyway, when the game ended, I would sit patiently by the pitch, waiting to meet my dad at the end of the match.

NEWCASTLE
UNITED
FOOTBALL CLUB
ST. JAMES' PARK · NEWCASTLE
GROUND CAPACITY — 70,000
RECORD ATTENDANCE — 68,386

WE WELCOME TODAY—

TOTTENHAM HOTSPUR

Saturday, 29th October, 1960 kick-off 3·0 p.m.

3D

OFFICIAL PROGRAMME

Newcastle United, where I crowdsurfed in front of 70,000 fans.

Iggy Pop has been credited with inventing crowd surfing during the Cincinnati summer pop festival of 1970 and other stars, such as Peter Gabriel and Billy Joel, have continued the tradition. But remember where it really started!

When I was little, there was also a very clear demarcation between children's TV and adult TV. During the 1950s, children's television began with just one programme a week on the BBC. The first *For the Children*, featuring the '*Hogarth Puppet Circus*', went out on Sunday 9 June 1946 from 3.35 to 4.00pm. Within two years, a weekly hour of programmes was being broadcast under the same title. By 1954, there was a daily hour or so of programmes; a 15-minute *Watch with Mother* film at 4pm, then up to 60 minutes more from 5pm. In the late '40s and early '50s, those making these programmes thought it was dangerous to have children watching too much television!

There were also TV programmes, which we, as children, were not allowed to watch. Popular American programmes such as *I Love Lucy* and *Dragnet* were off-limits. Today these same programmes would not even require a Parental Guidance certificate.

One of the TV programmes I *was* allowed to watch was *Billy Bunter*. Billy, described in the books as a 15-stone-12½-pound public school boy, was played by a comparatively slim 11-stone 29-year-old actor called Gerald Campion. The programme was based in the imaginary Greyfriars Public School, which had featured in the *Comet* comic from 1908 to 1940.

The live broadcast at 5.40pm was about a world of education that I did not understand or would never inhabit, though, admittedly, my grammar school did a fair impersonation.

However, radio was still dominant; my favourite character being Archie Andrews: Archie, a ventriloquist's dummy used by ventriloquist Peter Brough, starred in *Educating Archie* on the radio.

Radio should have been the last place on earth that a ventriloquist's dummy appeared. Even so, there was a remarkable gallery of stars who appeared on the show, including Tony Hancock, Max Bygraves, Harry Secombe, Hattie Jacques, Dick Emery, Bruce Forsyth and Julie Andrews.

Peter Brough was such a bad ventriloquist that many of us reckoned we could see his lips move, even on the radio! The strange thing was that, when the show transferred to TV, it didn't take off to the same extent. Despite the fact that Peter Brough had filed his two upper front teeth to help him throw his voice.

Archie Andrews and Peter Brough. Watch my lips!

My other favourite radio programme in 1953 was *Journey into Space*, a BBC Radio science fiction programme, written by BBC producer, Charles Chilton. In the UK it was the last radio programme to attract a bigger evening audience than television.

The first series, *A Tale of the Future*, was set in the far-off future of 1965 and described man's conquest of the moon. This was quite a remarkable prediction, as the first manned landing on the moon eventually took place in 1969.

When I became a headteacher, I would always be very strict on bad language. My usual comment was:

You wouldn't swear in a church or at your grandma's funeral, so you do know how to control your language.

Even this no longer seems a reasonable guide. A few years ago the vicar at the church of St Mary the Virgin in Herefordshire told his churchgoers to swear more, *'because it is how Jesus would have spoken'.*

Occasionally, the anti-swearing position is hard to maintain. A local primary headteacher, who later was made a dame for her services to education, invited me to give an assembly in her school. As I was talking to the children, a former student came in at the back with her 2-year-old child. Just as I had achieved total silence, a little voice piped up: '**** *off'.*

After the toddler had repeated the phrase half a dozen times the mother was asked to take the child outside. The management of 'bad language' is not easy. Quite often bad language for one person is just a part of the normal everyday conversation for another.

Many years later, I was sitting in my usual seat at Newcastle United, when the man next to me started swearing. I asked him to tone it down as my children were sitting next to me. He stopped. Then his wife leaned across to me and said: '*I'm sorry, the little ******* does it all the time'.*

So, what do we do in schools when children can hear bad language on the TV every night? The very clear divisions between what children and adults watch on TV have now gone. For many people swearing is normal behaviour.

Perhaps schools will have to accept that they are always likely to be just behind the ever-changing cultural norms. When I started teaching, we would always address fellow teachers as Mr or Mrs; now teachers call each other by their first names. Children would always call you either Sir or Miss, but in some schools, the use of teacher forenames is accepted or even encouraged. As a headteacher in the 1990s, and you may consider me old-fashioned, I always insisted we used the terms 'children' or 'pupils', rather than the term 'kids'.

Whenever I talked to parents when I was a headteacher, there was an absolute agreement that schools should make a stand on bad language. This was the case, despite the fact that the parents and children may be happily *cussin'* and *blindin'* in front of the telly at home. Most people accept that we should not allow behaviour in our schools that uncritically reflects that seen outside the school.

This is why being a headteacher has never been simple. As a child of the 1950s, all we brought to school were imaginary adventures in space, a ventriloquist's dummy and the occasional swear word from the match. Today the job is even more complicated because the range of influences brought into school by our culture is so wide. A teacher today is working with young people who bring all the advantages and dangers of social media. So, what is the answer?

Perhaps the answer is that schools should defend the values and behaviours that we all aspire to, or certainly that we remember from our own childhood, even though this means we might be labelled as out of touch and old-fashioned.

CHAPTER 10

SORTING THE INTELLIGENT

My father and mother believe in inherited intelligence and that a simple test can separate the artisans from the academic and the grammar school is *the* way out of poverty.

Seek consensus on how we measure the ability and potential of children, as it is a constant cause of turbulence within our education system.

To be fair, as part of the test, we are asking you all to climb the same tree.

It is always fascinating to me how our views on education are influenced by family background and childhood experiences. These views in turn are influenced by politicians and 'education experts'. But perhaps the major influence on my achievement at school was my own family's views on education. They firmly believed in inherited intelligence.

They also believed that a simple test would allow the authorities to judge whether I was a clever lad, inheriting my mother's side, or conversely coming from the Geordie Walton clan. Moreover, they had absolute confidence that with the support of a grammar school education I was going to avoid the pit and get a 'clean job'.

In 1952, I was a member of a happy family – two parents with two children. In addition, I was surrounded by my extended family, which included uncles and aunts and cousins. Some of my uncles and aunts were not blood relatives, but that seemed like a minor issue.

My extended family were 'interesting'. One uncle would secretly serve Winalot dog food at parties, then whisper to me that everyone would 'woof' it down.

Sometimes, when people left our local pub on a Saturday night, they would see candles glowing in rows of skulls along the church wall, put there by another 'uncle', who hid in the churchyard making wailing sounds. His other claim to fame was sucking lemons in front of a visiting brass band to put them off during the annual brass band competition.

A few years ago my mother's sister died at the age of 96 and was buried in the local churchyard. My wife, who had been regaled with tales of my childhood, had some final confirmation that they might possibly be true. When she praised the beauty of the churchyard, which was adjacent to the Durham moors, another 'aunt' then introduced her two sons, two bald-headed 50 year-olds. She said to them:

Remember when you two used to put sheets over your heads with little eye slits and hide in the graves? Then, when someone walked by, you used to jump up and scare them.

When was this? my wife asked.

Just last week, came the answer!

My family was both funny and optimistic. They also clearly saw themselves as working class and had very strong views about the inequalities in society. I would often sit and listen to the men – it was always the men – hotly debating such topics. Very rarely, if ever, did they discuss gender inequality and certainly there was no mention of racial equality. The inequalities they were concerned about were seen as a product of class inequality. It always struck me, even as a young boy in the North East, that the issue of equality was really much more about why working-class children generally attained less in terms of examinations than middle-class children, despite in many cases having similar measured intelligence.

What these family fireside critics did *not* challenge were the 'experts'. Experts were after all better educated, and, therefore, self-evidently more intelligent. Consequently, they were usually right.

In 1950, one such expert was Sir Cyril Burt, pontificating from his post as Professor of Psychology at University College in London.

Sir Cyril Burt: the experts' expert.

In 1909, he published his experimental tests on general intelligence. His studies had convinced him that intelligence was more than 75 per cent hereditary in origin. He did accept, however, that social and environmental factors could play a secondary role in intellectual development.

From the 1940s onwards, he published studies showing that intelligence among large groups of test subjects could be correlated with occupational groups. He claimed, on the basis of these large groups of test subjects, that such intelligence levels were then transmitted to these subjects' offspring. His data seemed to demonstrate that occupational groups and social class are determined mainly by innate, hereditary levels of intelligence. After Burt's death, most authorities concluded that Burt had manipulated and thereby falsified those IQ test results, even going so far as inventing research assistants and presenting impossible data.

My family and, indeed, most of UK society at large knew very little about the research background of Burt's theories, but, like the designers of the tripartite system, they swallowed this view hook, line and sinker. Burt served as a consultant on the various committees that restructured the English educational system after the Second World War. At its core was the eleven-plus examination, taken by children at age 11. Even when the eleven-plus was scrapped in 1969, and before the falsifications in his results were exposed, Burt continued his work by publishing articles purporting to show a decline in educational standards since the 1969 change.

All my family were fully supportive of the first major area of education policy in the post-war period, which was to address class and equality of opportunity. They were very proud of the recently established welfare state, believing the National Health Service and the State Education Service were there to address these inequalities. They wholeheartedly supported the new great advances, the provision of an entirely free state education, the raising of the school leaving age to 15 and the tripartite system, with its promise of upward mobility enhanced by the eleven-plus. They saw the tripartite system as an attempt to bring about greater equality of opportunity and to tap previously 'wasted' sources of talent, including that of my sister and me.

In short, the eleven-plus would be used to sort out the 'wheat from the chaff'.

Our class in primary school. Eventually, this group would be broken up.

My 'uncles' were not all so optimistic. They had strong political views, mainly supporting the Labour or Liberal parties. While my own parents saw education as a means of getting out of poverty, they were less optimistic about the likely impact of the new state education system. The male members of my family were more radical in their thinking, much more in the mould of those who believed real change would only come about through a fundamental change in the structure of society.

They also believed that getting a 'trade' was important, considering that becoming apprenticed fitters and mechanics was a safer bet than taking examinations. Even so, my parents were confident and happy about the reforms that were being brought in, including the opportunity for me and my sister to sit the eleven-plus exam and gain a better life. They believed that the eleven-plus exam would select those who had the ability and then the system would allocate jobs in accordance with their ability. Simple!

Even when I was in primary school, I began to have my doubts. By the age of seven, I could see that some pupils had advantages simply because of their backgrounds, no matter what type of school they went to. Indeed, the 'cultural capital', ideas and knowledge that better-off children brought to the school, became more and more visible. What my parents, who would be so proud of me for getting into a grammar school, failed to understand was the limited amount of 'cultural capital' I took with me. It would hinder me at primary school and was a severe handicap at secondary school.

As one of the first-generation grammar school boys, I would have to face the challenge of working alongside children who had inherited from their parents cultural advantages that I did not have. I would read Shakespeare alongside children who had been to see a play, any play. I would study Latin with the children of doctors. I would study French with children who had been to France. The furthest I had been on holiday was Scarborough, and that required four bus changes and a day-long journey. Enough said, I think.

My family's clear support for the Labour policies started to falter in the late 1950s, when the tripartite system was increasingly attacked by the Labour Party, arguing that the eleven-plus examination discriminated against working-class children. The Party began promoting a comprehensive system.

I often wonder what the ghosts of my past would have thought of the 1980s and 1990s. Ironically, they would empathise with the Conservative emphasis on the link between education and economic success. They would have been shocked by the anti-school culture of white North East lads in the 1990s, who acknowledged no link between getting jobs and school performance. They also would have denigrated and been mystified by a system, which saw young people taking qualifications that did not even lead to a job.

What they would never have conceived of was that government ministers would ever advocate a 'free market' approach to education. To them, this would have challenged the very principles of a National Education Service focused on reducing the inequality that resulted from class divisions.

CHAPTER 11

A WEEKLY MORNING OF MADNESS

The 'Flea Pit' cinema is truly comprehensive and ecumenical, where grammar and secondary modern, Roman Catholics and Methodists come together to boo and cheer, and where boys pee in the back rows and float lollipop sticks down to the front.

We all can stimulate, excite and inspire, as well as demotivate, suppress and inhibit creativity and imagination.

The only active thing about you, Walton, is your imagination.

In the mid-1950s I was about to get another opportunity to learn about the outside world – from the local 'picture house', usually on a Saturday morning. Reading American science fantasy had certainly stimulated my imagination; now I awaited what the local cinema would teach me.

It was sixpence in the stalls and ninepence in the circle. Going with my parents most Friday nights was an ordered affair. We entered in an orderly fashion, sat in our usual seats, watched the two films on show, then stood in silence at the end for the national anthem and finally made our way home.

The Saturday morning cinema was starkly and delightfully different. It was an absolute madhouse: kids pushing and shoving to get in, running around, all trying to grab the best seats, small kids being kicked out of certain seats by the older ones and then universally cheering at the top of our voices when the screen flickered to life.

The contrast with the cane-imposed behaviour in school was dramatic. The richer kids in the circle would throw down lollipop sticks on the rest of us in the stalls. Predictably, every week, Jake Wilson with his twin brother would flick peanuts into the projection beam and shout: *'it's snowing!'*

Billy Sterling was once thrown out of the cinema for peeing on the floor in the back seats and attempting to float a lollipop stick to the front row.

Perhaps it was this experience that reinforced our school's view of the matter. Without cane-imposed discipline, we would, like the children in William Golding's *Lord of the Flies*, descend rapidly into anarchy.

Cinemas were always called 'picture houses' or, later in the 1950s, 'the pictures'. Our village picture house was affectionately known as 'the flea pit'. Rather more than the

The 'flea pit', now a Tesco.

Co-op and even the Chapel, the picture house was the beating heart of our village. It was where most of the villagers went; its adherents were extremely diverse and un-segregated Catholic, Church of England, Methodist, grammar school, secondary modern and privately educated children all in the mix together.

There were three changes of programmes every week at our picture house. In addition, there was the children's cinema every Saturday morning.

The adventure serial was the highlight of the Saturday morning show. There were classics then which still occur in the cinema today. Names like *Zorro, Superman, Buck Rogers, Batman,* and *Flash Gordon* still ring bells.

Some names don't. *Captain Video, Guardian of the Safety of the World,* and his *Video Rangers* serial only appeared once. Yet, *Captain Video* was incredibly popular in the USA, where it ran to more than 1500 episodes. I remember that in one episode the first robot *ever* to be seen on American TV made its debut. I am unashamedly interested in *Captain Video* because some of the show's writers included the elite names of science fiction writing, including Arthur C Clarke and Isaac Asimov. Regrettably, these TV shows were never screened in the UK.

Most of the serials ended with the frustrating and yet exciting words:

... to be continued

or simply, by begging the question with a question mark:

The End?

These were known to us all as 'cliffhangers'. The term 'cliffhanger' is considered to have originated from Thomas Hardy's novel *A Pair of Blue Eyes,* in which Hardy left one of his protagonists, Henry Knight, hanging on a cliff.

Since their appearance in the 1950s, we have got used to cliffhangers in TV series. Possibly the most famous of these was *'Who Shot JR?'* in the TV show *Dallas.* The film endings in our Saturday morning serials had actually taken the idea a little further. Incredibly, we would see the hero thrown off a cliff, being shot by some Nazi-impersonating baddy, or crashing his car unavoidably into a wall. However, the next week we would find that our hero had survived. Yet, we would all clearly recall that the week before he had actually *fallen off* the cliff. However, in the new episode, here he is standing a good 20 feet from the edge or we see that he has just jumped from the car before the explosion and in the nick of time.

Children's matinee performances have in fact been shown in British cinemas since the 1920s. Not surprisingly, in the cerebral hothouse after the Second World War, educationalists raised objections to the nature of the films being screened, leading to the *Wheare Report,* which investigated juvenile cinema-going in 1950.

In 1946, the County Councils Association recommended that the British Board of Film Censors be replaced by AB Independent Censorship Body, appointed and supervised by local authorities. The authorities thought the film industry was not sufficiently interested in the public's moral concerns.

Four new certificates were proposed in 1954:

- **X** – films aimed at adults only, from which children under 16 should be absolutely excluded;

- **C** – films aimed specifically at children;

- *Advisory U* – films suitable for all; and

- *Advisory A* – films suitable for all, but dealing with more adult subject matter.

The creation of the X certificate replaced the H certificate, which was introduced in 1932 and stood for 'horrific'. However, somewhat predictably, this led to many of us in our teenage years seeing entry to an X film as a rite of passage. Some tried to get in well before they were 16 years old.

I remember well the Wilson twins making one valiant attempt to get into the X-rated Japanese prison camp film, *Camp on Blood Island*. Despite wearing long macs, sporting false moustaches and gamely standing on stilts, they never made it.

To me and my Saturday morning cinema gang, it was incredibly frustrating to know that *Killers from Space* and *Menace from Outer Space* were both rated X certificate. Today, I guess, these two films would only be rated as requiring a Parental Guidance (PG) certificate.

Released in 1958, *Camp on Blood Island* was one of the most divisive films of the 1950s.

The 'X' certificates were applied to films for many reasons. For example, *The Battleship Potemkin* was rejected altogether for its 'inflammatory subtitles' and 'Bolshevik propaganda' in 1926 and then rated X in 1954, finally becoming 'PG' in 1987.

My father, mother, sister and I would go to the cinema every Friday night without fail. We would shuffle along the upstairs front row, waiting patiently as Auld George unscrewed his wooden leg so that we could get into our seats. Sometimes, often at a tense moment in the film, the wooden leg would fall into the stalls and occasionally cause minor head injuries.

Everyone would have their own favourite seats. For example, Fred, our local shop-keeper, always sat in the back row downstairs. One night, as my father was locating our seats, he accidentally knocked George's wooden leg over. It fell off the balcony and hit Fred on the head, which wouldn't have been so bad, but Fred fell off his seat, catching his watch strap in the bra of a local beauty. The house lights then went on, accompanied by the usual stamping and shouting. It was a slight problem that Fred was also well known as the church choirmaster and he was now being turned into a figure of fun. Without doubt, if the incident had been made into a film, it would have had to be X-rated.

The Saturday cinema was more than a window on the world. It was, in fact, a window on our village. As the opening line in L P Hartley's *The Go-between* has it:

The past is a foreign country: they do things differently there.

The local village cinema was purpose-built. It even had a pay booth, which was very impressive. In many other remote villages, films were simply shown in the local village hall.

Many years later, as a student, I took my newly acquired friends back to the Dales Village which my family came from. My Uncle George and his friends were playing in the local dance band in the Town Hall. Then, just before 9pm, as I was wandering across the floor to ask a girl to dance, I heard my uncle announce over the microphone that the band was having a break. He also announced over the microphone: '*Leslie, before you make your choice, have you seen the bonnie lass sitting in the corner?*'

Stanhope Town Hall.

Everyone in the hall, including my sophisticated student friends, then began placing all the chairs in rows facing the front. We then sat down to watch Popeye cartoons. Some of our more traditional locals thought that Saturday should be 'strictly dancing' and that the cartoons exemplified the destruction of tradition and a lowering of standards.

Even today, when a visitor enters a classroom and the children are watching films on the electronic whiteboard, there is a little voice inside the visitor's head, which is saying:

this is not proper learning.

It is actually common for parents and grandparents, when we see our children playing with a computer, to think that this isn't the real deal. But this is almost certainly wrong and we should remind ourselves of those long dull days of endless 'blackboards, chalk and talk' and learn to embrace the present.

During my own primary years in the 1940s and 1950s, with the exception of the practical subjects, the classroom only contained a blackboard. Then the only tool a teacher had was a box of chalk and our only access to the outside world was provided by books.

Even in the 1960s, as a young teacher, all I had access to was a Bell and Howell projector and an epidiascope. The epidiascope was a machine that projected pages from books onto a screen. In a desperate attempt to harness better resources, I would book films every week throughout the '60s and '70s from the Durham County Film Library. This was not without opposition: even then some of the older teachers considered that showing films was a diversion from the real job – meaning 'chalk and talk'. Films provided no more than entertainment.

Without doubt, one of the most significant changes in schools over the last quarter of a century is the increasing access to multi-media resources. Have no doubt that this *is* 'proper learning' and it signals a sea-change in our thinking.

We no longer queue up on a Saturday morning to watch spaceships and control centres constructed crudely from cardboard and ray guns made from ashtrays and spark plugs.

In the 1950s, and for a long time afterwards, I always felt a little let down by the poorly designed film and TV scenery and sets. The Walton imagination, so stimulated by earlier reading and listening, is gradually being replaced by cardboard, leaving less and less to the imagination.

CHAPTER 12

WHEN PATHWAYS DIVIDE

A number of things are working in favour of me being designated a failure by a simple test and a primary headteacher, who causes such resentment and anger, that many years later one of my classmates tells me he set his own dog to kill the headteacher's dog.

We should always be uneasy that children's aspirations and future pathways may be determined by simple tests and early judgements.

This is the test for the test which will test you to see if you are ready for the test.

In 1956 my sister, Sheila, had been ill with encephalomyelitis since the age of nine. Encephalomyelitis is defined as an inflammation of the brain. When she sat her eleven-plus exam, a couple of years before me, the symptoms of her illness had already begun to appear. She was a tall, beautiful girl and was very athletic, but I remember that on a holiday in Scarborough she would occasionally stumble. She failed the eleven-plus and her illness was not taken into account when making the assessment.

It was then decided that Sheila would go to the secondary modern school. Unfortunately, she was never able to attend. At the time I was suffering from a very real dilemma, because I knew that, if I passed

Sheila.

the eleven-plus, I would go to a different school from my sister. So, at the age of ten, I had decided that failing the eleven-plus would not be such a bad thing, after all.

There were three factors favouring my failure:

- my age;

- my class; and

- my headteacher.

In due course, in 1955, I sat my eleven-plus during my final year of primary school. I was ten years old, my 11th birthday being in June of that year. The eleven-plus was in effect a basic arithmetic and English test. Some of my fellow pupils had been 11 since the previous September, so in order to balance out this difference in ages, younger pupils were given extra points. It is questionable whether the additional points were ever enough to counterbalance the fact that, ever since starting school, kids like me would be in classes with children who were mainly older. For example, one of my friends who sat the test with me was a good ten months older. Later, in my studies to become a teacher I would discover that children born in the summer months dominated the so-called lower ability groups in all schools.

My primary headteacher was known as 'Two Canes Smith'. The accepted wisdom in our class was that Smith used the long rattan cane as his weapon of choice. But he also had a much smaller cane, which he sported when the Inspectors were visiting. There was no doubt in my mind at the time that the beatings were mainly delivered to the children coming from poorer backgrounds. While occasionally caned, my own suffering was nothing compared to some. A good friend of mine, Alan Skipton, was beaten by Smith regularly every week.

A few years later Alan described how Two Canes walked into our local public house with his small dog. Alan was sitting with his Alsatian, a large and vicious beast. When Two Canes left the pub, Alan followed him and loosed his dog, which immediately attacked and killed Two Canes' pet. Regrettably, a suppressed anger that Alan must have felt regarding the constant beatings the headteacher had given him had reached the surface. The headteacher's view, that caning was quick and soon over, never leaving a lasting mark and easily forgotten, was possibly a wrong one.

Two Canes had created two classes in his head. He called them the 'goats' and the 'sheep'. From my time in Sunday school, I knew that the parable of the sheep and goats is a parable found in the New Testament. On the day of reckoning, Jesus will separate the sheep, who will be blessed and given an inheritance, and the goats, who will be cursed with eternal hell-fire. Guess who was the goat!

Yes, I was in the group that was not considered capable of passing the test. Even then I recognised that the pupils from the better-off class came from more affluent backgrounds – doctors, dentists and so on – while I and all the other 'goats' came from modest backgrounds. The group who were considered capable of passing the test were provided with extra tuition. Sometimes this was on top of the private tuition they were receiving at home.

Results day eventually came around, bringing with it bewilderment. I was the only child in my neighbourhood who had passed to go to grammar school. I am not sure who was more shocked, me or Two Canes!

My primary school was a real neighbourhood school: it was in effect a truly comprehensive school, as indeed most primary schools still are today. It is also true that my other 'seats of learning', Sunday school and the flea pit, were also all-embracing and all-inclusive.

Now, within the space of three months, I would be separated from my neighbourhood friends, most of my Sunday school friends and probably all those lads who threw peanuts in the pictures. Worst of all, in my mind, it was settled that I would never go to school with my sister again. My parents were truly delighted with my success. I, in the end, felt sadness.

My parents were fully supportive of the eleven-plus. They also firmly believed that society could accurately be separated into two types – the 'academic' and the 'practical'. Passing the eleven-plus, using arithmetic and English tests, had now proved for them that I was an academic child. At the time one might have expected that the rest, the practical group, would be given the choice of either a secondary modern or a technical school place. However, this was a problem in our area, because there were only secondary modern schools available. The fact was that the percentage of pupils attending grammar schools varied across the country. The further north you went, the fewer such places were available. So, while in south-west England up to 35 per cent passed the eleven-plus, in the North East it was between 10 per cent and 14 per cent.

As a result, in the following September, I would be walking through my neighbourhood, wearing my distinctive school uniform, to get the bus to the grammar school, while the majority of my long-time friends trudged down the road to the local secondary modern. An inevitable separation from my old friends was being put in place by a bureaucratic system.

The eleven-plus and the choice between academic or practical were very attractive to my parents. They understood the model because of its simplicity. It also seemed to fit in with their world view and the class divisions in society. They liked the idea of very clear pathways for the academically successful into fields like medicine, the law, accountancy and teaching, matched by equally clear pathways for the 'non-academic' children into unskilled, semi-skilled and skilled employment as craftsmen, hairdressers and plumbers.

So, at this point my pathway seemed to be clear. Pass O levels, then move on to A levels and afterwards enrol for higher education. Grammar school students could also enter examinations to enter the civil service, banking and other professions.

For my friends, who were going to the secondary modern, the future was much less clear. They were destined to leave school without an examination certificate and either look for work immediately or go into an apprenticeship, which was a lottery. This lack of clarity over what should happen to the 'non-academic' majority would continue throughout the whole of my life in education. While my education future was more or less mapped out with a clear pathway forward, my friends, some of whom had more challenging, complex and unstable lives, were about to be faced with complicated and ever-changing pathways to education, employment and training.

Now, as I came to the end of my primary phase in the education system I asked myself some simple questions.

● *Will the potential of the 'Genius Walton Foetus' be developed to the full?*

● *How well will I be prepared for life?*

● *Will I have my horizons expanded?*

● *Will I do well?*

Well, my personal report card shows a mixed picture:

Leslie Walton
Early Years' Experience
Final Report

- My parents taught me that we should have aspirations, as long as they are not too high.

- My infant school taught me that being instructed in the skills of reading and writing was something you put up with in order to progress.

- My junior school taught me that the purpose of education is to select young people for their appropriate place in society.

- My radio listening stimulated my imagination.

- My television viewing generally dimmed my imagination.

- My Sunday school experiences widened my horizons.

- My involvement in sport reinforced my Geordie tribalism.

- My experience of the flea pit taught me about life – 'but not life as we know it'.

General Comment: Could do better

So, I am about to enter the grammar school. I am in the top 10 per cent of the region. I play a reasonable tune on the piano. I love drawing and painting. I have an insatiable appetite for learning. Most of all, I have a belief that God will look after me, no matter what.

What next?

CHAPTER 13

I DON'T BELIEVE IN FAIRIES

I enter a grammar school where I meet bullies who 'nut' door lintels with their heads and learn new skills, including peeing at competitive altitudes and spitting through smoke rings.

Some children consider it is cool to demonstrate a dislike of learning and that, sadly, they have learned how not to learn.

The staff stopped believing your fairy stories years ago.

At my advanced age, I am still hanging on to the belief that all children are born to learn and want to learn. However, this view has been sorely tested over the years. My early experience was that joining the grammar school meant that I now met a superior sort of bully. Compared to many children, I don't think I was unduly bullied at school but as an average-sized, useless footballer, I certainly had my share.

The biggest bully I ever met in the grammar school was called 'Beezer'. I met him in my first year and, to put it bluntly, he would punch and 'nut' anyone that upset him. Beezer was a Teddy Boy and a specialist in 'nutting', sometimes called the 'Glasgow kiss'. This was a situation in which Beezer's hard forehead would crunch into the nose of his unfortunate victim. Beezer would, on occasion, even nut the lintel of the door when entering the classroom. This could go wrong and my favourite memory is when, having mistimed his head butt, he knocked himself out and ended up lying flat out on the floor of the classroom.

I learned from long experience that the four most dangerous places were:

- the school yard;
- the toilets;
- the journey to and from school; and
- school trips.

There were also other forms of bullying – possibly with more serious consequences. For example, I came across, for the first time, the word 'swot'. This was the insult thrown at you if you were considered to be too keen on learning. As a result, children who studied hard and did well in examinations were attacked by the bullies. Some of the pupils, myself included, were very conscious of being seen to work too hard. Then, the culture of the school yard had a significant effect on performance within the classroom. Coming from a background that did not value or understand academic study, I was easily influenced and persuaded by the *Anti-Swot Brigade*.

Bobby Dazzlers in our uniforms.

In 1956, I started grammar school, fully equipped with my new blazer, which my mother had made from a billiard table cloth, in the closest match she could get to the official school colours. She had also hand embroidered the school badge. Despite her efforts, I must admit that I did stand out, compared to the other children in their Raymond Barnes shop-bought outfits.

It is hard to imagine today the sight of 11 year-olds walking to school in short, grey trousers and wearing school caps. Just to complete the picture, we also wore black shoes, long socks, a blazer, a white shirt and a tie.

The school yard was the place where my daily ritual humiliation took place when the football teams were being chosen. I would stand waiting patiently for my name to be shouted. Eventually, I was the one not picked at all. An argument would then ensue:

You can have him ... No, you have him.

Eventually, one of the captains would concede defeat and accept me on strict terms:

... as long as you stay on the wing and keep out of the way.

For most of the football games I played in, I would wander aimlessly up and down the side line, constantly praying that the ball would never come near me. It rarely did.

Many years later I made a speech in London and talked about this experience of being argued over in the schoolyard. I asked out of curiosity if anyone in the room had suffered the same fate. Among the small number who remembered similar experiences were: the Editor of the *Times Educational Supplement,* the Chief Executive of the Education Funding Agency and Lord Hill, the Minister for Schools.

So, perhaps it's true that what doesn't kill you makes you stronger.

The outside toilets or 'netties' were certainly dangerous places to venture into. Of course, I was used to outside toilets at home and I always remember being very frightened of sitting alone in the outhouse with its candle flickering in the background, aimed at stopping the pipes from freezing. By the end of my first day at school, my cap had been pushed down the outside toilet and my tie had proved useful for garrotting me in the playground.

In those days, every headteacher would keep a '*punishment book*'. One notable entry recorded: '*Peter Smith, caned four times for urinating at competitive altitudes over the toilet wall.*'

In fact, when I was an 11-year-old boy I always thought that this banned activity was really impressive and deserved more positive recognition.

Then there was the dreaded journey to school. As the only grammar kid in my village, I was forced to walk in the opposite direction to all my previous friends and enemies, wearing my new uniform. I really did wish at the time that the uniform could have been camouflaged in green and grey. As I walked to school, I was often faced with the likes of Ike Charlton. Ike had discovered he was a vampire at the age of six and on most nights, as I walked back from primary school, he would jump out of a convenient bush and try to bite my neck. Regrettably, the onions I used to hide in my pocket didn't seem to work. Nevertheless, I had a secret admiration for Ike, particularly when it became known that he had played truant from school and then turned up in the audience of the *One O'clock Show*. The *One O'clock Show* was shown every weekday on Tyne Tees TV. It was impressive for all of us, as Ike actually met 'Wacky Jackie' and the rest of the crew! Jack Haig, who played Wacky Jackie, was later to play Monsieur Leclerc in BBC's *'Allo 'Allo!*: fame indeed.

And then there were the school trips! One of our school trips in primary school had been to see *Peter Pan* at the Theatre Royal in Newcastle. Peggy Cummins, who later became a girlfriend of John F Kennedy, played Peter Pan and Frank Thring took the part of Captain Hook. He later became very famous as Pontius Pilate in the film *Ben Hur*.

I remember, Tinkerbell was dying and Peter Pan had just told us that if anyone says they don't believe in fairies, then a fairy dies. I was going through a severe case of guilt and shame as I recalled my own doubts as to their existence. Peter Pan called to the audience to shout out:

I believe in fairies.

As we all started to shout:

Yes, we believe!

Ike, in full view of the hovering teachers and packed auditorium, shouted:

Die, yer bastard.

I have always had a belief that children are essentially good and want to learn. Of course, there are always exceptions that prove the rule.

Children today are still dealing with all the issues surrounding bullying and isolation. There are still children today who live in fear of physical and verbal assault, including being disparaged for studying hard. I also know that schools work much harder today to address these issues than they did in my day. It is an established fact that today the majority of schools have much stricter processes in place for dealing with bullying in all its forms. School visits are also governed by strict guidelines. High-standard toilet facilities, where children can be safe, are increasingly being provided. Nowadays, even the playground is seen as a positive environment to aid learning.

However, it is critical to remember that bullying, in whatever form it is manifested, is unacceptable. It is a debilitating and damaging experience for all those involved. Bullying is *not* simply a rite of passage, nor is it inevitable. It can and should be tackled in all its forms to rescue both victims and perpetrators.

CHAPTER 14

CHILDHOOD BEREAVEMENT

My sister dies of brain disease and my father is killed when our new car falls on him in the garage and Laddie, my dog, is drowned in a dustbin by my grandfather.

Those who are wrapped up in the noise of discussion about standards, structures and systems may not hear the voices of children dealing with the transition from childhood to adulthood.

In July 1958 important things were happening. Colonel Saddam Hussein and the Iraqi army had just overthrown the monarch in Iraq. Also, the USA had just tested an atmospheric atomic bomb on Bikini Atoll and in the UK the first woman life peer entered the House of Lords. On the streets the first parking meter was being installed.

Conversely, in the world of education, local education authorities were still reluctant to develop expensive new secondary technical schools. Despite widespread support for the tripartite system, less than 4 per cent of the secondary school age group were in secondary technical. Indeed, there was active opposition and the Carr Committee, in 1954, reported that employers were overwhelmingly opposed to vocational instruction provided by schools.

The Walton family.

However, as a boy of 14 years, and an important customer of the education system, these significant events were irrelevant. More significant personal events had intervened. Sadly, my sister, Sheila, died just after I started grammar school following the point at which we had moved to a wonderful detached house in a more affluent part of the area. Retrospectively, I have always presumed we could afford this because of the considerable amount of overtime my father was accumulating. As Sheila's health deteriorated, she was brought down to sleep in the downstairs front room. I still have a vivid recollection of watching TV and being interrupted when my mother and father came back from the hospital to tell me my sister had died. My immediate response was to ask why God would allow such a thing to happen. I never got a satisfactory answer.

On a Monday morning a couple of years later, on 28 July, my father was preparing our Ford Popular car for our first family holiday after the death of my sister. By this time I was in the third year of the grammar school. I remember that the car had a single windscreen wiper, no heater, painted bumpers and semaphore signals instead of lights indicating right and left. In a fateful moment, the bricks that were propping up the car slipped and my father was crushed to death.

A few weeks later my Grandmother Walton bought me a dog, Laddie, thinking, I guess, that this would help me to get over the death of my father. However, I wasn't allowed to keep it at home, so I would visit my grandparents every weekend to take Laddie out for a walk. Then, one weekend, when I arrived on my visit to my grandparents, I learned that Laddie had been killed by a bus. It was many years after this, when my grandfather was dying, that just before he died he said he wanted to confess to me. He then described how he had filled a dustbin with water, put Laddie inside the bin and sat on the lid until he drowned. Despite the stress of the surrounding circumstances, I could not forgive him – at least not until many years had passed.

It was much later on, when I researched my family tree, that I discovered my grandfather had started working at Medomsley Pit at the age of 12, cleaning the toilets. His own father had died at the age of 47 from a mine-related lung disease. To my grandfather, the death of a dog must have seemed no great shakes.

In my youth, it seemed that death was more openly discussed, certainly among adults, and seemed to be just part of everyday life. When my other grandfather was about to die, he asked my cousin Dennis and myself to take him for one last drink of whisky at the Working Men's Club. It was a Friday night and he held court, as all his old mates popped in for a drink with him. He died on the following Sunday morning.

My 'uncles' were a mixture of real uncles and friends of the family. When one of these uncles was dying, the rest visited him on a Saturday night in the hospital and I watched as they all told him to hang on until Monday morning so that they could 'put a bob' on the insurance. *'No bloody way am I doing that',* he said. *'I'll die tomorrow just to upset you all.'*

Sure enough he died on the Sunday.

To me, death was less of a taboo than among many in my extended family. Grieving, among the men, was even seen as a sign of weakness. This was, of course, true of male adults talking to adults about adults dying. The practice of talking with children about death was a whole different ball game. The stock approaches seemed to be:

- *death is adult territory, it's not a place for children;*

- *don't talk about it in front of the child, or at least whisper about it to other adults;*

- *assume the child has a long life ahead and will eventually get over it;*

- *encourage the child to get on with 'normal life';*

- *protect the child from the realities of death.*

So, it seemed a natural response, when my father died, to straightaway put me with the Graham family next door to play with their son Viv. Much later, on New Year's Eve 1993, Viv Graham, who was to become the most notorious gangster on Tyneside, was shot three times at point-blank range by an unidentified gunman. He died at the age of 34.

As was common practice in those days, I attended school rather than go to the funerals of my father and sister. Both these events were particularly difficult times for me as a pupil, the first occurring at the end of my first year at secondary school and the second at the beginning of the fourth year O-level examination courses.

In my last year of primary school, I had won the English prize. In the Second Year of the grammar school, my report described my work as 'increasingly unsatisfactory' and commented that I 'lacked concentration'.

Indeed, I was never to win another prize at school. The mental, emotional, physiological and behavioural impact of these two family deaths on me as a child was not seen as relevant in a school focused on academic and sporting success. The conclusion I drew from this was that, while my attitude had deteriorated, the only remedy was for me to work harder.

Without doubt, my school was unable to respond to, or cope with, or even engage with my bereavement. As I went from class to class on the day my father was buried, I was constantly being rebuked for not doing my homework. Not one teacher had been informed that this was the day of my father's funeral. Being a 'Geordie male', my attitude to death was a major factor in why I never cried or showed any emotion about the deaths within my family. Certainly, I would not do this in school. The first time I cried was in my mid-20s. To this day, I cannot remember what triggered that unusual event.

Many years later I would be prominent in the development of the pastoral care movement within schools, focusing on child-centred education. My motivation for engineering the establishment of Gateshead Pastoral Care Association and subsequently the National Association of Pastoral Care was to address the continuing need for schools to place the child's needs at the centre of whatever they provided.

Child Bereavement UK provides some very powerful statistics for thoughtful people. For example:

- **a parent with children under 18 dies every 22 minutes in the UK, totalling around 23,600 a year;**

- **this equates to around 111 children being bereaved of a parent every day;**

- **one in 29 young people aged from 5 to 16 has been bereaved of a parent or sibling – that's a child in every average class.**

Without a doubt, there is still insufficient focus on child bereavement.

In fact, it is always so important to remember that children are dealing with far more than just studying, and schools are not simply examination factories. The death of a family member – and that includes pets – is a significant event for children. I know that it is difficult within schools to identify and address the immediate emotional needs of children. The school curriculum, through Personal and Social Education, should explore issues such as bereavement, but that is not enough on its own. We will need a culture of care in the school. It is a crucial role for teachers, a role that involves everyone being alert for signs of vulnerability.

The teacher in the classroom is the child's first line of defence.

We are all there in the school to support one another, whenever that support is needed.

CHAPTER 15

EXTRA-CURRICULAR ANTICS

Part-time working on delivery vans, packing dried blood and fish manure and playing the piano every weekend in the local pub, have a significant impact on my self-confidence and ability to relate to people.

Value personal and social education, always stressing the importance of extra-curricular activities and creative subjects for the development of the whole child.

He used to be a pub pianist before he played in school assemblies.

In my third year at grammar school, I had to make choices regarding my subjects for O level. In addition to the core subjects, I also selected music, art and religious education. As well as being very good in these areas, they were also subjects that I loved. I was then told by my form teacher that I should drop art and take physics, because art, he intimated, was not all that important. I hated physics.

After O levels, I exercised more freedom and at this point selected music, history and religious education at A level. This fitted in well with my long-term ambition to be a teacher of religious education (RE) and continue with my love of music. Disappointingly, I was then informed I couldn't take RE, as it clashed with history. So I then substituted English for RE. I was then told I could not take music, as I was the only student who had opted for it. I subsequently changed music to geography.

This all makes a point, doesn't it? We can easily forget the limited option choices available in a small grammar school in the 1950s. The school also held an underlying, prejudicial view that the creative subjects such as music and art were intrinsically less important. So it was that the personal and social development of the individual in school was delivered largely within physical education. Since the death of my father, I had increasingly lost interest in the school side of my life. My mother had taken a job as a wages clerk at Vickers-Armstrong and we had also sold the beautiful house we'd moved into only a few years earlier. Our new address meant that I had to catch three different buses to get to school. Indeed, there were a number of factors, which had built up over the years, that made the school experience even less fruitful.

I continued with the strong belief that the school cared more about *their* grades than *my* development. I found myself now returning daily to an empty home where there was no back-up, or focus on what I was doing at school. My outside interests, beyond the ambit of the school, were now becoming much more important to me. I worked

Put yourself in the picture about the

new coal industry

Coal is Britain's biggest industry—and the North East's most important. And the new age of automation offers a challenging and satisfying career to young people with ambition—and ability to match.

A career in the new coal industry means an assured future in a basic industry—an industry vital to Britain's economy. It means interesting, stimulating work in your choice of many different, rewarding branches. It means quite exceptional training facilities—really good promotion prospects—and a generous pension scheme.

All types of engineering and most professions are open to you in the Coal Board. Ask about the 100 N.C.B. University scholarships available every year.

Much of coal extraction is now mechanised—on the technical side you can be accepted for practical training and further education under the many apprenticeship schemes available. Boys and girls interested in the non-technical side enter at clerical level with opportunities for studying for professional qualifications.

CAREERS AVAILABLE

Accountancy
Administration
Building
Coal Preparation
Coal Carbonisation
Draughtsmanship
Electrical Engineering
Estates Management
Fuel Technology
Marketing and Transport
Mechanical Engineering
Mining Engineering
Personnel Management
Physics and Chemistry
Purchasing
Surveying

Enquiries to: DIVISIONAL CHIEF STAFF OFFICER,

NATIONAL COAL BOARD

(Durham Division), Team Valley Trading Estate, Gateshead, 11

The school magazine sponsor promoting working for the National Coal Board.

at weekends and in every holiday period to support my mother's income. I also became wrapped up in the amateur music scene. By comparison, achieving at school was secondary.

From the age of 15 onwards I had taken Saturday and holiday jobs. I was, for a time, a van boy for Fenwick's in Newcastle and also found work in local market gardens. In addition, every Saturday and during many holidays, I sat in a dark and dingy cellar beneath Finney's Seed Shop in central Newcastle. This was *not* a glamorous job: I would pack dried blood, fish manure and John Innes compost into brown paper bags, which I had to make from single sheets of brown paper.

After a couple of years at Finney's, I rose to the dizzy heights of working on the shop floor. Every morning I would wax the floors and all the wooden counters before starting to serve customers. Occasionally I would take a trip with Alan, Finney's buyer, who would go out to farms in Northumberland to sell equipment. Alan would often give me 'important life lessons'. For instance, on one occasion he revealed that in the boot of his car was a box of mini pork pies. Before meeting customers in the pub at lunchtime, he would take a few moments to scoff some pies.

This is the secret of selling, he whispered to me.

Eat a pile of pies and you will never get drunk. The lining on your stomach will be protected by the pies and, while the customer gets quietly sozzled, you will be able to keep sober and sell them anything.

I also earned a little money playing the piano at a 'Go-as-you-Please' every Saturday and Sunday night in the Bay Horse in Whickham. I absolutely loved it. The compere, Dave, was a brilliant presenter. His favourite phrase, I remember, was: '*It's nice to be nice*.' So, most of my Saturday nights were full of fun, song and laughter – each 'turn' produced their favourite song and repeated it every Saturday.

The real skill in playing piano for Go-as-you-Please entertainers is to know how to slow down, speed up and even change key in sympathy with the singer. My two favourite performers were Billy, who sang '*If you were the only girl in the world*' and George, who would give a masterly rendition of the German tenor Richard Tauber's song '*Only a Simple Little Melody*' – delivered, of course, in a German accent.

Then, every New Year's Eve, just before closing time, Billy would grab the mike and sing his '*London Medley*'. At the same time, George would stand on a chair and sing German army songs from the back of the room. In the meantime, I would try to accompany both singers, in different keys, while listening as Dave pleaded: '*It's nice to be nice*'.

This growing experience of playing in bands in various clubs and pubs certainly expanded my understanding of the world outside of school and college. Many years later I took a party of German teachers to a working men's club in the East End of Newcastle, hoping the visit would widen their horizons. Having negotiated with the doorman, he announced to them loudly:

We forgive you for bombing us and you mustn't resent us beating you in the war and the World Cup (language slightly modulated for the sensitive).

Anyway, I managed to get them seated at the back of the concert room. Then came the acts:

The first to come on was a woman, who sang Tom Jones songs, including all the hip and leg movements. This was soon followed by 'Marvo, the Mystic', who did card tricks. Unfortunately, the cards he used were normal-sized, so when he revealed the magic card, we couldn't see it.

Marvo was immediately followed by a man in a wheelchair who, having moved the obstructing footrests from the chair, proceeded to tap dance.

The final act eventually killed off the German contingent – it was the final straw in the wind.

It was a man, who was introduced as the 'Ronnie Ronalde of Byker'. Ronnie Ronalde was a famous actor on the radio. He would impersonate different bird songs. The Byker Ronnie didn't quite have his skill and would repeat the same whistle for all the different birds he revealed. He would say:

Imagine yea were waalking through Wallsend Graveyard and ye heard this spuggy.

Then from his mouth came the same whistle we had heard before – it could have been an eagle, or a parrot or even a sparrow. The Germans left with a confused sound in their ears. The prospects for a united Europe would have suffered a severe setback that night, I expect!

Currently, the pressure on students to get good examination grades is bringing about the death of the Saturday job. According to a recent report by a government-funded UK Commission for Employment and Skills (UKCES):

The number of teenagers taking on part-time work has halved in less than two decades, as they concentrate on their studies instead. Just 18% of 16 and 17-year-olds had Saturday jobs in 2014, compared to more than 42% in 1997.

Underlying this report is an implied suggestion that extra-curricular activity, such as part-time employment, works against the education of our children. Yet, thinking through my experiences, I consider the variety of part-time jobs to be an important part of my personal and social development. Part-time work provides an invaluable access to 'the outside world'. What did I really learn as a dried blood packer or pub pianist that was important?

Well, I simply learned that context is everything when you are working with others. Having an O level in music or English does not necessarily impress people in our cellars or pubs. Learning to empathise with others and relate to them was an important experience, which has helped me immeasurably in managing my future career.

CHAPTER 16

ME AND MAURICE CHEVALIER

So why, having been born with the predisposition to speak more than 3000 languages, will I struggle to pass my French O-level examination, particularly as there is a possibility that I am the love child of Maurice Chevalier?

We know not only for our children, but for ourselves, that the accumulation of cultural capital is the key to social mobility.

How many times do I have to tell yea, I'm a Geordie, and 'am taalkin' English.

Learning a foreign language in my grammar school was a challenge, both for me and my teachers. Yet, a decade earlier I'd emerged from the womb with my synaptic links and potentialities buzzing in my brain, and a readiness and capacity to speak any language in the world.

Over the previous ten years or so of my life up to this point I had developed a manner of English pronunciation that is peculiar to the North East of England. Being able to speak in any language involves producing a wide range of complex and subtle distinctions of sound and articulation. Japanese children by the age of 11 will find difficulty in pronouncing 'th', while English children will have a similar difficulty in saying 'f', as in futon. I had difficulty pronouncing English. There is a standing joke in these parts about a Northumbrian barber who was asked if he would give his customer a perm. His answer was:

I wandered lonely as a clood.

On reflection, the education system's decision to delay my opportunity to learn another language until I was 11 seems irrational; somewhat too late for me. In September 2014, it was deemed necessary for all maintained primary schools across England to teach a modern or ancient foreign language to children aged 7 to 11. The DfE also argued that teaching primary children provided the opportunity to explore more creative and playful ways to open minds to the learning of foreign languages.

This was music to my ears because without a doubt my own experience of learning a foreign language at school was short on creativity and certainly *not* playful.

Apart from Latin, the only language I studied was French, and French has always remained a foreign language to me. The three worst French pupils in the class were Geoff and Doreen (both my good friends) and yours truly! Geoff spoke with an appealingly broad Geordie French accent. Not one single person in the whole of France would have been able to understand him. However, I understood every word. He sounded *perfect* to me.

Doreen, who was in love with James Dean and other assorted American film stars, spoke with a nasal American accent, edged cunningly with a breathy Marilyn Monroe intonation. While the teacher announced that Doreen would not be able to communicate with a normal Parisian, I reckoned she would go down a bomb in Quebec. She was also very sexy. I could listen to her for days.

By coincidence, while studying for my French O levels I actually met Maurice Chevalier, the incredibly popular and charming French film actor and singer. It was in 1960 that my mother and I went to the Victoria Palace Theatre in London to see the Crazy Gang in their show *Young at Heart*. And there, sitting next to my mother was Maurice Chevalier! When I heard him speak with her, I realised that I sounded more like him than he did. From that moment on in my French classes, I spoke like Maurice Chevalier. For that lesson (*Stars in Your Eyes* please note) I *was* Maurice Chevalier. My accent was very much French. I even introduced the odd Gallic shrug and raised an eyebrow.

Maurice Chevalier was a good friend of the headmaster of Whickham County School, Front Street, Whickham. There were also local rumours circulating that

Maurice frequently went to Whickham, where my mother lived, in order to meet a secret lover. Years later when I was principal of a further education college, I mentioned this rumour to the staff. Afterwards, a colleague told me his mother had also talked about Maurice Chevalier visiting Whickham.

Surely too many coincidences! I was born in 1945 at the end of the war. My mother sat with Maurice Chevalier in the theatre. He visited Whickham to meet his secret lover and I spoke with a Maurice Chevalier accent. There is really nothing more to say.

The only real problem with my theory of me being the love child of Maurice Chevalier is that in 1944, a year *before* my birth, when the Allies freed

The mysterious and secretive Maurice Chevalier.

France, Chevalier was accused of collaborationism. Even though he was acquitted by a French court, he was refused access to a visa throughout the 1940s.

To the absolute surprise of my French teacher, I passed French O level. I have always believed that there was a link between me playing the piano and learning French: I had achieved a reasonable level in playing the piano and was now beginning to extemporise. This boiled down to playing a crude form of rhythm and blues without preparation, just improvising. My confidence in ad-libbing on the piano seemed to influence how I spoke and wrote French. Never perfect, but good enough to be understood. Somehow this is me through and through. I have been 'winging it' in French ever since.

In the late 1960s, my friend Tony and I decided to hitchhike to the south of France. This was the first time I had had the opportunity to try out my French on the French. Tony had A-level French, but I had only scraped an O level. Surprisingly in the face-to-face situations, I communicated better than Tony. I had that special self-confidence born of ignorance. I made up words, I waved my arms and I raised my eyebrows. Tony, on the other hand, was anxious to speak 'properly' and consequently spoke very little to avoid making mistakes. In a peculiar way, Tony's school, by insisting on written and spoken perfection and instilling in him a fear of making mistakes, limited his ability to apply the very skill he was being taught.

Many of my teachers lived out the Latin motto of the school, believing there would be '*no gain without pain*' or in the education context '*no learn without burn*'. Of course, there is some truth in this. Studying and learning new things can be hard and challenging, but pupils also need the self-confidence to enjoy learning and applying their new knowledge. Of course, in my grammar school, there were always some teachers who recognised this.

Again, I return to a core function of a school, which is to develop the personal and social confidence of children and allow them to acquire the skills and knowledge to live successfully in our modern society.

CHAPTER 17

TEENAGERS

I am now designated with a newly invented title, 'teenager', though I am far removed from the James Dean American style 'rebel without a cause'.

Remember and understand that childhood and youth are a period of multiple transitions, not a uni-dimensional, simple transition to readiness for examinations and assessment.

Do you think we'll ever be asked to do a TED talk?

As a child in the 1940s and 50s, my simplistic human world simply consisted of two species – adults and children. I soon became used to being described as a baby boomer or a war baby. I was certainly raised on strict rations and under the benign care of the welfare state.

There were three phrases that were often used as axioms and applied to us as young people:

- *'Children should be seen and not heard';*

- *'Spare the rod and spoil the child'; and*

- *'There's nothing wrong with him that two years' National Service wouldn't cure'.*

Before my childhood, the word teenager was not part of everyday language. However, the word teen-age had been around since the late nineteenth century. Only after the Second World War did the adjective *teen-age* become the noun, *teenager*.

So, by the late 1950s, I would be reclassified as a teenager. Then, in 1951, J D Salinger's *Catcher in the Rye* supposedly delivered an accurate depiction of teenagers in American society and ours, too. Many considered that Salinger had an unerring understanding of the feelings of teenage angst, vulnerability and anger, and that he articulated clearly what it was to be young and sensitive. As young teenagers in the 1950s, we were divided into those who identified with Salinger's thinking and those who did not. My own transition from child to teenager did not seem to have the great highs and lows that were portrayed by Salinger. The deaths of my sister and father and the belief that we should not express feelings of loss in public led to a quiet numbness, hiding the depth of sorrow I was feeling.

My own Geordie experience was also different from the young Americans in numerous ways – in the cinema, young people would drive open-top cars and, most radical of all, go on dates. For most of my teenage years, I considered a date to be a fruit that grew on a palm tree and was one of the best presents I ever received at Christmas.

My secondary school was small and divided into three streams, enforced by a strict discipline, which included the wearing of school uniform, and firmly backed up by the cane. The chance of us developing our own culture was very limited indeed. My big personal rebellion was loosening my tie on the way back from school. But my Raleigh bike did not compare to the American automobile. While American teenagers were holding hands at the drive-in cinema, I was flicking peanuts in our flea pit picture house.

However, for me, the impact of American cinema and television programmes was small when compared to the impact of rock and roll. When rock and roll came across the Atlantic, it certainly changed how we behaved. In 1954, two years before I officially became a teenager, Bill Haley and the Comets recorded 'Rock Around the Clock'. It was not the first rock and roll record and I still consider that Big Joe Turner's 'Shake, Rattle and Roll' was the first.

On 17 February 1957, Bill Haley and the Comets played at the Newcastle Odeon. 'Rock Around the Clock' had suddenly become an anthem for youth across the world. Haley used the word 'teenager' to signify a more rebellious kind of young person.

Bill Haley and the Comets.

Soon, Elvis's 'All Shook Up' and Jerry Lee Lewis's 'Whole Lotta Shakin' Goin' On' would begin to replace Bing Crosby and Gracie Fields in the charts.

It was odd for me and my friends to be part of a group of people who were described as rebellious and sex mad. For a start, I was no rebel and I thought sex was something you carried coal around in!

And yet, we did make strenuous attempts to have our own language, our own technology and our own political views. True, our own unique language was a parody of Americanisms: when things were good, they were *cool*; having *a blast* meant a great time. We also had our own technology – we were using transistor radios rather than the wireless and buying extended play records rather than the old-fashioned 12-inch 78 singles.

In 1954, Elvis's famous 'That's All Right Mama' came out and within two years he was an international phenomenon. Critics described him as vulgar and animalistic. There were serious concerns expressed regarding the effect this man would have on 'impressionable teenagers' like myself.

A year later James Dean's film *Rebel Without a Cause* was screened. This time the authorities had a mechanism by which they could easily control our access to this film. So, *Rebel Without a Cause* was given an X certificate and this wonderful depiction of angst-ridden teenagers was forbidden to me and my fellow angst-ridden teenagers. For me, James Dean's performance carried a number of messages. One was about living for the moment, taking risks and being true to yourself. James Dean challenged us to:

Dream as if you'll live forever. Live as if you'll die today.

He managed to reflect the sense of impotence we sometimes feel in an adult world:

There is no way to be truly great in this world. We are all impaled on the crook of our own conditioning.

So, would I be great or limited by my upbringing?

To James Dean and Elvis, my little rebellion would have appeared quite 'square'. I wore denim and made my first guitar in my woodwork classes and then formed a skiffle band. To accompany the homemade guitar we had a washboard, comb and paper and one drum.

This inelegant skiffle group was later transformed into a rock band. Amazingly, we even played a rock song in our local church. One Sunday night, our band, now three guitars and drums, performed a rock version of the Lord's Prayer. Pretty impressively, this was more than a decade before Tim Rice and Andrew Lloyd Webber brought out *Joseph and the Amazing Technicolour Dreamcoat*. This was quite a bold step for our little Methodist chapel. *The Evening Chronicle* reported that this was '*a first*' in the 97-year history of the church. Perhaps Tim Rice and Andrew Lloyd Webber read the article?

Challenging tradition?

Nevertheless, a generation gap was forming between adults, parents and teachers on the one hand and ourselves on the other. This gap was the space that my parents and teachers were trying to control and, as they thought, protect us. But the gap was also the space in which we started to push hard to create our own world, on our own terms. We filled in this gap with our own culture – our own youth culture.

As baby boomers, we were characterised as the first generation that went against everything our parents had previously believed in a host of areas – music, values and political views. It is true that we certainly did feel we were developing a new culture by meeting up in youth clubs, playing our own music and wearing our own style of clothing but also, more seriously, by supporting the Campaign for Nuclear Disarmament (CND), which had formed in 1957.

In schools today, we still have teenagers adopting their own personal agenda and unique set of challenges. I don't know whether it is harder for today's young person to go through the transition to adulthood, or not. The range of choices and plans to be made remains vast and intimidating.

In my grammar school, the teachers stressed matters like: learning a language, studying Shakespeare or solving algebraic equations. The problems of growing up, managing physical and emotional change, earning a living and establishing relationships with the opposite sex were for them of secondary importance. This narrow emphasis is still with us today. In a class of 15 year-olds, the combined experience of love and sadness, discovery and loss, friendship and divorce, birth and death, good fortune and poverty is beyond comprehension. A good teacher sees these experiences as one of their greatest assets, a group from which to learn.

Perhaps all my fellow teenagers should have been celebrated and commended for making their way in this brave new world. We were at once daft and yet wise, we were also radical and yet, quite often careful and conservative. We could be cynical and at the same time optimistic. We parroted things we learned in class, while at the same time frequently challenging any imposed view.

The bottom line is that we were in intense learning mode and maybe our parents and teachers failed to recognise this.

CHAPTER 18

YOUTH VOICE

I am about to leave full-time schooling and start to move a long way from the 'voiceless child', entering the new 1960s 'Culture of Youth', quietly pasting a CND sticker on my guitar.

Listening to the voice of the child will help the teacher and the child to learn together and improve the quality of education.

In the 1960s an idea was growing that 'youth culture' was somehow subverting the beliefs and standards of schools. All young people were being attracted to other values, which rejected the regimented imposed education that schools were providing. The new expresso coffee bars were often seen as focal points of this rebellious change. The reality was the impact of the new youth culture varied considerably according to who you were and where you lived.

For the 'Swinging Sixties' youth of the UK, there was an alternative to rebellious change – the coffee bar. This came about largely because, following the privations of the 1939–45 War, people had started going abroad for their holidays, mainly to France and Italy. One thing they brought back was the idea of the coffee bar. The fast growth of coffee bars that followed was the result of Achille Gaggia's invention of the espresso coffee-maker in Milan in 1946. Teenagers were soon made to feel at home in the coffee bar.

My first contact with an espresso coffee shop was second hand at our local flea pit, where I saw *Expresso Bongo* in 1959. In this, Cliff Richard played a teenage singer named Bert Rudge, who is 'discovered' in an espresso coffee shop.

These coffee bars, when combined with burgeoning television, skiffle and rock and roll, were a powerful force. Some social commentators even said they were leading us towards a new world order – a formidable new youth culture.

But it seemed that this was not for us! During the 60s the new-fangled coffee bars were just beginning to gain a foothold in the North East, mainly in Newcastle. Even so, there was a feeling that the coffee bar was for cosmopolitan Londoners and not for the likes of us.

Indeed, the coffee bar never made it anywhere near our village. All we had was our Youth Club.

I had never been a member of the Cubs or Scouts. My father would never let me join. He considered that Baden Powell, the founder of the movement, was a fascist supporter. Certainly, Powell did suggest that Hitler's *Mein Kampf* was:

A wonderful book, with good ideas on education, health, propaganda, organisation, etc.

However, my father would have been happy for me to go to our Methodist Youth Club. It is hard nowadays to imagine that the main social network for young people in the 50s and 60s was through the Youth Club. Looking back at what we did in the Youth Club, everything appears to be quaint and rather innocent. Strangely, the concern today is that the more time we spend interconnected via the numerous online links, the less there is available for developing those true friendships that I experienced as a young man.

In 1961, I was a member of the Methodist Church Junior Fellowship. This was the Methodist get-together for young people and it happened every Sunday evening. The enrolment fee was 2/6, half a crown, or one-eighth of a pound. As time went on, from the enrolment fees and weekly subscriptions we managed to buy a record player for £14 13s 4d.

In due course, I became the Chairman of the Junior Fellowship Club Committee. The Youth Club met in the church hall every Wednesday night. We held debates, invited speakers and ran sports events. It was certainly very different from the social scene in *Expresso Bongo*.

Some of the debates that took place reflected the key issues of our time. For example, we debated the motion *'The age of chivalry is not dead'*. This was seen as an important debate at a time when the idea of giving up your seat on a bus for an older person was fading out.

We also discussed really contentious issues like nuclear disarmament, which was very high on our agenda. The 'Ban the Bomb' debate divided the group and the nation. In 1960, at least 60,000 protesters gathered in Trafalgar Square, making it the largest demonstration London had seen since the beginning of the century. Bertrand Russell, the philosopher, and Canon John Collins spoke. The church link with this issue was clear right from the start. Some of those involved wore Campaign for Nuclear Disarmament (CND) badges and would later take part in the growing CND campaigns including the Aldermaston Rally. The CND organisation, which was formed in 1957, advocated unilateral nuclear disarmament. Nevertheless, in 1961 the USSR detonated a 50-megaton bomb in the largest man-made explosion in history. It was only 15 years since the first atomic bomb had been dropped on the Japanese city of Hiroshima by the United States. It seemed as if we had learned little from such events.

While the events of the 'Winter of Discontent' and the miners' strikes were many years in the future, one of our debates was prophetically:

Starving and strikes. Who's to blame?

The 'colour bar' was another focus of our discussions. Post-war immigration attracted, for the first time, large numbers of workers and their families from outside Europe. People came predominantly from the Caribbean and from India and Pakistan. All was not sweetness and light, and bed and breakfast establishments would often display signs saying boldly:

No coloureds allowed.

It wasn't until 1968 that the Race Relations Act was introduced. It was the same year that Martin Luther King was assassinated at the age of 39.

On 18 January 1961, the Youth Club debate was more parochially concerned with debating the motion that:

Comprehensive schools are better than grammar schools.

Even then, almost predicting my later career, I chaired this education debate! Comprehensive schools were predicated on not selecting their intake on the basis of academic achievement or aptitude. They had been introduced, on an experimental basis, in the 1940s and were to become much more widespread after 1965. The move towards comprehensives impacted the North East later than the rest of the country. In fact, the school I would eventually teach in did not become comprehensive until 1971.

This process, of gradually changing the norms of the time, was to be reflected in our ongoing debates. Some of these would have been considered rather risqué by our parents. One really adventurous debate was:

There is too much indiscriminate snogging among young people.

Another was:

This house believes there is an increase in immorality among teenagers.

We also had talks: I remember one, entitled 'One man's view of Palestine', was delivered by an ex-Palestine Police Force Officer. Mandatory Palestine, a geopolitical entity under British administration, had ended in 1948. The All-Palestine Government, a Palestinian Arab state proclaimed by the Arab League in September 1948, was situated in the Egyptian-occupied Gaza Strip. Later, in 1959 it was to be absorbed into the United Arab Republic.

Our annual talent show clearly reflected the change in the culture of youth in the 1950s, before the invention of teenagers and the introduction of rock and roll. We performed songs mainly from cinema musicals, such as: 'We're a Couple of Swells', 'Oh What a Beautiful Morning' and 'Getting to Know You'.

We also scripted and took part in short comedy sketches. In addition, table tennis matches were played against other youth clubs, including the rival St Barnabas Catholic Club.

To a modern young person, we would have appeared a very strange bunch, when we went to the Methodist Association of Youth Clubs event at the Albert Hall, sponsored by the Halford's brand famous across the land: 'For all your cycle accessories'. The highlight of the programme was being entertained by Pearl Fawcett, the Junior Accordion Champion.

Standing outside WH Smith & Son at Newcastle Central Station, waiting to go to London, we would have appeared distinctly odd to the modern teenager – all the girls were wearing skirts and cardigans and the boys were clad in jackets and ties. This dress code was the norm for us and, indeed, I recollect another outing to Alnmouth when once again the girls wore dresses and cardigans and the boys wore jackets. However, we did feel able to remove our ties, especially for the beach. In modern parlance, I guess we were beach ready.

However, some things never change. I remember, pasted on a window in one of the compartments, was the following:

Special Notice to British Railways passengers: Owing to engineering work on the main line between Peterborough (North) and Barkston Junction (North of Grantham) in connection with our programme of modernisation, your train will be diverted via Sleaford.

In reality, the Youth Club, rather than providing a counter-culture to the culture of the school, was almost an extension of the school ambit. At the time, I was feeling the tension between wanting to be part of the new rock and roll generation, while wishing to adhere to the norms and values of church and school.

Amidst all this 'innocent' tradition of 50s youth, a revolution was surely coming. One of our flock, Keith (Digger) Graves, started a rock band called 'The Grave Diggers'. Also, at about the same time the Beatles performed for the first time at the Cavern Club in Liverpool.

So, the rock and roll years were about to begin, and for me would never end. There is, of course, a danger that we look back at our youth romantically as a time of innocence. But be careful, as this may be a self-deception. Perhaps, many of us had no innocence to lose?

CHAPTER 19

COLLEGE

I grow my hair and arrive in college as part of a new self-confident youth culture, while at the same time child-centred education challenges the traditional ways of teaching. I also plug the lead into Jerry Lee Lewis's piano.

We need constantly to seek harmony in the endless struggle between the traditionalists and child-centred education.

The difference between the day-to-day life of a school and the domestic community in which children are brought up is often striking. As a student in the 'swinging sixties', almost overnight, the gap between the experience of those in education institutions and the experience of the students in the outside world suddenly appeared enormous.

The new 'style' teachers.

I have to say I enjoyed my time at college and I was surprised and delighted in the way many of the lecturers treated me as an adult. I was now focusing hard on my increasing love of history and operating among some very able fellow students. I saw this phase as a fresh start. This was unlike school, where your reputation, whether good or bad, followed you from one year to the next. *Here* was an opportunity to begin again.

There was also a very positive attitude to the profession of a teacher in the wider community. More than twice as many teachers were being trained in the 1960s as compared to 1947. On the other hand, there was a continuing debate about the importance of academic expertise and professionalism. These discussions were particularly centred on primary school teachers and how far training should be child-centred rather than subject-centred.

Because of my mixed experiences at grammar school, I strongly favoured the need to be more student-centred. So, I was pleased that, during my Education Theory sessions, we concentrated on theorists like John Dewey and Jean Piaget, who focused on *how* students learn. Soon I became a life-long advocate of the thinking of Carl Rogers, who considered that the only process which significantly influences learning is self-discovery. Later, when I eventually studied for my Master's degree, I incorporated the thinking of Carl Rogers into my thesis. He was to be a profound influence on me.

The College had a long and dignified history of 'instructing' students, most of whom were treated as passive receptors. Like many higher education institutions in the 1960s, the College was struggling to adapt to a new wave of more liberated and demanding students. The move was underway to shift away from 'training teachers' to providing teacher education.

The challenge to the traditions of our College came from the thinking of the 'new educators' and from the students themselves. Somewhat strangely, the transition from the old order to the new one is possibly best exemplified by what happened to the College dances and the introduction of rock and roll.

When in 1963 I arrived at college, I had already been acting *almost* like a grown-up since my mid-teens. For a number of years, I had been going to see rock bands at the Club A'Gogo and I even stayed up late on the weekends! So, my College and its rules were a culture shock. For example, there was a 10pm curfew in our hall of residence and there were limited hours when friends and families could visit. Moreover, the Student Common Room was inhabited by strange, studious characters wearing tweed jackets and ties.

The first social events I attended could best be described as 'tea dances' and they took place on Saturday nights. The music was provided by an old record player. Refreshments included cakes, but there were no signs of any alcohol-fuelled Student Union events like those that are common today. With one exception of course, which was during the 'Rag Week' celebrations. For this high point, we would go out to collect money for charity – of course, wearing our college scarves. I, like all real students then, wouldn't dream of being seen out and about without my scarf.

Prior to arriving in college, I played in a rock band called The Hustlers. We had started out as a skiffle group with a homemade guitar and a bass made out of an old tea chest. A washboard substituted for drums, which were out of our league. We then advanced to proper guitars, drums and amplifiers, augmented with a Watkins Echo Machine. We all wore obligatory Beatle jackets and thought we were the veritable bee's knees. We had exactly the same impact as the Beatles did – whenever we sang, the girls screamed – but in our case, they were screaming to be let out! It was obvious that many students coming to our College had had a very different social experience from that of the College hierarchy and it showed.

The Hustlers: 'Sach' Saul on the right is our cartoonist.

I can remember going to hear and see the Beatles at the Majestic Dance Hall on Westgate Road in Newcastle. It's a venue now called the O2 Academy. The Beatles were clearly so different from other bands around at the time. By 1962, they were playing eight hours per night, seven nights every week. By 1964, which was the year they burst onto the international scene, the Beatles had played over 1200 concerts together. By way of comparison, most bands nowadays don't play 1200 times in their entire career.

This demonstration of the Beatles' dedication and hard work makes me think about the ideas in Malcolm Gladwell's book *Outliers*. In this, he claimed that it takes roughly 10,000 hours of practice to achieve mastery in any field. Natural talent is not as important. Based on this thinking educational theorists may legitimately say that we can help children *more* by praising their hard work than by over emphasising their 'innate intelligence'.

The club scene in Newcastle at that time was, I firmly believe, the best in the UK. The resident band in the Club A'Gogo at that time was The Animals. In 1964, the band's revolutionary first folk-rock hit, the 'House of the Rising Sun', had just made number one. Nearly every Saturday night we would watch many fantastic bands and drink rum and blacks, while the women consumed their usual snowballs. On a regular basis, we would go to see high-level American artists like Chuck Berry and Jerry Lee Lewis. One night I was standing by the piano when Jerry Lee Lewis played at the Club A'Gogo in February 1963. He actually let me plug the lead into his piano!

For those of us who loved the new music scene, the College approach to socialising seemed anachronistic to say the least. As an attempt to influence the situation, I decided to stand for President of the Student Union. After my election, my new committee and I proposed major changes to the Saturday dances. We then did a very simple thing – by using our contacts through the various entertainment agencies, including Jack Wright in Newcastle, Terry Blood in London and, of course, Brian Epstein in Liverpool, we began to book our favourite bands. These were acts like 'The Big Three': Heinz and the Tornados; the Foremost; Tony Rivers and the Castaways.

Also, the iconic Johnny Kidd and the Pirates – this is a band that still has the reputation for producing the best UK rock and roll record ever, 'Shaking All Over'. Tragically, shortly after performing at our college dance, Johnny was killed in a car accident on 7 October 1966.

Of course, we had disappointments, too. Often we would book an artist and then they would have a hit record. Their agents would then inform us that they were no longer available. This happened to us with Alan Price when he made 'I Put a Spell on You'.

Our biggest *miss* was when my good friend Tony Coleman decided to book an unknown folk singer from the USA. The week before he was due to sing we were told we were going to have a replacement. The replacement turned out to be a country singer dressed up like a cowboy. We discovered that the act we had originally booked had just had his first big UK hit, 'I Am a Rock'. His name was Paul Simon. So, my greatest claim to fame, apart from plugging in Jerry Lee Lewis' piano, was nearly seeing Paul Simon.

To be a student during these seismic cultural shifts in music was incredible. Our challenge to the traditional social life of the College simply reflected a set of parallel challenges to the traditional ways of teaching and instructing children.

The College had started to adapt and the student's voice grew louder. We began to move from the traditions of instruction to a new style of education. Not everything changed overnight and, when I eventually started teaching, I was required to get my hair cut and was compelled always to wear a tie. In addition, I could only use surnames when speaking to my fellow teachers. Female teachers were expected to wear bright colourful dresses. As far as my first headteacher was concerned, rock and roll was dead.

Even today we still continue to maintain the unhelpful gap between school life and the outside world. Perhaps it is necessary? And perhaps young people would not want it any other way? After all, who really wants to see groovy headteachers or vicars on motorbikes come to that?

CHAPTER 20

THE SHEEP

I am in danger of repeating the approach to teaching that I experienced when I was at school, particularly as I am forced to go to elocution lessons. My friend is banned for taking a sheep into the classroom.

A serious challenge to us all is Einstein's view that it is a miracle curiosity survives formal education.

If anyone asks, just say we're in the goats' class.

At College we were allocated schools for 'teaching practice'. I was now about to be unleashed on the unsuspecting children of the nation. I am reminded of the Philip Larkin poem about parents:

They fill you with the faults they had,

And add some extra, just for you.

Would I be like the teachers who taught me? Of course, unlike my own special parents, I had many different teachers. As a result, I experienced many different approaches: teacher-centred, direct instruction, student-centred, inquiry-based, collaborative, autocratic and an almost endless list of minor variations. My approach to teaching was going to be based on my unique set of experiences of learning, my own personal values and my developing thoughts about the nature of education.

Throughout my primary and secondary years as a pupil, I had been critical of the pure 'instructional' approach to learning. So, this would be my chance to rectify things and focus on the real needs of the children. I wanted to inspire them, rather than instruct them. I wanted to build on the child's interests rather than forcing them to learn things which didn't seem to be relevant to their own lives. To put it another way, I clearly wanted to operate differently and to replace the dominant approach of 'chalk and talk', which I had experienced throughout most of my school life.

In 1963, I learned that I was to be placed on a teaching practice in a secondary school together with my friend, John. It was a nervous time because we both had natural doubts in our minds. What type of school would we be allocated? Would we be welcomed by the staff? Most important of all, we wondered, would we have credibility with the children?

This was a period when students were often seen as bringing in new teaching styles. They were less authoritarian and hierarchical than the traditional pattern in which teachers were mostly seen to be scribbling on a blackboard. Today, tastes may have swung back somewhat and it is fashionable to denigrate the alternatives we were advocating as so much hippy nonsense.

Certainly, in the 1960s, it was a time when these new child-centred approaches to teaching, rather than traditional methods, were being stressed. We were given clear directions by the College on how we should speak and behave in the school. In particular, male student teachers were expected to wear a jacket and tie. The female student teachers were encouraged to wear bright colourful dresses, probably in order to 'cheer up the child'. In most schools, they were warned, it was completely unacceptable for a female teacher to wear trousers. So there we were, all ready to go.

Of course, a regional accent was to be deplored. Together with my good friend, John, the son of a Yorkshire hill farmer, we were required to attend elocution lessons.

John had a strong Yorkshire accent and I was, as usual, spouting my pure Geordie. After John had tried to defend his right to maintain his accent he was told to be bilingual and speak the 'Queen's English' when in school. John argued that he was already fluently bilingual, defending himself with the words:

Thou should hear me when am at yem.

I, of course, switched into a version of sophisticated Geordie, which consisted of maintaining the same accent but injecting occasional big words such as 'iconoclastic' and 'antidisestablishmentarianism'.

For example, when I was asked about the influence of my family, I would say:

Aa've been browt up wi an iconoclastic attitude.

This worked a treat!

Surprisingly, the lecturers considered that I was the sensible one of the two and I was put 'in charge' of John and placed in the same school for teaching practice.

One of our lecturers had made a big thing of the different ways in which children learn. This would surely have been considered revolutionary to my old teachers at the grammar school. She reckoned that the vast majority of children are visual learners who need to be shown something *visually* in order to have an understanding of it. Then she claimed there were the auditory learners, children who need to be *told* how to do something. Kinaesthetic learners would learn best by *moving, doing* and *touching*.

Before we were sent out into the field the key demand made by our education lecturers was that we prepare appropriate 'visual aids'. The emphasis was on our ability to *teach* rather than on how much the children learned. This seemed to be a secondary issue!

On the first day at school, I arrived with my carefully prepared visual aid. I was loaded down with flash cards, flannel graphs and flip charts. I ignored the cynical comments of some of the older staff in the school:

You can always spot a student by their visual aids.

And then, John arrived at school – with a sheep. I had never been up close to a fully grown sheep before. This wasn't just any old sheep. It was a Swaledale sheep. A thick-coated, black-faced, curly horned, off-white, smelly, sticky beast. John had followed to the letter the College views on how children learn.

A teaching practice visual aid from Swaledale.

John reckoned this was an ideal visual aid for the children. They could see it, hear it, touch it and even smell it. John had succeeded in leading the sheep into the school and was waiting in the classroom, excited to show the children his surprise visual aid. As I entered the building, crowds of children were jostling outside the classroom, trying to get a glimpse of the sheep. Unfortunately, John's brilliant 'visual aid' did not go down too well with the headteacher. Within ten minutes of our arrival, both John and I were packed off back to College. I never saw the sheep again.

On the last day of the College term, John announced he was going around the world. Teaching, he said, was not for him. Certainly, the kind of teaching that the College and schools demanded was not. A year later, to everyone's surprise, he walked into our pub. After chatting with me and other friends, mainly teachers, he announced that he had just decided to go around the world again. Apart from one postcard from Hawaii, like the sheep, I never saw or heard from John again.

I have often tried to work out what makes a great teacher. Too often I have seen teachers figuratively and literally chasing after children, forcibly distributing knowledge like castor oil. Wouldn't it be great if this was reversed and it was the other way round? Indeed, I have met teachers who were almost like magnets to children, arousing their curiosity and stimulating their desire to learn.

Great teachers are those who can make children think rather than simply teaching them things. I have observed English teachers read books to children in such a way that the children would yearn for the lesson to continue forever. I've come across mathematics teachers who so love their subject that the children will voluntarily strain every part of their brain to understand the complexity of the task they are facing.

So where are we today? The DfE's description of a good teacher in its publication *Teachers' Standards* says:

Teachers make the education of their pupils their first concern, and are accountable for achieving the highest possible standards in work and conduct. Teachers act with honesty and integrity; have strong subject knowledge, keep their knowledge and skills as teachers up to date and are self-critical; forge positive professional relationships and work with parents in the best interests of their pupils.

The DfE then goes on to say the first thing a teacher must do is to:

Set high expectations which inspire, motivate and challenge pupils.

I was delighted to see the word 'inspire' in this guidance. But still there remains a little niggle in my mind that, at the beginning of the twenty-first century, we are beginning again to focus increasingly on transmitting knowledge and skills and rather less on stimulating and challenging our pupils' minds.

Perhaps we are increasingly treating our teachers as technicians, to be scrutinised, analysed and then put into categories?

● *Teaching is more than imparting knowledge; it is about inspiring change.*

● *Learning is more than absorbing facts; it is acquiring understanding.*

I would much prefer a system in which children are being taught *how* to think rather than *what* to think. Schools should be creating young people equipped and capable of doing new things and thinking new thoughts, rather than simply regurgitating the deeds and thoughts of past generations. William Butler Yeats, no mean thinker, summed this up perfectly.

Education is not the filling of a pail but the lighting of a fire.

How many fires did my friend John light when he brought that sheep into the school? Without a doubt, the curiosity of the children would have been awakened and I guess that many of those pupils remember this event to this very day, when they will be in their mid to late 50s.

Einstein always considered it was a miracle that curiosity manages to survive formal education. If teachers can teach students to learn by exercising their curiosity, they will continue to benefit from this learning process as long as they live. Curiosity leads us to open new doors, create new paths and do new things.

Are you, yourself, not just a little curious about what John's abortive lesson would have been like with the sheep standing defiantly beside him in front of the class? After 50 years I am still wondering.

CHAPTER 21

1966: DUBLIN AND THE IMPORTANCE OF HISTORY

My apprehension that teachers must not simply be transmitters of knowledge, but help our young people to challenge and question the received wisdom of adults, is reinforced by my study of Irish history and a group of Irish nuns.

A fundamental question we should all ask is: 'Who controls what we learn?'

It's just fake news written by people who were not there.

A critical question today is how we go about choosing what history to teach in our schools. While battles rage about structures and systems, too often we forget about the importance of *what* is taught in our schools. Napoleon Bonaparte said:

History is the version of past events that people have decided to agree upon.

There are serious questions about what sort of history should be passed on to English learners in the second decade of the twenty-first century.

In my final year at College, I specialised in twentieth-century Irish history. Genius that I am, I never considered the implications of this for a teaching career in England. Unfortunately, Irish history was not to be an agreed part of the English syllabus for most of my career.

In Easter 1966, I sailed to Ireland with around a dozen other students. Our arrival coincided with the 50th anniversary of the Easter Rising in Ireland. We were not at all sure of our welcome, particularly against the backdrop of Ludlow's new number one Irish hit record, containing the words:

The sea, oh the sea ... long may it stay between England and me.

We were led by our history tutor, Tom Corfe, a Cambridge graduate whose enthusiasm for history continued right up to the end of his life. One of his claims to fame was that he won the *Brain of Britain* competition. His many books included *The Phoenix Park Murders*, which was published a couple of years after our visit.

Around 200,000 onlookers and 600 'Rising' veterans watched a military parade organised to commemorate the storming and taking of the Post Office on O'Connell Street in 1916. The armed rebellion, which started on Easter Monday 1916, ended in surrender a week later. About 500 people, including 40 children, died during the Rising. More than 100 British soldiers also lost their lives. President Eamonn De Valera and Taoiseach (Prime Minister) Sean Lemass addressed a large crowd and took the salute in a military march past.

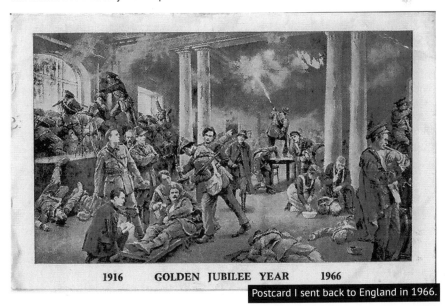

1916   GOLDEN JUBILEE YEAR   1966

Postcard I sent back to England in 1966.

At the time, in 1966, I never really considered the theme of the events as simply celebrating the past. Looking to the future was equally important. Sean Lemass made a point of announcing that the descendants of the Rising leaders were now the students enrolling in the technical colleges. To me, it seemed that he was more concerned about shaping contemporary Ireland than living in the past. And yet, it was only a month before we arrived in Dublin, on the morning of 9 March, that Republican terrorists had blown up Nelson's Column on O'Connell Street. The Dublin City Council then ordered the demolition of the remainder a fortnight later. By the time we arrived in Dublin no trace of this monument remained. This explosive incident accentuated the fear that the IRA would commit further violence during the celebrations. In the event, violent incidents were few and the week of celebrations passed off peacefully.

During our time in Dublin, we visited Kilmainham Prison. We were taken to the Stonebreaker's Yard where 14 leaders of the Easter Rising had been shot. James Connolly, who had been wounded, had to be tied to a chair to support him during his execution. The execution of 16 of the leaders mobilised large swathes of the Irish population behind the campaign for independence from Britain.

Later, as I was examining the bullet holes still visible on the General Post Office columns, a group of nuns realised I was English. They suggested we should pray for forgiveness for what the British had done during the Rising. Without a doubt, we felt very anxious about the reaction of ordinary people when they discovered we were English. On the other hand, when people found we were studying Irish history, they were keen to talk to us and congratulate us on our choice.

A couple of months after this salutary experience, I was appointed as a history teacher to my first school. The irony that I could not teach Irish history was not lost on me. It was simply not on the curriculum. For many years afterwards, as the 'Troubles' in Ireland began to develop and people discovered my specialist area of study, I was often asked:

What do you think is the solution to the Irish situation?

For many years my response would always start with the words: *'Well, it's complicated.'*

In 1992, I was invited to Northern Ireland to advise the Lisburn Safer Towns Organisation on how schools could develop their links with communities more effectively. In the run-up to this, there had been 88 conflict-related deaths during that year. When I visited local schools, some brilliant headteachers were apologetic about the violence taking place in Belfast and wanted to demonstrate that their schools were doing a good job. Whenever I entered the schools they were havens of calm and learning. When I asked teachers what the solution was to the situation, the answer always began with the words: *'It's complicated.'*

Much later, in 2013, I was asked to facilitate a conference in Sarajevo, ten years after the Third Balkans War. The conference involved delegates from what we would have once called the Eastern bloc. There were delegates from Bosnia and Herzegovina, Serbia and Croatia, as well as Russia, the Czech Republic, Slovakia, Ukraine and Kazakhstan. One night a Bosnian delegate showed me the bullet holes in the walls of a church in Sarajevo. They were of course very similar to the bullet holes in Dublin. Again, when I asked about the causes of the Balkans War, his answer began with the words: *'It's complicated.'*

I believe there is a case for expanding the history curriculum beyond the narrow confines of English history. This would reflect England's greater cultural diversity nowadays and also recognise that history does not exist purely within a national context. Studying our own national and local heritage is important. But allowing this to blind us to the complexities of the history and heritage of *other* societies is positively dangerous.

History tells us that things are complex. It is the job of all history teachers to help learners to understand the complexities of the past, use arguments based on evidence, develop empathy for the position of others and expose bias in writing and reporting. Simplistic solutions to complex problems rarely work, do they? Throughout my life in education, I have witnessed a pattern whereby the more complex the problem is, the more simplistic is the solution offered to us. Indeed, history is littered with so many one-dimensional answers to multi-dimensional challenges.

I remember that just before my grandfather Thompson died, he reminded me of the dangers of central government control over the teaching of history. As he put it:

One of the first things the Nazis did, when they came to power, was to take control of what was taught in history lessons.

So, undoubtedly, what we teach in history lessons and how we do it is particularly important. When I started teaching in 1966 there was no central control over *what* was taught in schools. I was unaware that the history of my region would in the not too distant future be marginalised.

I never dreamed that someday, what is taught in schools and how it is taught would be so strongly controlled by the government in power. It is a warning from history.

REFLECTIONS

Looking back soberly over the previous 20 years, my memories of school are largely negative. I do recognise that this will not be the same for all children and young people. I know many children will have a very positive view of their school life. I did have some good experiences, though my memory is dominated by the bad ones. However, I have been talking about my overriding memories, those that have influenced my view of life. Up to the age of 11, I enjoyed the care of a happy family and the comfort of the Methodist community. I also suffered an uncaring and sometimes abusive schooling system.

My memories of my secondary years are overshadowed by the disintegration of my family and a school which cared more about results than children. My attention is increasingly 'extra-curricular' and concerned with the rites of passage surrounding growing up. Memories of being separated from my friends at the age of 11; visits to the cinema; going to youth clubs; playing the piano in pubs; and dealing with changes within my home life built up a bulwark of experience.

I do absolutely understand that other children will have had a much more positive experience of school. The grammar school had its strengths. If you were bright, with lots of cultural capital to invest and did not suffer any significant problems outside school, the school would certainly offer a lot. However, for many secondary-age children, my own story is not unusual. Time does not run smoothly and events outside our control interfere. *For many of us just growing up is hard enough.*

By the time my secondary school career came to an end, I had achieved good enough A levels to go on to college. The truth remains that my vivid memories of this period do not include school lessons and supportive teachers. There were, and always will be, exceptions. There were some teachers who listened to students and incorporated our views into their lessons and others who didn't. What the school system did achieve was that it set me on a mission to address what I saw as an imbalance in our education system. Importantly, we should all recognise:

● **the importance of creative arts; and**

● **that the personal and social development of children is critical for development.**

And most of all:

● **that the right to a rich childhood experience is sacrosanct.**

My college years were transformational. They allowed me to reflect on my childhood experience of schooling. I began to understand that my own experience of education did not reflect the experience of everyone else. I started to develop an empathy for the teachers who taught me and why they taught me in a certain way. I also began to understand that I was not entirely to blame for my own failures. Most of all I was being introduced to a different way of approaching teaching and learning.

I regained my innate joy in learning! I am now ready for my mission in life – to put right all the wrongs I suffered in school by becoming a teacher. The big question is – will I have learned anything or will I repeat the sins of the past?

PART TWO

Teaching: caring, capable, child-centred

Ready to go

CHAPTER 22

THE TALE OF THE POT

My first school has no examinations, no prescribed national syllabus and celebrates our regional traditions and identity, by adapting the curriculum to the needs of our own children living in North West Durham.

Advocate for a curriculum that recognises the importance of a child's heritage.

An early Geordie playing 'Boulder Ball'. Doesn't move when you kick it.

I have had my hair cut and am now about to join the teaching profession, bringing an intense dislike of my own school life. I am also part of a new youth culture that challenges some of the fundamental views of 'how things should be'. I meet the 'new educationalists', who challenge traditional teaching methods. I also work within a system that changes to a comprehensive system, that treats special needs children as second-class citizens and believes the world will fall apart if we stop using corporal punishment to control children.

Sometimes I accept the norms of the day. Other times I challenge received wisdom. I am putting in place the building blocks to my own educational philosophy. At the end of this period, I will be appointed as a headteacher. Most of my values and principles will have been formed through my experience as a pupil and a teacher.

I will, of course, continue to learn, sometimes.

I joined a school that had a local curriculum and a clear sense of the importance of passing on the values and traditions of the region. As a result, it was easy for me, within a few months, to start up a folk club, which met every month in the school hall. At that time the folk scene in the North East was enormously active.

I played guitar accompaniment for a colleague, Maureen, who had an incredibly beautiful voice. We sang mainly American and North East folk songs. Some of the North East songs were well known nationally, for example, 'Bobby Shafto', 'The Keel Row', 'Blaydon Races' and 'Dance to Your Daddy'. The last of these was made extremely famous by the TV Series *When the Boat Comes In*. Others were already very well known in the area – 'The Lambton Worm', 'Cushie Butterfield' and 'Keep Your Feet Still, Geordie Hinnie'. Then came what I considered the most beautiful of them all, 'Waters of Tyne'.

Increasingly today we stress that children should have a wide and all-encompassing view of the world in which they live. They should also understand and appreciate their own regional heritage. This regional heritage is often related to the sites, buildings and landscapes that are perceived to be valuable. However, it also includes the history, stories and customs that are constantly being recreated and transferred from one generation to the next, creating an authentic sense of identity and continuity.

Regional heritage value can be found in a museum, a national park, a street or a family home. Our North East heritage is one of the richest in the world, yet paradoxically, in our schools, it is nowadays increasingly neglected.

In 1966, as a young history teacher, I was handed a priceless treasure. In my classroom there was, displayed in a cabinet, an object of great antiquity. It was a Bronze Age beaker. The pot had been discovered by schoolboys in 1930 when they found it tantalisingly concealed in a stone burial chamber. The Bronze Age in Britain spanned the period from 2500 BC until 800 BC and the beaker was an object of awe! Every September from that point onwards, I would hold a ceremony in which all my new 11-year-old pupils would get a chance to hold the pot for a few precious seconds. The object, always safely protected by my own hands, was a thrilling demonstration of our history for these children.

I soon developed a local history and industrial archaeology programme for the older children. This enabled me to bring the recent past alive for them too. My classroom 'museum' contained another important, though possibly less valuable, item than the beaker: it was a Cowen brick. This object had been made in the Blaydon Joseph Cowen Brick Works nearly a century earlier. Throwing bricks of another sort, I remembered Sir Joseph Cowen, who was a leading advocate of parliamentary reform and became a Member of Parliament for Newcastle in the 1860s.

Sir Joseph's son, Joe 'The Brick' Cowen, later took an active role in the family business and devoted much of his time to politics and particularly to improving social conditions for workmen in the region. As chairman of the Northumbrian Education League, he helped push for greater availability for education and higher standards of schooling for all. Geordie party-goers in Newcastle will often walk by his statue in Fenkle Street without realising what a benefactor he was.

Joe Cowen also became associated with reformist movements abroad. When Giuseppe Garibaldi, the Italian general and politician, visited Tyneside, he and Joe became firm friends. It was even rumoured that Joe sent radical pamphlets and leaflets abroad, smuggled inside brick consignments. In my classroom, I hinted to the children that the Cowen brick might contain a secret message for Garibaldi. Every year, I asked the children to decide on what we should do with the brick. We could break it open and possibly find a message to Garibaldi, or should we leave it intact? There always followed a heated debate but, in the end, the children always decided to leave the brick alone.

Now, over the last couple of years, the Cowen brick and the Blaydon beaker have both become talking points again with my own family. The brick has certainly had a haunting presence over the years. So, when I first took my own children to Rome, we walked around the Circus Maximus, the ancient Roman chariot racing stadium. While there, I discovered a brick sticking out of the ground and I noticed it had the word 'Cowen' imprinted on the side. Unfortunately, at that moment, I did not have the time to investigate further. Despite this, I always intended to return and look for it. Then, a couple of years ago, one of my grandchildren – because her mother is Italian – had to attend a hospital in Rome. While there, I mentioned the brick to my son and between hospital visiting times, my son and I wandered around the Circus Maximus again, looking for the Cowen brick. In truth, I never really expected to find the brick, partly because I was becoming less and less sure that I had seen it in the first place. Unfortunately, we never did find the brick. But, imagine if we *had,* proving at last by doing so that there was a link between Italy and Tyneside's Joseph Cowen!

However, not all searches of this kind end in failure. A couple of years ago, I picked up my granddaughter after school. She told me she had been learning about the Bronze Age. I told her all about the pot and added that, in 1971, a new headteacher had come to my school and insisted that the pot was handed over to the Hancock Museum, later renamed the Great North Museum. He reasoned that more people would have a chance to view the pot there.

At the time I was very upset. I argued with the headteacher that, if the pot entered the museum, it would disappear into a store cupboard, after being labelled by an antiquarian. As headteachers normally do, he won the argument. Subsequently, a rather grandiose ceremony was held and the pot was ceremoniously handed over to the Mayor of Newcastle. My granddaughter immediately empathised with my long-held resentment regarding the removal of the pot:

It would be terrible if the pot were hidden away in a dark cupboard.

Let's go and find out.

It was 3.15pm but there was still time to get to the museum. For 50 years, I had been wondering what had happened to the pot. For 50 years, I had never tried to find out. On arrival at the museum, I asked to speak to the archivist. I described the pot, decorated with horizontal lines, bordered above and below by cross-hatch cuts. There were also cross-hatch cuts on the base, I explained. Half an hour later, the archivist returned with the ledger containing details of pots held in the museum. In Section 13.1, the actual 'Summerhill Blaydon Beaker' was recorded. I then asked if the pot could be taken out of storage so that my granddaughter could see it.

My granddaughter, Maia, was proud to show off her regional heritage.

The archivist then announced that the pot had not simply been stuck in a cupboard but was currently featuring in a new major display in the museum. And there it was, lying beside the skeleton that had been found near it and inside the original burial chamber.

Regional identity and continuity are important. Our regional heritage is not necessarily in the past – it is alive in the present and, hopefully, it will remain so in the future.

CHAPTER 23

THE STAFF ROOM

As a probationary teacher with 'new-fangled' views about child-centred learning, I am soon pressured to ignore modern pedagogical stupidity. I enter a school with two staff rooms. One dominated by a powerful Senior Mistress and the other full of men, the majority of whom had been in the armed services.

Consider the views of all colleagues, while not being afraid to introduce new thinking and challenge old orthodoxies.

If you can read this, you don't need us.

In 1966, as a newly qualified teacher, I applied to Durham County Council for my first teaching post. I was then placed in the 'pool' and allocated three interviews. Prophetically, I was offered a post in a school which was right next to the graveyard where my father and sister were buried and where eventually my mother would be placed. I did think about mentioning this issue at the interview but, as it was rare to be re-allocated alternative schools, I decided in the end to take the job.

My first school had two staff rooms at opposite ends of the school. One for female staff, the other for males. The male staff room was a place of wonder, shrouded in tobacco smoke, which billowed from the lungs of various pipe-smoking and fag-puffing men. Certainly, the female staff room was rarely visited by the likes of me.

The headteacher was a firm believer in discipline and the cane. He was ably supported by his deputy, who never caned and believed it was through providing an exciting education that self-discipline would emerge. This balance of 'imposed discipline' and 'learning-centred self-discipline' was to be a central theme throughout my career. Like all balancing acts, it was hard to get it completely right.

The headteacher rarely entered the male staff room and almost never the female equivalent. There was one memorable visit he made when he asked about the pervasive smell in the staff room. He commented that it smelled like someone had 'peed on the fire'. When challenged about how he could identify the fragrance of electrified pee, he admitted that he used to pee on electric fires when he was in the army. The majority of the men in the staff room had either been full-time soldiers or had undertaken National Service. Personally, I had missed National Service by a couple of years. Unaccountably, the fact that he had fought in the war *and* peed in electric fires increased my admiration of him beyond belief!

On first entering the male staff room, I met the most singular bunch of teachers I have ever had the pleasure to work with. For example, 'Jumping Jim' was the weakest link in the discipline hierarchy. He was to be seen, always wearing a gown, running around his classroom, hopelessly trying to keep order. The one science teacher would sit in the corner all by himself as everyone tried to avoid him. As one colleague put it, 'he bores for Britain'. On the other hand, the behaviour in his classroom was immaculate. Basically, I suppose, he bored the kids into submission.

When a tall good-looking track-suited PE teacher took the place of Jumping Jim, the science teacher then became the weakest link. Put simply, the pupils then targeted him, having reached conclusions of their own. I was also a little put out by the new PE star, because, when I did the odd PE lesson, my usual gear consisted of wellies and an umbrella.

There was also the brilliant art teacher. His lessons were simply a haven and a heaven for pupils who loved to be creative. When we later introduced monthly folk evenings, he would cover the walls of the school hall or gymnasium with newsprint to advertise the event. Then, on the day of the folk event itself, the walls would be transformed into Paris, the Arizona desert or an African jungle. These folk evenings were an example of how the school had successfully begun to merge formal with informal education.

Then, sitting in the corner of the staff room, was Jack Royal, a quiet pipe-smoking man with hidden depths. Both Jack and his classes were always under control.

Paradoxically, many years later, Jack would be twice tried and acquitted, first for murder and then for manslaughter. At the age of 57, he was himself murdered.

Then there was 'Decimal Bill'. It was he who led the charge to convert the staff and students to the new decimal coinage, when it was introduced in 1971. Following an impressive publicity campaign Decimal Day went smoothly enough. The pupils took to the new money very easily. Actually, it was much harder for the staff many of whom, like me, would be saying for years to come: *'How much is that in old money?'*

The mathematics teacher was Don Robson. Many years later, as Leader of Durham County Council, Don was searching for a home for the Durham County Cricket Club, when he received the historic approach from a Chester-le-Street farmer that led eventually to the establishment of the first Durham County Cricket Ground.

There were other formidable characters in that staff room, too. As an example, the Head of Mathematics who was later destined to be head of the local primary school; this was, somewhat strangely, viewed as a normal career move in those days. Then there were John the 'Hippie' and Don the 'Ladies Man'. Once, when Don heard that the Senior Mistress in the female staff room had been passing comments about his night-time adventures in the Newcastle Oxford Galleries Ballroom, he did the unthinkable. He entered that forbidden space and challenged the Senior Mistress directly. On his return to safety he recounted how he had been thrown out with:

the violent sound of knitting needles clicking in the background.

The female staff room was indeed a terrifying place, dominated by the Senior Mistress. She would visit my lessons armed with her 12-inch ruler – the Decimal Bill had had a 0.0 effect on her. She would then proceed to measure the indentations of my pupils' paragraphs. If these were more than ¼-inch from the edge, then my pupils would have to rewrite the whole paragraph. How many senior members of staff today would be so concerned with such hands-on quality control!

As a young 21-year-old innocent, I at least had the good fortune to meet my two new best friends, Ian and Maureen. The three of us ran a weekly youth club, organised skiing trips, set up weekend camps and basically lived for the kids. I think we were probably a breath of fresh air in a school dominated by older, much more experienced and perhaps rather austere teachers, many of whom had served in the forces during the war. At break-time, Ian and I would be out playing football on the rather unsuitable 45-degree sloping yard. We were all committed to a 'new way' of teaching, which involved gaining interest first, believing that involvement in learning and discipline would follow. Of course, the more traditionalist teachers in the staff room would argue that we could only work like this because they maintained discipline in the background, mainly through a fear of the strap.

After a career that has lasted for 50 years, do I still hold on to the belief that education should focus on the needs of children and young people? Of course, I do! Were the teacher disciplinarians right about the background of support they provided? Possibly not. Had I made the right decision to become a teacher? Absolutely yes! To be a young teacher was the greatest thing on earth.

CHAPTER 24

THE THUNDEROUS WHISPER IN THE DINNER HALL

Teachers eat with the children, eat the same meals and demand the children dine in silence, They teach me the point of education is how to achieve 'dead silence', by whispering loudly.

Provide opportunities for positive personal and social experiences for both children and staff.

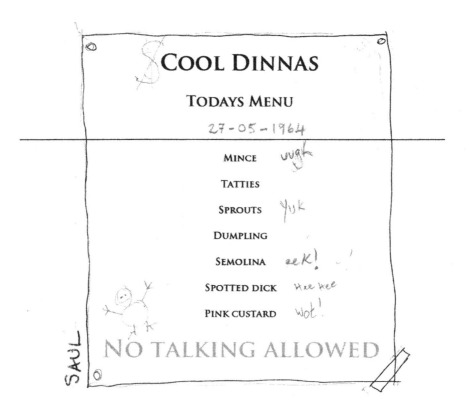

Each day bottles of milk were delivered to the school. All the big lads in Year 4 – what we call Year 10 today – would meet me, guzzle a couple of bottles and then hand out the milk. This served two purposes. The big lads were well occupied with this task at break and the health of the nation was safeguarded.

Dinner time was an important event. All the pupils filed silently into the mobile class-room which served as a dining room. The meals had come from the Central Kitchen, situated elsewhere. In my previous school, I had had responsibility for marching the children from the school to the Central Kitchen, which served a number of schools in the area, and then marching them back again.

The meals consisted of the classic combination:

- **a first course of meat and dumplings;**

- **followed by either semolina or chocolate cake with pink custard;**

- **roly-poly pudding and spotted dick were usually reserved for special occasions.**

We would, of course, say grace before the meal, sometimes using the Selkirk Grace by Robert Burns:

Some hae meat and canna eat,

And some wad eat that want it;

But we hae meat, and we can eat,

Sae let the Lord be thankit.

In 1966, I took up my first teaching post in a secondary school. My induction was thorough, to say the least, and necessarily included dinner duty training.

It was clear from the first day that, while I would have absolute freedom with regard to designing my own curriculum within a broad framework, there would be clear and unchallenged rules on how I and the children should behave.

The Senior Mistress – now there's an interesting title – would never direct me on *what* I should teach, but on the details of *how* I should do it and the protocols involved – like the paragraph indentations of my pupils' work – she was adamant.

The senior mathematics teacher, Ron, who later became a primary headteacher, was my dinner duty trainer. Ron was a heavyweight in the traditional school of discipline. However, this didn't mean that he relied solely on the cane or strap and Ron rarely used such means. His main form of control was his voice. He reckoned that he had based his accompanying *glower* on Winston Churchill, but he would never emit a loud shout, it was always a loud whisper. This thunderous whispering was highly effective and he had the parallel ability to glower with the intensity of four atom bombs.

At the beginning of lunch, Ron simply stood in the middle of the mobile classroom that doubled as our dining hall and glowered, always staring at one child in particular. When the children stopped talking, he would turn to me and say:

That is first stage silence.

He then continued to glower, staring intensely at *all* the children at the same time, no mean feat. He then would ask me if I could hear the clock ticking and birds singing outside:

That's the achievement of dead silence, the one skill you need to know...

and that's what education is all about.

Later on, the PE teacher gave me another piece of advice:

If you can get them through the showers you can get them through life.

Thus began my lifetime admiration for PE teachers, who not only taught the children but had the additional responsibilities of dealing with the kit, handling dangerous equipment, coping with bad weather and reading endless sick notes.

After the Newcastle riots in the 1990s, I was asked by Sir John Stevens, the Chief Constable of Northumbria Police – later he was to become the Head of the Metropolitan Police Service in London – to speak to the annual police conference on how to manage juvenile discipline. Sir John had visited my school and was particularly interested in why children, who had been involved in rioting the night before, were to be seen behaving well in school on the following day.

When I walked onto the platform, I faced hundreds of policemen, who were wondering what on earth a teacher could really teach them on the matter. This is a question most teachers are asked throughout their lives.

There is a real skill in holding the attention of a school hall full of young people at 9am. Indeed, it takes the combined expertise of Martin Luther King, Nelson Mandela, Winston Churchill, the Archbishop of Canterbury and all the top comedians on British TV to run a really good school assembly.

My personal role model was Dave Allen, the famous Irish comedian. I once saw him in Greys Club in Newcastle in the 1970s. Traditionally comedians had always attacked audiences by trying to be louder than the noise coming from the audience. Dave Allen was different, he whispered loudly, so the audience had to make an effort in order to hear and engage. So it was that loud whispering that became a core aspect of my school assemblies.

I showed the police a slide of a policeman on a white horse controlling crowds at the 1923 Cup Final. My caption for the slide read:

Teachers don't need horses to control crowds.

I then 'whispered loudly' to a policeman in the second row, while staring at him intently. Then I waited for silence. When silence descended, I waited for second stage silence. Then, once the police could hear the clock ticking in the hall I began. I then spoke about the methodology of achieving silence in dining halls by glowering and loud whispering.

Perhaps my dinner duty training helped me to understand that part of the teacher's skill is to control groups by using group management techniques. The teacher's voice is their key tool. For too long, partly because of my own schooling experiences,

I had associated imposed discipline with corporal punishment. The fact is that there may be a need for both a learning-centred approach supported by a sensitively imposed discipline.

A big issue recently has been whether there should be free meals for all school pupils.

Many politicians will, of course, continue to argue hard about whether there are sufficient funds to provide these meals and whether the impact of these new requirements will have a beneficial effect on the attainment and educational routine of children. Leaving aside all the financial implications of these changes, it has always been my view that school lunchtimes are a critical part of any child's education.

For the record, I would never argue for the return of silence in the dining halls of British schools. School meals should be more than the simple provision of a balanced diet for young people: they should be seen as a positive social and educational experience. Our children's health and well-being are dependent on our commitment to promoting food access and influencing good eating habits at home, in the school and within the community.

I once asked our chief school cook if she would arrange for flowers to be put on the dining tables at lunchtime. This, I said, was in order to:

... enhance the lunch-time social experience.

She looked at me as though I was mad, exclaiming, with widening eyes:

Don't do it. They'll eat them – stalks and all!

Jamie Oliver, please take note.

CHAPTER 25

KAHLIL GIBRAN: THE 1960s AND CUSTODY BATTLES

Like many schools at the time, the headteacher might as well have posted a sign saying 'parents and caring services keep out'. A Lebanese poet becomes very popular among young teachers, reinforcing the importance of professionals collaborating for the sake of our children.

Leaders place children at the centre of everything they do, then seek to create a co-ordinated and comprehensive approach to education and social care.

I don't want to stay with either of you. Is there a third option?

As a young teacher, my main preoccupation was the struggle about who 'controlled' the classroom: was it me or was it the children? At that point, I was losing interest in the bigger questions, like who controlled what they learned.

Nevertheless, the world outside education did start to intrude on my thinking at this early stage. I experienced a dawning realisation that the children were *also* at the centre of other, sometimes almost invisible struggles for power. I had met this frequently with the parents I had to deal with. Mothers would angrily confront me when a divorced father would turn up at the gates of the school to meet their children. I would also meet fathers and mothers at annual parents' meetings, who would use it as an opportunity to subtly criticise each other about the way their children were being brought up. This game always dismayed me.

One of the saddest phrases I came across in the context of schools was 'custody battle'. When relationships have broken down between people who may have once declared their love for each other, they are often represented as 'battling over the children'. The imagery is poignant.

In the 1960s, custody battles were frequently fought out between social services and education authorities. Teachers at this time tended to have a fairly limited relationship with, or understanding of, the caring services. It was as if many schools were saying 'keep out' to both the parents and the caring services. This was the period of the 'institutional school'.

As my first headteacher once said to me:

When they enter here, they are mine.

He had a great suspicion of the 'caring services'. He considered they pandered to the children and undermined his own attempts to bring discipline to the undisciplined. In a situation like this, the child would often fall through the middle, for example, by being expelled from a school that would refuse to work proactively with the social services who were trying to pick up the pieces.

This type of battle, concerned with who has custodial responsibility for the children, may also occur when a national or local authority is seeking to reorganise its schools. Some parents of children within the schools will begin to 'battle for their school'. In fact, it is very difficult to separate the concept of care and responsibility for children from the idea of *ownership* of them.

Take a careful look at the motivation for change that a national or local authority, which almost certainly truly cares about the children within its schools, may have. There may, for example, be an urgent need to reorganise schools for the sake of *all* children, even including those who have not yet been born. But for parents, the perspective is different and much narrower, as they are likely to be concerned only about the here and now. Some might even say:

I agree with your desire to reorganise my children's school ... but not while they are attending it ... maybe afterwards.

Whenever I am faced with this sort of custody battle, I refer to the writings of Kahlil Gibran.

This man was not an author who would have been introduced to me at my school or college. Although, in the interests of many children in schools, he should have been.

Kahlil Gibran.

Gibran is said to be one of the world's best-selling poets. His seminal work, *The Prophet*, was published in 1923 and immediately struck a chord in the minds of a whole generation of readers. This certainly included me and many other like-minded young teachers in the 1960s.

Since its publication, *The Prophet* has never been out of print. This perennial classic has been translated into over 50 languages and is a staple on the international best-seller lists. It is thought to have sold tens of millions of copies.

Although it was practically ignored by the literary establishments in the West, lines from *The Prophet* have inspired many people in many fields. Song lyrics and political speeches celebrate him. His words have been read with feeling at weddings and funerals all around the world. The Beatles, John F Kennedy and Indira Gandhi were all among those who have been influenced by Gibran's words.

The book itself is made up of 26 prose poems. They are all delivered as sermons by a fictional wise man called Al Mustapha. He is about to set sail for his homeland after 12 years living in exile on an island when the people of the island ask him to share his wisdom with them by addressing the big questions of life:

Love, family, work and death.

The book's popularity peaked in the 1930s and then rose to a second peak in the 1960s when I came across it. In the passage about children, Gibran says the following:

Your children are not your children. They are the sons and daughters of Life's longing for itself.

Despite the immense popularity of his writing, or perhaps because of it, *The Prophet* was panned by many critics in the West, who thought it simplistic, naive and lacking in substance. I am not presenting an intellectual argument for it here. All I am suggesting is that Gibran's views are worth considering and contain the seeds of wisdom. To this day in Lebanon, where he was born, he is still celebrated as a literary hero. However, some political leaders have considered his thoughts poisonous to young people. In fact one of his books, *Spirit Rebellious,* was burnt very publicly in the marketplace in Beirut soon after it was published. It is important to consider such a person's views seriously.

So what are the key messages we can take from *The Prophet*?

- **That the children in our care are not owned, they are not possessions.**

- **If we truly care for children we must all work together in their support.**

- **We should avoid the temptation to try to control the thoughts of children and allow them to have their own thoughts.**

- **Understand the truism that our children are likely to live in a future world which we can barely comprehend.**

- **Recognise that the best help we can give them is a stable present and then encourage them to fly into the future.**

We may need to remember in the end that we have to let them go and allow them to live their own lives. Those responsible for children will accept that children should not be part of a tug-of-war. We must all do the best we can to provide a stable and harmonious platform, focused on the needs of children and not the needs of either the government or the parents.

Is this too much to ask from those who love their children?

CHAPTER 26

THE DURHAM DISPUTE

I enter a profession, purporting to place the child at the centre of everything, and then take part in one of the most acrimonious industrial disputes in modern education history.

Maintain a positive and constructive professional dialogue with all colleagues, whether we agree with them or not.

There was a very popular slogan that was often seen being paraded, whenever teachers took industrial action in the 1960s. It read as follows:

If you can read this sign, thank a teacher.

When I joined my first school, the majority of the male staff were members of the National Association of Schoolmasters, the NAS. I had already been recruited to the union as a student and, therefore, it was natural to continue my membership, once I joined the teaching force. At that time the teacher unions were very influential.

Student demonstration in London 1972. March of 10,000 organised by the Schools Action Union and the National Union of School Students.

Even pupils had begun joining unions. In 1968, the National Union of Students allowed full-time students over 15 years of age to join the union as 'Associates'. In May 1972, the newly established National Union of School Students held its founding conference.

As I progressed in my career the teacher unions became less and less influential. There is now a mixed view as to whether the unions have a positive or negative effect on schools and therefore on the lives of our children.

However, like my family, I was very clear about the relevance of trade unions in the 1960s. It was a simple matter. If teachers' rights were protected and teachers were well rewarded with good working conditions and pay, then in turn the children would benefit from a fulfilled and contented profession. This fitted nicely with my view of young children. If we removed the obstacles to the pupil's and teacher's natural desire to learn and to teach respectively, then things would be OK.

One of my contractual requirements as a teacher was to supervise children at lunchtime.

In 1969, during my third year of teaching, the National Association of Schoolmasters was involved in an industrial action in County Durham which, to say the least, was widespread and highly acrimonious. This action was also supported by the recently formed Union of Women Teachers, created with similar perspectives on education. The original cause of the action was disaffection over pay. However, this initial cause was soon lost in the bitterness of the ensuing dispute.

The teachers' action primarily involved a withdrawal from lunchtime supervision. I remember that in County Durham it began in Milton Hall and Acre Rigg schools.

In response, the Council ordered their officials to visit the schools personally to discipline NAS members. The union members were then issued with letters of suspension and ordered to leave the premises. As a follow-up, the members were visited in their homes by Local Education Authority officials and formally suspended.

As a result of these procedures, all Durham members, excluding probationary staff, were called out on a half-day strike on 20 February 1969. Over 800 of them then met in the Palladium Cinema in Durham. Following another breakdown in negotiations, the Durham NAS instructed its members that, from 24 February, they should refuse to handle any school dinner money for a period of two weeks.

This was a perfectly legitimate action because there had been a High Court judgment in 1956, which secured the right of teachers to decline to undertake such voluntary duties. The Director of Education and senior staff then toured the schools, attempting to collect dinner money between lessons!

On 5 March, the LEA clamped down on all leave for teachers to attend in-service courses. At this point, two more schools joined in the action, Clegwell School in Hebburn and Hermitage School in Chester-le-Street.

On 15 April, when I attended the NAS Conference in Eastbourne, the Durham delegates were given a heroes' reception.

By this time the dispute was beginning to impinge on preparation for public examinations, for the GCE and the Northern Counties CSE. Partly to deal with this, the Director of Education chose to make a distinction between 'suspension' and 'exclusion'. Paradoxically, this apparently meant that excluded teachers could return to work. Following a further breakdown in talks, four more secondary schools joined the action and 32 members teaching at schools in Murton, Whickham, Heworth and Sedgefield were immediately suspended.

In addition, four headteachers were suspended for obstructing staff in the collection of school meals money. In order to undermine the action, teachers from other unions were now being sent to replace those who were suspended. As a direct result, one NAS deputy head and three NAS teachers were then suspended for refusing to work with these 'blacklegs'. In one case, County Durham sent a teacher to take charge of the class of a NAS teacher at Chopwell School. The acting headteacher, incensed by this action, refused to allow the teacher into the school and he was immediately suspended from his post.

The *Newcastle Journal* of 29 April reported that:

Attitudes had hardened on both sides.

Sixty-three of the suspended NAS members were finally given notice of dismissal to take effect from 6 May, 'unless they returned to normal work'. At this point in professional solidarity, the other main union, the National Union of Teachers, announced that they were prepared to strike in all those schools with the suspended NAS members.

At the same time, a national levy of £2 per member was raised, which would be used to ensure that those excluded would receive full reimbursement of their net pay. Following a series of meetings between the NAS and Durham County Council, it seemed at first that some progress was being made to resolve the dispute. However, one of the key obstacles, the restitution of salary for reinstated teachers, still remained unresolved.

Meanwhile, the Secretary of State, Ted Short, despite his earlier career as a headteacher in Northumberland, refused to intervene:

Unless the service was threatened with disruption.

As a result of this, the NAS decided to escalate the action and over 10,000 schoolchildren were faced with having their education seriously disrupted. At the beginning of June, the *Newcastle Journal* carried the headline:

County schools on brink of breakdown.

A few days later, on the 18 and 19 of June, 35 members teaching in the four voluntary Roman Catholic schools, which had recently joined the action, were suspended. The number now suspended had reached nearly 200 and included some women members.

By July, with just three weeks of the school term remaining, Barbara Castle and Ted Short, Secretaries of State for Employment and Education, announced that they would jointly sponsor an inquiry into the dispute. The NAS issued a press statement indicating that they would welcome such an inquiry. The NAS then instructed its suspended members in four primary and four voluntary secondary schools, who were engaged in the action, to resume normal working. They also said they were prepared to instruct their members at the 14 other secondary schools involved to return to duty if the LEA reinstated them without penalty. The County Durham LEA turned down this offer. But the Roman Catholic Authorities accepted it.

The Court of Inquiry published its findings on 22 August. It concluded that the central nub of the residual dispute lay in the question of payment for the period of suspension. It was unequivocal in its judgment. They concluded that the initial decision to suspend the teachers had been unjustified. Thus, they should be fully paid for their period of exclusion. Both sides were then criticised on other points and offered some well-meaning advice on how to improve relations.

In due course, the NAS agreed to accept the report. The NAS accepted the inquiry's judgment that work-to-rule tactics:

are not suited to the advancement of stable joint relationships in the teaching profession.

Durham accepted that the excluded teachers should be reinstated under the terms specified within the Agreement and be paid for the period of exclusion.

The Chairman of the Durham Education Committee was later to issue a statement saying:

We have not been looking for success or defeat. We are glad it is all over.

Both sides have had to make concessions and this was the only way that the decision would be reached.

After the final discussion between the NAS and Durham LEA in Durham County Hall, everyone on all sides agreed the dispute was over.

These events were to leave an indelible mark on all those who were involved, on all sides. The headteachers who were suspended were honourable, highly principled people. They truly believed that what they were doing was in the best long-term interests of children. I am also certain that they would never wish to be involved in such a situation again. Could we ever return to such an unpleasant, uncivilised climate again? Personally, I do hope not.

CHAPTER 27

PERLS OF WISDOM

I am beginning to work out my personal educational philosophy, which is so mixed up I end up combining the views of Fritz Perls and Popeye. Popeye, because of his self-confidence in his own ability and Perls because of his advocacy for high self-esteem and not depending on the judgement of others.

Leaders must not simply operate as technicians without being able to elucidate their own personal philosophies, values and beliefs.

Popeye: I yam what I yam.

Unlike Popeye, for a lot of my time in education, I have struggled with my lack of confidence over what I believe in. Over the years, I have met so many people in education, who are absolutely self-assured in their views of how things should be in schools. I suppose the one thing I really do believe in is *continuous learning*. In order to learn, one must constantly be challenging one's own beliefs, as well as positively responding to new thinking and ideas.

In 1969, in my third year of teaching, the world that I knew seemed to kick into another gear. It was a year in which everything seemed to be changing under our feet. While we now had Concorde and the Boeing 747, and England were still world champions at football, the optimism of the 'swinging sixties' was being replaced by realism and some sadness. US troops had massacred 109 villagers in My Lai. The Beatles' last performance took place at the Apple HQ and Woodstock seemed to signal the end of 'the summer of love'. For me, I was particularly saddened that Kenneth Horne, the compere of the funniest show I have ever heard on the radio, had died at the age of 61.

On home turf, the 'Troubles' came again to Northern Ireland and this was followed by the deployment of the British army. Those who knew that I had studied Irish history would start asking the question that would last for the next 50 years:

What is the solution to the Northern Ireland problem?

My answer was always the same:

I don't know, I am not clear about the best way forward.

Towards the end of the 1960s, *other* troubles were looming too. Relations between the Labour Party and the trade unions were becoming strained. Then, in the 1969 White Paper 'In Place of Strife', the Secretary of State for Employment and Productivity, Barbara Castle, argued for the replacement of voluntary collective bargaining by more vigorous state intervention. This proved very confusing for my parents, who had always had a clear view about the importance of the unions and their relationship with the Labour Party. The industrial unrest that resulted was soon to engulf the school in which I worked and began to cloud my views on the professional responsibilities of teachers for children.

This lack of political clarity was also reflected in my own philosophy of education. Now I was trying to articulate my own values and beliefs more clearly and consistently.

I *was* clear about what I *didn't* believe in. I didn't believe that education should be limited to instruction – education as a training model. Neither did I believe that education was simply a matter of passing on subject knowledge, although I did understand that society will only make progress if it hands on what it has learned from one generation to the next. In addition to doubts and anxieties, I also had a set of new and developing beliefs.

- I believed that education should be concerned with the personal and social development of children as well as their academic development.

- I believed that we learn best if we discover answers ourselves rather than simply being presented with 'solutions'.

- I wanted to celebrate the individuality of all our children.

- I wanted it to be recognised that group collaboration is capable of delivering tremendous opportunities for young people.

While I had not by this point developed a fully formed philosophical and values basis for how I approached teaching, at least I was in the continuing process of learning and developing my own thinking.

In the 1960s my approach to education, like most teachers before and since, was profoundly influenced by the philosophers and psychologists who were prominent at the time.

Among the most influential of these thinkers were the Gestalt theorists. They had been around since the 1920s and they struck a chord with many 1960s students. We were all heavily involved in discussions about the need for individual liberty and working together to create a better world. The most popular phrase associated with Gestalt psychological theory is:

The whole is greater than the sum of the parts.

For example, the whole – say a picture of an aircraft – carries a different and altogether greater meaning than its individual component elements – items like paint, doors, windows and wheels. However, quite often this phrase is, in my view, wrongly used to suggest that the group is more important than the individual.

In 1969, I read that Fritz Perls, the noted German-born psychiatrist, had coined the term Gestalt Therapy and published the 'Gestalt Prayer'. You may like to note that he translates Popeye's mantra into a simple formula and then penned the prayer, which inspired so many of us:

Fritz Perls: *'You are you and I am I'.*

I do my thing and you do your thing.
I am not in this world to live up to your expectations,
And you are not in the world to live up to mine.
You are you, and I am I,
And if by chance we find each other, it's beautiful.
If not, it can't be helped.

Fritz Perls, Gestalt Therapy Verbatim, 1969

This prayer clearly reinforces the great importance of individualism within the group. It also forms a basis for learning by discovery. These thoughts struck a chord with many young teachers like me, who were particularly attracted by the concepts of individualism within our communities.

Of course, over the years, many new influences and new ways of thinking have influenced educators. However, when I and my fellow 'gadgees' are sitting in conferences listening to debates about national strategies, national testing regimes, national inspection and the National Curriculum, our minds will often wander back to the glorious days of individual freedom of expression and peace and love!

The truth is that the thinking of Gestalt theorists like Perls still challenge our thinking today. How can you develop leadership skills in young headteachers without giving them a chance to fail? Perls would probably comment:

Nobody can stand truth if it is told to him. Truth can be tolerated only if you discover it yourself, because then the pride of discovery makes the truth palatable.

How frequently is a school's judgement of itself seemingly dependent on the views of external inspectors or those who seek to judge from afar? Perls would question the wisdom of this externalisation of judgment.

Our dependency makes slaves out of us, especially if this dependency is a dependency of our self-esteem. If you need encouragement, praise, pats on the back from everybody, then you make everybody your judge.

Many years later Professor Tim Brighouse, a living legend in the world of education and a fellow oldie, reinforced this view by indicating that organisations should always judge themselves by their previous best, not by the best of the rest. We really don't want to create schools that are simply copies of a national model. Don't let us create teachers who blindly teach by an authority-driven formula, nor do we want children who learn by numbers.

I leave you with the final word from Frederick Salmon Perls – a 'pearl' of wisdom, indeed:

A thousand plastic flowers don't make a desert bloom. A thousand empty faces don't fill an empty room.

Learning is the discovery that something is *possible*, not that it is impossible.

Fifty years later, in October 2014, I attended a national education conference. The discussions throughout the day focused on structures, systems, planning, marketing, financial management, network management and leadership. Not one speaker took time to elucidate their own personal philosophies, values and beliefs. This was in stark contrast to the atmosphere generated in the conferences we all attended in the 1960s.

All the discussion at this 2014 conference was centred on presenting a response to possible future government policy. Sadly, it is now rare to hear different views on the philosophical or the psychological bases of education at events ostensibly aimed at developing the education necessary for tomorrow.

CHAPTER 28

ANOTHER BRICK IN THE WALL

I discover Paulo Freire, who brilliantly articulates what I have been thinking for so many years. Mode 3 CSE allows me to involve children as 'co-designers' of their curriculum. We disadvantage our futures by not incorporating the views of children.

Recognise that children have a human right to be actively involved in their learning, and are not just empty vessels to be filled.

I expect you to be independent, innovative, critical thinkers who will do exactly as I say.

In the 1970s, with half a decade of lessons under my belt, I continued to wrestle with the idea of child-centred education, and my ongoing experience of a school that heavily emphasised the need for control and the instruction of children. The best way I can describe how I managed the situation, like most things in my life, is to avoid taking an extreme stance one way or the other and look for the middle ground.

Indeed, this could be the central plank of my educational experience. I have held to the belief that, If education is to evolve and develop in a positive way, it requires all education leaders to seek consensus – this is so, whether they are politicians, school leaders or leading members of communities. It goes without saying that this would be a consensus that places the child at the centre.

Conversely, many influential educational thinkers at the time were challenging the very idea that education was there essentially to serve the needs of children, or even the economy. To many of these new pedagogues, the education system was just another way in which the present elite could maintain itself while oppressing the poor. This was certainly new thinking to me. Can we truly have child-centred education within a system, which exists primarily to maintain the power of privileged groups? As a teacher, was I just fooling myself? Do our schools, by their nature simply reflect a particular position in the continual struggle about who controls what our children learn?

In the 1960s and 1970s popular songs that were frequently critical of the controlling influence of teachers had begun to appear. These new 'protest songs' contrasted with the Beach Boys' very pro-school song in 1963, abjuring us to:

Be true to your school. Just like your gal or guy.

A year later Tom Paxton sang '*What did you learn in school today?*', a song about the American school system. It expressed doubts about the way that schools were misinforming children by presenting an optimistic outlook on history – a view that they claimed was just not true.

The ultimate school protest song came along in 1979 in the Pink Floyd rock opera *The Wall*. So it was, that 'Another Brick in the Wall' became a serious protest song rejecting rigid schooling in general and boarding schools in the UK in particular. One song struck a serious note:

We don't need no thought control.

With this one track, Pink Floyd provided a voice for millions of students across the globe. In this way during the 1970s the big protest began, targeting the controlling influence that teachers had over children.

In 1972, the English translation of one of this period's most influential books about education was published. Every so often I have had the good fortune to read a book that not only transforms my thinking but more importantly affects my day-to-day experience.

Pedagogy of the Oppressed was such a book. It was written by the educator Paulo Freire and has achieved near-iconic status. The publisher sold almost one million copies, which is a truly remarkable number for a book operating in a crowded educational field. I have never thought it was a coincidence that Pink Floyd came along so soon after Paulo Freire. Freire calls our traditional pedagogy the '*banking model*' because it treats the student as an empty vessel or '*tabula rasa*', in effect simply a vessel waiting to be filled with knowledge, like a piggy bank.

However, Freire argued for a new pedagogy, which would treat the learner as a co-creator of knowledge. In addition, he argued the banking model will stimulate and reinforce oppressive attitudes and practices in society. In his ideal world, the child would be an *active learner*. The transmission of mere facts should not be the end goal of those responsible for educating our children.

When new CSE examinations were introduced in the 1960s, control had moved away from the universities. It was the teachers who were now the designers of the curriculum. The days when politicians became curriculum designers, would come later. Teacher con-

PEDAGOGY OF THE OPPRESSED
PAULO FREIRE

New revised edition of this international classic

Paulo Freire, a Brazilian educator and philosopher, was a leading advocate of critical pedagogy.

trol over the curriculum content was an important feature of CSE administration in all its three modes – even for CSE 'Mode 1', which was externally set and examined. The subject committees which determined the content of syllabuses were dominated by teachers rather than university academics. Perhaps this was a move in the right direction. Clearly, it meant that the design of what was taught and examined would be closer to the child.

The new CSE 'Mode 3' examinations allowed individual teachers to devise their syllabus, get it approved and then examine and mark it, supported through moderation by other teachers from outside the school involved. This was a popular option for enthusiastic and innovative teachers. However, the thought that *pupils* could co-design the syllabuses was very rarely even considered. The teacher still decided what was to be taught and the pupils accepted what was given. There was also one major drawback during this period. While CSE Mode 3 offered much in terms of innovation, pupils at that time weren't entitled by law to receive a broad and balanced offer.

I attempted to apply aspects of Freire's thinking to our Mode 3 Social Studies syllabus. I made sure that the pupils were involved, albeit in a very limited way, at the design stage. Part of the syllabus encouraged the children in my school to understand why they were described as deprived and understand the barriers standing in the way of their success. So:

- **we examined the health and economic limitations they faced within the North East; and**

- **we analysed why they had fewer opportunities for employment, poorer health and even lower life expectancy.**

We believed that, if our pupils understood why poorer white children from their part of the North East did not succeed and recognised their own part in this process, then they might be able to do something about the blockages.

This sort of thinking became a critical building block in my personal educational philosophy. I continue to reject the idea that we routinely need to compensate for the individual failings of our poorer children. I refuse to use the phrase 'disadvantaged children'. It is our society itself that is disadvantaged by not accessing the tremendous potential that these children possess. I am delighted to say that my own children have, in their turn, taken up the mantle of supporting children in need. Our poorer children must not be treated as unfortunates nor should we present middle-class children as models to which they must aspire.

Today we believe it is both the art of teaching and the duty of any teacher to engage the young people in their own learning and make the subject matter relevant and interesting.

Education should be a *shared* journey, rigorously taught and rigorously assessed. I would go even further than this. We also need our children to examine their own role in how *they themselves* can limit or expand their own opportunities. The school should be a partner with children, helping them to overcome the barriers, which mask and limit their opportunities.

Protest songs about the controlling influence of teachers over what is taught in schools are rarely heard nowadays. Ironically, with the increasing autonomy of schools in organisational terms, control over curriculum design has moved progressively further away from the pupil and the teacher. Curriculum matters now lie firmly in the hands of the central government, or more worryingly, in the hands of individual government ministers.

The voice of the child in the design of the curriculum was rarely heard in the 1960s and 1970s. Today it is the teachers' voice that is increasingly silent.

There is now not only another brick in the wall ... there is now another wall altogether.

CHAPTER 29

THE PASTORAL HEAD

As a pastoral head in one of the new comprehensive schools, I realise that the headteacher wants me to mainly 'sort out' non-academic children. What this really means is 'don't interfere in the curriculum or how lessons are taught, just discipline them and make sure they turn up for school.'

Positive relationships with parents and other agencies are the prerequisite to building positive relationships with children.

More truancy equals less overcrowding. I'm just doing my bit to help.

As we sat expectantly in the grammar school hall, the Director of Education and the headteacher from the grammar school, together with the designated head of the comprehensive school, entered the room. The headteacher was carrying a blackboard, which he held closely to his chest and then placed on a stand. It revealed a staffing structure chart.

Unfortunately, the blackboard was too far away for us to read and the headteacher had partly rubbed out some of the words with his jacket, which he then spent several minutes furiously rewriting onto the chart.

I was Head of History & Social Studies within the secondary modern school and I desperately searched for my job on the blackboard. My job simply wasn't there. Instead, there were new titles such as Head of Humanities along with several heads of year.

The next day the headteacher called me in and said 'I was a very lucky young man.' He announced that I was to be appointed to a Grade 4 post. I was to be the only promotion from my school. Moving from a Grade A, head of department, to Grade 4 produced an enormous leap in salary. He also said that he was to become a head of year, along with his two deputy heads, in effect all on the same grade as me. It was hard for me to be pleased with this massive promotion when I realised that my former seniors, who would take over the roles of heads of year, were essentially facing demotion.

Much later I would, in my turn, be asked to reorganise and merge schools as a director of education; then, later still, to outsource a local authority and merge two FE colleges. The clear lessons I learned from my own early experience of a comprehensive restructure suggest that change management requires empathy and a shared understanding of the reasons why the change is necessary. These were elements that were clearly missing from my first experience of reorganisation.

At this time the concept of a year head or a pastoral head was brand new. After two weeks in the job, the headteacher asked if I would explain what is involved in his local round table meeting. When I asked what I should say, he admitted that he hadn't a clue, as he wasn't quite sure what my job entailed, either. Accordingly, I decided to describe my role as working with parents and other agencies in order to improve their children's chances in school. To a former grammar school headteacher, this was all very new, because he had been used to working with parents, most of whom were supportive of education. His experience of working with parents who were not so positive was non-existent.

A couple of years ago a headline in the *Times* suggested rather a punitive action:

Fine parents who don't read to children, says Schools' Chief.

Sir Michael Wilshaw was then the Chief Inspector for Schools and he recalled that:

When I was a headteacher, this was what I did.

This kind of talk broke with an unwritten agreement; indeed, many of my colleagues who are serving or former headteachers have a mantra they privately use about communication:

Never say ... this is what I used to do.

Why was this? Well, probably because, if we are honest with ourselves, we didn't.

What Michael Wilshaw was trying to say, in his own way, was that we should challenge parents who clearly don't care enough about their children's education and see nothing wrong with permitting their children to stay off school unnecessarily, or taking them on holiday in term time, or not turning up regularly to parents' meetings.

So, our former Chief Inspector was partly right. We *do* need to challenge parents who do not value education. I believe firmly that parents should turn up for school meetings and should insist on their children attending school every day.

However, things are never quite that simple. Right from the start, in my new pastoral role, I considered that educators must also take some responsibility for encouraging parents to be concerned about the education of their children. My mother never attended the schools I went to. She was actually too apprehensive and overawed by the power and importance of the headteacher and the staff. Schools in my day did not positively encourage parents to turn up at school. The staff considered themselves to be acting '*in loco parentis*' – literally to be 'in place of parents'. The school might just as well have placed a big sign outside the school gates saying 'Parents keep out'. Certainly in my early days in education, many headteachers would have loved to have had a keep-out sign for *everybody*.

It's different now: schools make remarkable efforts to engage with parents and the community. As well as the traditional open days and parent-teacher associations, there are new closer manifestations. These include celebration assemblies, parents in the classroom learning alongside their children, homework clubs open to parents, e-newsletters, text messaging, Twitter and parent feedback sites. I could go on and on, with almost endless creative variations.

Along with my appointment as a pastoral head in a newly formed comprehensive school came a new and unfamiliar responsibility, the establishment of links with other professionals, such as local authority advisers, social services, education welfare officers and educational psychologists. My first meeting with the educational psychologist was rather embarrassing, as I didn't really know the difference between a psychologist and a psychiatrist. This was a difficult meeting, as I had just left the truant officer, or 'wag man', who was telling me that he was now to be called a welfare officer.

Then I had a humbling shock. I discovered that social workers, education welfare officers (EWO) and psychologists had a much deeper insight into many aspects of my children's circumstances and the varied contexts within which they lived, compared to my own very partial understanding,

The first educational psychologist I worked with was great fun. For example, I would rather innocently say '*good morning*' to him and then, looking at me straight in the eyes, he would say '*and what do you mean by that?*' I grew to admire and respect these indispensable colleagues. I particularly admired those EWOs who were out and about 'in the field' dealing with a myriad of complex and challenging issues.

When our welfare officers visited homes they often heard wonderful and creative reasons for the child's absence.

● *She is off with her leg;*

● *He's under the doctor;*

- *There was a wasp in the bathroom and he couldn't get dressed;*
- *His cat was on the roof.*

Over the years the excuses would become more sophisticated and hi-tech.

- *Her alarm clock is solar-powered and it was cloudy.*

On one occasion, one of my EWO colleagues noticed a pattern of absence was occurring every week. A number of pupils were off on Thursdays but only if it rained or looked as if it might do. Eventually, a mum admitted that Thursday was washing day and, if it looked like rain, her kids were needed at home to be ready to take in the washing.

On one particularly memorable home visit, the child continued to hide upstairs, while the welfare officer sat in the front room talking to the mother. Halfway through the explanation for her son's non-appearance.

- *Because the bedroom door was jammed.*

At this point, a dog wandered into the front room. The dog then stood by the fireplace and, oblivious to the situation, left a rather smelly 'deposit' on the carpet. Eventually, unable to put up with the smell, the EWO excused himself and left the house. The mother then called after him: *'Aren't you going to take your dog with you?'*

This story tells us a lot about the relationships between some homes and school, particularly about the power and the self-confidence of many parents. Would threats of prosecution or fines have worked in this case? Some parents may need the threat of a fine or court. However, this must always be the last resort.

Parents and pupils cannot be treated as a homogeneous group that will respond to a single strategy. Remember my own grandparents: both were working class but couldn't have been more different. One worked down the pit from the age of 12 and could barely read, the other was a quarryman who loved Dickens and opera.

CHAPTER 30

CARETAKERS

I am now about to come across a new focus at the beating heart of education. The support staff, without whom the education system would implode. I also take the 'Archbishop of Santiago' on a tour of the school.

Use every ounce of intelligence we can find and listen to all staff, not just teachers, as we need their insight and wisdom to continually learn and improve.

Muttering 'who takes care of the caretakers' doesn't help.

In my short career, I had heard arguments for the centrality of academic subjects, children and also teachers. As a new pastoral head in a comprehensive school, I was to discover the importance of working with parents and other agencies linked with the well-being of children. I was now about to come across a new focus at the heart of education, the support staff and systems which removed so many barriers to children's learning.

As a trainee teacher, I had never really considered how the school operated. We never discussed the managerial aspects of the job, such as finance, equipment, services and building management. After all, we were teachers and we taught lessons. All the rest was the responsibility of the headteacher. Things are very different today. Good school leaders understand that the way management relates to *all* employees has a critical impact on their performance and the success of any organisation.

I soon began to realise the importance of good relationships with 'support staff'. I was taught very early on to be especially considerate to the caretaker and the cook. For example, good relationships with the caretaker meant that you would be let back into school at night if you had left something behind in a classroom that you needed urgently. Being nice to the cook meant you got extra pudding.

The first caretaker in my first school, in the 1960s, was called Fred. Every Wednesday he helped out at the youth club. He would prepare the school hall for our weekly activities. Nothing was too much trouble for Fred.

Then I met Jack in 1971. Our secondary modern school had moved half a mile down the road to merge with the grammar school to become the comprehensive school. Jack, the grammar school caretaker, was a former pitman and resented the secondary modern staff joining *his* school. It was a matter of status. In his view, being the caretaker in a grammar school was of much higher status than working in a comprehensive school. Before the establishment of the new comprehensive, he was used to having morning meetings with the headmaster in his study. Now he was being invaded by all these secondary modern kids and teachers. Neither the kids nor the teachers compared favourably to Jack's mental image of grammar school students and teachers. The latter were, in his view, much superior, both academically and socially. He would say:

Remember, if it wasn't for all these little b******s, the school would be perfect. Every day they come in and make a mess of my place.

Jack ran the school with a rod of iron and with the occasional help of the headteacher. If a member of staff stayed late to work, he would kick them out. If a football match went into extra time, he would declare '*time*'. If the art teacher dared to leave some paint stains in the wrong place, he would have a blue fit. To give Jack his due, the school was immaculately kept. Certainly, in his view, it would have been even more perfect, if all children had been banned:

This place is great in the holidays without all the bloody teachers and kids.

One day I was away being interviewed for a post in another school. When I returned, I was in a pretty good mood, even pleased to see Jack standing by the school gate. Behind the school was what appeared to be a beautiful red sky. I was transfixed by the glow surrounding the school:

Jack, have you seen the lovely sunset?

In response, Jack shouted:

That's not a sunset, the ****ing school's on fire.

And sure enough, just at that point, a fire engine came rushing along the road, siren screaming.

When I announced I was leaving the school, Jack came to see me and said he was arranging a leaving do for me at the local rugby club, where I played. But, and he gave me no choice, it was only for the men. At the event, he also gave a speech. Basically, he said that all teachers were 's**t' and I was no different. Compelled by the circumstances, I 'wittily' responded by saying that, whenever he was cleaning a corridor, he would literally '*sweep lady teachers off their feet*'. Jack immediately retorted that he never did such a thing and that he always treated lady teachers with proper respect! It's curious but, in a funny way, he was one of the things I was to miss most about the school when I departed.

My next caretaker's speciality was that he only cleaned up to 11 foot from the floor. The result was that, after some time, the school was beginning to look as if it was decorated in two different coats of paint. Apparently, this decision complied with union guidelines. One classic remark from a colleague at the time was:

if Bill goes on refusing to clean above 11 feet, you will have to take steps to sort it.

When the policy of Local Financial Management was introduced, the school took on control of the repairs and maintenance budget, previously managed by the local authority. I decided to make use of the expertise available and I brought in Chris, a professional builder. Chris managed all the maintenance and had transformed the school within a year. Chris was proactive and listened and consequently addressed many of the long-standing repairs, which the school so badly needed.

Later on, when I became the principal of a further education college, I would always give a yearly presentation to the staff. I would include an item I called 'Quote of the Year'.

One year, Alan, the building manager, won hands down. He issued a classic weekly email bulletin to the staff. One of these contained his winning announcement:

I am notifying staff that they cannot enter the staff room this morning, as I have taken off the door.

I think I knew what he meant.

Too often, we don't value those who clean our buildings and ensure that the basic services work well. One day, I was involved in a conference in a Durham hotel. I was wandering around looking for reception. I asked a cleaner, whom I encountered, and she pointed me in the right direction. I then noticed a sign for the reception, which pointed in the *opposite* direction. The cleaner pointed out that the sign had been wrong for months:

Nobody asks us for our opinion, so we just let the problem continue.

The lesson from this is that good school leaders listen to *all* their staff, not just the teachers.

One day our very flustered headteacher asked me into his office. When I arrived, the Archbishop of Santiago was standing there dressed in his full regalia. He introduced himself as Cardinal Raul Silva Henriquez. I then took the cardinal on a tour of the school, introducing him to all the staff including Jack the caretaker and, eventually, Doris the school cook. It was quite an experience for us all.

On meeting the cardinal, Doris bent forward and kissed his large gold stone-set ecclesiastical ring. A few moments later, Doris took me aside and whispered to me that the cardinal was wearing his ring on the wrong hand. When we quizzed the 'cardinal' a little more, he eventually admitted that he was in fact a waiter from Hexham in Northumberland.

Konosuke Matsushita, the one-time Head of Matsushita Electric, commented that:

Organisations' continued existence depends on the day-to-day mobilisation of every ounce of intelligence.

In educational matters, this *intelligence* must include all staff and, of course, the school cook!

CHAPTER 31

NUTTY SLACK AND TV

I meet Basil Bernstein, who tells me that working-class children are disadvantaged because they use limited vocabulary, unlike teachers, books and exams, which use a more explicit and complex language. I side with William Labov, who says working-class speech is just as complex. I am actually starting to question received educational wisdom!

Question and challenge theories about why children fail and refuse to blame them for the shortcomings of the education system.

The DfE have issued new 'Education Jargon Guidelines' just in time. Unfortunately, parents have started to understand what we have been talking about.

To many people, the effects of television on children are self-evidently noxious, like cigarette smoke. They say TV makes you dumb. Of course, the actual TV is still a simple box in the corner of the room. What is important is the information that it transmits. Whenever I watch old TV programmes, in hindsight they look so *slow!*

Perhaps, if my childhood family could have been transported in a time machine to the present day, they would have been totally overwhelmed by the fast-moving images and graphics which appear on our screen. They would also have been utterly confused by individuals in the family talking on phones without wires and watching programmes on a slim little device, while mum and dad continually flicked between hundreds of programmes.

In 2014, Reg Bailey, the government's childhood tsar, said that British parents were the most likely in Europe to neglect their children. He thought that the screens take over unduly from family time. He also considered that the proliferation of smartphones and tablet computers were reducing the amount of face-to-face time that families experience. Citing a recent UNICEF study, which examined the behaviour of families from the UK, Spain and Sweden by recording them in their homes, Reg said:

it was clear that British parents spent far less time talking to their children – and far more time in front of the television than their European counterparts ... What was really noticeable was how few of the British families had a dining table or a kitchen table ... instead, they tended to eat meals around the television on their laps, whereas Swedish families had a meal around the table and spent a lot of time just talking.

He continued:

I think it perhaps tells you something about the amount of face-to-face time which is spent in British families. People talk sometimes about 'quality time', and actually I think most children don't really need quality time. They need you to be there to talk informally all the time.

These debates about spending quality time with children and the impact of television have been going on for years. In 1972, I shared a platform with a very distinguished member of Her Majesty's Inspectorate, who noted the poor and restricted social interaction within working-class families, which often limited their conversations to comments about popular TV programmes. He also reminisced about the good old days, pre-television, when families sat around the fire and were engrossed in conversation.

The year before this, Basil Bernstein had published his magnum opus *Class, Codes and Control*, which spoke about two types of language, the so-called *elaborated* and *restricted codes*. At the time, his ideas were mind-blowing for the teaching profession, many members of which still considered education theory and research to be important. Bernstein argued that members of the working class are more likely to use a restricted code for most communication, whereas the middle class demonstrate a better balance between the restricted code and the elaborated code in the way they communicate.

Restricted code speech is very predictable and limited and based on easily shared understandings: it does not tend to concern itself with communicating new ideas or sharing information. By contrast, the elaborated code uses more complex vocabulary and ideas and is likely to be more discursive and sometimes argumentative.

However, I profoundly disagreed with the idea that families with TV had more elaborated conversations than families without TV.

In fact, my most compelling memory of a pre-television childhood in the 1950s was of helping to shovel the free coal, dumped outside our house weekly, into the coal house, rather than about the conversations we had. We would have detailed and decidedly restricted conversations about the amount of nutty slack in the coal. Nutty slack consisted of small, hard and shiny pieces in with the coal, which had extremely poor burning qualities. For those of you who are not aficionados of the nutty slack situation, it is hard to comprehend the significance of the discussions about it when I was a child.

Nutty slack was even debated in the House of Commons. On 2 February 1953, Gerald Nabarro MP asked Geoffrey Lloyd, the Minister of Fuel and Power, the calorific value of the nutty slack that was currently being marketed to domestic consumers, ration-free, by the National Coal Board. He went on by asking:

... whether nutty slack is to be a permanent, ration-free feature of our domestic economy?

Mr Hamilton, another MP, pressed the matter by asking:

What steps he proposes to take to reduce the price of nutty slack, in view of its extremely poor burning qualities?

On reflection, the Walton family was rather impressively going beyond the restricted code in discussing issues of national importance that were being debated in the House of Commons.

Unlike my friend, the HMI, I considered that conversation actually improved when television arrived in our household in the mid-1950s. We were able to talk about *Robin Hood*, *William Tell*, *the Lone Ranger* and *Champion the Wonder Horse*. Then, when *Coronation Street* came along, our family had more arguments going on than the Oxford Union! What made me concerned about the HMI view of the restricted code was that he appeared to be promoting it as an excuse for poor teaching. He also failed to recognise that most schools themselves were employing a rather restricted code.

The teachers at my grammar school were certainly limited in their use of language, using words such as 'swotting' and 'prep'. In addition, they also slipped easily into using terms unclear to myself, my family and most human beings, such as UCAS, clearing houses and redbrick universities. Plainly, the latter description is distinguishing the brick structures from those made of wood.

This was a new kind of restricted code, generating mystery and considerable confusion. Today, it is hard to be a school governor, when terms like 'three levels of progress'; 'requires improvement'; and 'assertive mentoring' are all bandied about. To some extent, this is language – *designed to exclude*.

Without a doubt, language codes are alive and well within education – even the Chief Inspector has now re-defined the word 'satisfactory' and has restricted its use to non-educationalists.

So, where am I going with this? Well, I'm really making three points.

1. There is an ever-present danger of the misuse of educational theory and research because it is often accompanied by a rather shallow understanding of the theory.

2. Too often the very theories that encourage us to challenge our own limitations in supporting young people can then be used to provide excuses for our failure.

3. We are in danger of developing an educational 'mystifying code', which can increasingly isolate the education system from other parts of our society and from the students it is designed to serve.

To see how easy it is to be seduced by specialist, mystifying language, try this: if you really want to impress the educational community, simply link any of the verbs within the left-hand column with any of the adjectives on the right and then add the word 'learning'. They may not make any sense but they sound really good!

Verbs	Adjectives
Advocate	Assessment-driven
Drive	Child-centred
Embrace	Collaborative
Empower	Cross-curricular
Expedite	Data-driven
Facilitate	Interdisciplinary
Optimise	Mission-critical
Recontextualise	Multidisciplinary
Triangulate	Outcome-based
Unpack	Thematic

Oh, by the way, many of these mysterious words are featured in this book, so beware. I may also be found to be:

deploying brain-compatible, compellingly diverse and impactful language.

Forgive me, I apologise. I just wanted to sound good!

CHAPTER 32

ROSLA: THE RAISING OF THE SCHOOL LEAVING AGE

The raising of the school leaving age eventually happens in 1972, following the introduction of the comprehensive system. As usual, the O level pupils continue their studies, uninterrupted by the change.

Understand that pupils with the most stable and supportive background are provided with the most constant and secure education pathways; those with the most unsettled backgrounds are subjected to the most change and disruption.

Frankly, Walton, if I had had work experience when I was at school, I wouldn't have ended up teaching you.

Margaret Thatcher at the National Union of Teachers Conference 1972.

On 4 April 1972, Margaret Thatcher announced to the National Union of Teachers Conference that she had considered over 1400 proposals to establish new schools, close others, significantly enlarge some and change the character of many established schools. The majority of these proposals related to the introduction of the comprehensive system of education.

Like many around the country, our school had just been through a major comprehensive reorganisation, while at the same time dealing with a dramatic rise in the school population. While managing the fall-out from merging three schools – the nuclear war imagery is strangely appropriate – we were now faced with a new and extremely difficult task. We had to announce to the children, many of whom, like the staff, had only reluctantly joined the newly reorganised school, that they would also have to face staying on for a compulsory extra year.

Margaret Thatcher described in glowing terms the 'enthusiasm and careful planning' which had gone into preparing for the children to stay on. Every one of the 140 local authorities had submitted plans, which had been approved by the Secretary of State.

I happened to be head of a fifth year cohort with more than 250 pupils. More than a hundred of these had been expecting to leave at 15. This was not a happy scenario for them.

In 1964, early preparations began for the implementation of raising the school leaving age to 16. This was not about specifying and raising the participation age: it was hard and fast that, eventually, all pupils would have to stay at school until 16, come what may. The preparations for ROSLA were delayed and delayed until the decision was reached in 1971 that the new upper age limit would be enforced from 1 September 1972 onwards.

This was not totally new. The school leaving age had been raised at various times over the previous century. It was increased to 11 in 1893 and 13 in 1899. The Fisher Education Act in 1918 made education compulsory until 14 years old. Then, in 1939, the government considered raising the leaving age again to 15 but this was delayed owing to the War. Subsequently, the 1944 Education Act did succeed in extending compulsory education to 15, although it took until 1947 for this to come into effect.

The educational service was part of what was supposed to be a:

National system, locally delivered.

Unfortunately, at this time the government, local education authorities, schools and teachers all jealously guarded their autonomy. The outcome was that the response to ROSLA varied a great deal from school to school.

While I am sure there was a degree of forward planning in preparation for the extra numbers of pupils staying in school, my distinct impression was that teachers in the schools were largely left on their own to sort out what the children should do during their extra year.

I had the 'good luck' to be in charge of the fifth year – nowadays called Year 11. This was in the year when around 60 per cent of all our pupils were, at a stroke, required to stay for an extra year.

Two new ROSLA posts were created for, and taken by, the Head of Woodwork and Metalwork and the Head of Home Economics. Can you spot the clear message in these appointments? The management team in our new comprehensive school was dominated by former grammar school staff and their ideas and they simply handed the problem over to the former secondary modern teachers, 'who were good with this type of kid'. The presumption was that, in order to address the requirements of ROSLA, the answer would simply be to increase the amount of time given over to practical subjects.

As a result of this, in our case, the 'ROSLA kids', as they were known, received a time-table which was filled up with extra PE and woodwork and metalwork for the boys, and cooking and textiles for the girls.

I felt it was essential to take this thinking further. Consequently, I arranged an extended studies programme for these ROSLA children. This consisted of a year-long programme involving a number of elements: work experience, the Duke of Edinburgh Award Scheme and a personal and social education programme. As things progressed, we even introduced a film studies programme; for example, I remember taking the whole group to see the recently released Franco Zeffirelli's *Romeo and Juliet*.

Without a doubt, during the 1970s, there was an increasingly sharp focus on work-related education. So, as well as raising the school leaving age we also saw the introduction of the Education (Work Experience) Act.

I was fortunate to have come from a school in which work experience and a community-based learning programme were already part of the curriculum. Indeed, we had been running our work experience programmes since 1966. I had taken over the programme from a far-sighted teacher, who enthusiastically involved as many local companies as possible in the scheme. It was simple, then, because most companies were locally run and controlled and this included the local Council offices. Because of this, it was relatively easy for me to arrange to meet the bosses of local organisations and agree on placements for my students. At this time there was little bureaucracy and few health and safety constraints or criminal record checks. In this benign situation, every pupil in the final year of my then secondary modern would have one full week of work experience.

The lack of paperwork and health checks meant that all this was relatively trouble-free. The only really memorable incident was when our Tommy Smith spent some time at a local chicken farm. We placed all the children with some care and, knowing Tommy's reputation for mishaps, we thought a chicken farm would be a safe placement for him.

Unfortunately, one morning Tommy threw open the doors where the battery chickens were housed. When the daylight streamed into the building, the hens immediately took fright and panicked. Tommy ran from the building, shouting:

The chickens are rioting!

Looking back on this, it was actually a period of educational innovation and creativity. We had the freedom to introduce a new curriculum. This freedom was not granted because what we were doing was important. No, it was because the school authorities were concerned that the ROSLA children were being occupied and were not disrupting the whole school.

At the end of the year, the Head of ROSLA retired. During the year, Bill and I had become firm friends. Then, one fine day, I proudly drove my new Toyota Celicia into school. It was pretty rare to drive a Japanese car in those days. Bill did not collapse with admiration; he went berserk and exploded:

Why are you driving a Jap car?

Bill then calmed down and retreated to his woodwork room. He then removed his shirt and showed me the Japanese flag which had been burned onto his back with cigarettes. Bill was, in due course, to share with me his quite shocking experiences of being a prisoner of war during the Second World War.

Today, when many people talk about the need for continuing education, they focus on the idea of 'lifelong learning' and the need for a better and more competitive workforce. Bill's thinking contrasted with the modern idea that if we simply increase the amount and level of education, we can better compete with countries such as Japan and Germany. His view was that there was much more than this simple equation suggests. This may well be true. I certainly would like to think that education has other, wider purposes. Some of us can still remember the teaching of peace studies in schools. While I am not suggesting the return of such a programme, I do believe that education has a major part to play in improving international understanding and relations. I know that Bill would have agreed with this. His was a simple philosophy. The more educated people are, the less the likelihood of war and the atrocities sometimes associated with it.

To Bill, there was some moral purpose behind the raising of the school leaving age. It was not raised to simply ensure the children could get better qualifications and subsequently go on to higher education or better jobs. Bill's clear view was that the core purpose of education was to develop a society in which people would behave in a civilised way towards each other; also, that they would understand and empathise with other people from different backgrounds and different cultures.

When Bill eventually retired, it was very hard to persuade him to even attend a little staff celebration on his last day. But, eventually, he reluctantly attended and accepted his gift.

He then asked the staff to wave goodbye to him from the staff room window. As he drove his Ford Prefect out of the school, he gave a two-fingered salute from the window. I miss him.

CHAPTER 33

PARTY GAMES AND THE DISCO

There are certain pivotal moments in education. James Callaghan in 1976 calls for a 'Great Debate' about the 'secret garden of the curriculum'. There is also the 'Great School Parties Debate' about party games, the Gay Gordons and disco.

Great shifts in school practice are sometimes a result of bottom-up creativity, not just the delivery of top-down policy.

The party finished – my teacher started to "get down with the kids" and he couldn't get up again.

The mid-1970s were a pivotal point in the development of post-war education. At the beginning of the decade, Edward Heath had needed to make cuts in expenditure. In supporting his new Secretary of State for Education, Margaret Thatcher, he offered to abolish the universal provision of free school milk. Following the 1971 Education Act, which achieved this objective, the chorus of dissent gained a powerful sound-bite:

Thatcher, Thatcher, milk snatcher.

This soon became a popular and often repeated chant.

Subsequently, in 1974, Harold Wilson formed a minority Labour administration and, about a year later, in 1975, Heath was replaced as leader of the Conservative Party by Margaret Thatcher. Events came thick and fast and Wilson resigned in April 1976, replaced by Jim Callaghan. Then, in September 1976, Callaghan appointed Shirley Williams as Education Secretary. In this period, I had the pleasure of dancing with Shirley Williams at a teachers' conference and I can still remember her beautiful eyes!

At this time, many in the teaching profession were committed to the idea that, if we increase prosperity, then we can *then* invest more in education. This, in turn, would foster greater social unity. With mounting inflation, rising unemployment and endless bitter industrial conflicts, we increasingly began to disagree among ourselves as

James Callaghan calling for a 'great debate' on education.

to the purpose and practice of schooling. In 1976 Jim Callaghan gave his famous Ruskin College speech, in which he called for a 'great debate' about the nature and purposes of education. For the first time in my career, I began to sense there was an increasing disenchantment with the belief that education provided an answer to society's problems. Also, for the first time, politicians were increasingly calling for teachers to be more accountable for what went on in schools.

I was rising in the profession and, in 1975, I was designated a senior teacher in my comprehensive school. The 'great debate' in our school was not really about key issues of principle: the issues we saw were about pay, maintaining the traditions of the education service and making decisions about what type of Christmas parties we should have.

The original idea of senior teachers was that they would become the 'lead professionals', presenting a role model for teachers within the school. They were not to be teachers encumbered by management responsibility. However, like most other senior teachers in the 1970s, I didn't really know how to help other teachers to teach. In fact, this was not seen as a function of a school at the time. There was an assumption that Qualified Teacher Status was enough. So, like many other senior teachers, I gradually morphed into an administrator. For example, I was put in charge of probationary teachers and students in training, among other things. One of these 'other things' was the responsibility for the school Christmas parties. Because I was in essence becoming a bureaucrat, I decided to introduce a 'Christmas Party Policy'.

My memories of Christmas parties, as a pupil in my old grammar school, were not very positive. In fact they filled me with horror. Every year in December, instead of PE, we would all be taught to dance. The very PE teachers who had been shouting at me for being useless at football, cricket and athletics were now barking at me for my extremely clumsy attempts at dancing.

We would learn the Gay Gordons, the Dashing White Sergeant, Strip the Willow and, of course, the Waltz. For me, it was the activity from Hell. The worst part was having to hold a girl in close proximity. Up to this point, I had pretended girls didn't really exist. Also, most of the girls at the time were taller than me and they weren't too keen on having their feet stamped on by a totally uncoordinated hoofer. Then came the instructions:

Hold the girl's right hand with your left and place your right hand on her shoulder blade. Then stand in front of her and a little to the right. Step on your right foot, pivot on the ball of your foot, so that now you are facing the wall bars in the gym.

These commands had all the complexity of modern-day computer programming classes for me.

My own school decided to make matters worse by inflicting the dreaded 'Moonlight Saunter' on us all. This involved turning the lights down low and shining a spotlight on certain couples. For us all, avoiding the spotlight became a real art. The dance reminded me very much of a scene from a British prisoner of war film, when the prisoners, crossing the compound, trying to escape, would be caught in the guard's searchlight. It was comforting to reflect that they at least were put out of their misery by being shot. This sauntering pain, for me, continued right until the day I left school.

Around the same time that Callaghan was indicating that education was at a significant turning point in its development, those at the chalkface were also debating a momentous stage in the development of education. Should 1970s schools still continue to have Christmas parties, keeping alive the customs of pass the parcel and musical statues and traditional dances? In light of this, don't let anyone suggest that we didn't adapt with the times. We had become modern, even cool by having pass the parcel and statues set to pop music.

The particular tradition that physical education staff would provide the dance instruction was alive and well in the 1970s. In December the PE staff would again have the honour of teaching the children to dance. Instead of focusing on football and netball, there would be a shift in the direction of dancing lessons. The children were aware of being carefully trained to be 'party ready' by Christmas.

But enough of this, let me tell you about my Christmas party policy. On the whole, the 11 year-olds were well used to party games in primary, so they were happy to continue the tradition. But Year 11 badly wanted disco music. Following some lengthy and tough negotiations with the pupils, a ground-breaking agreement was reached. Year 7 pupils would have 100 per cent party games; Year 8, 75 per cent party games with 25 per cent disco; Year 9 would get a balanced 50/50; Year 10 would enjoy 75 per cent disco and 25 per cent games, and then Year 11 would have a free choice. I naively thought this was a brilliant solution. This was a proper school policy with firm rules and regulations.

Every Christmas we always presented a prize to the winner of the Christmas charity raffle.

The prize was usually the record that was headed Top of the Pops. I was desperately hoping in 1975 that it would not be a Bay City Rollers record.

In fact, in 1975 the winner's record was to be Queen's 'Bohemian Rhapsody'. At the time this was the most expensive single ever made, the first live performance having only taken place in November.

The headteacher was to present the prize and admitted that he quite liked the record because it: *'didn't sound like the usual rubbish you hear on the wireless'.*

However, I was asked to change the prize. Queen, at the time, were surrounded by controversy and were considered 'not a good role model for young people'. Consequently, having just produced the highly complex and revolutionary Christmas party policy, I was impelled into serious negotiations with the headteacher.

Part of the discussion related to the meaning of the lyrics. I argued fervently that the record would encourage children's love of opera. In fact, 'Bohemian Rhapsody' parodied many different elements of opera by using bombastic choruses and distorted fragments of Italian operatic phraseology. Also, were there not lyrical references to figures such as Scaramouche, Galileo, Figaro and Bismillah?

Eventually, common sense and profoundly intellectual reasoning won and 'Bohemian Rhapsody' was duly presented as the Christmas raffle prize.

Our great debate about Christmas parties had apparently achieved a 'new consensus'. Possibly this is best summed up as: rock and roll meets the White Heather Club.

The supposed post-war harmony with regard to the purpose and practice of education was about to break apart.

CHAPTER 34

THE WARNOCK REPORT AND SPECIAL NEEDS

The terms 'backward and educationally sub-normal' are still being used. The children with what we now term 'special needs' are put into remedial classes. I always have a feeling that the school never quite knows what to do with these 'difficult to educate children'. The approach is confused and often negative; they are simply children who cannot be 'properly educated'.

Value and respect the level of commitment and expertise in special schools or provision, where the concept of 'institutional pessimism' is rarely seen.

So what do you prefer to be called, disabled, physically challenged, special needs?

It is quite shocking today to recall the descriptions we used for certain children. In 1886, the Lunacy Act made no clear distinction between learning disability and mental illness. Subsequently, the Idiots Act introduced, for the first time, legislation relating to the educational needs of those with learning disabilities.

By 1924, the Geneva Declaration of the Rights of the Child was adopted by the League of Nations and clearly stated:

The child that is hungry must be fed, the child that is sick must be nursed, the child that is backward must be helped, the delinquent child must be reclaimed and the orphan and the waif must be sheltered and succoured.

There was clearly a desire, expressed in this declaration, that education should be *inclusive*.

Nevertheless, even as late as 1950, the most common terms used to describe learning disability were 'mentally defective' and 'mental deficiency'.

The 1944 Education Act clearly stated that the responsibility for such children lay with the local education authority. But, at the same time, the Act labelled children with learning disabilities as 'ineducable'. The National Association of Parents of Backward Children, which existed at this point, was to be succeeded by MENCAP and the Royal Society for Mentally Handicapped Children and Adults. In 1955, in a clear step forward, the Guild of Teachers of Backward Children was founded.

When I started teaching in 1966, the terms 'backward children' and 'educationally sub-normal' were in common use. However, things were beginning to change. Only a year after I started teaching in 1966, Stanley Segal's book *No Child is Ineducable* paved the way for the achievement of education for all. Five years later in 1972, the Education (Handicapped Children) Act made education a universal right.

In my new comprehensive school, the idea that no child is ineducable was clearly not part of the ethos of the school. Despite this, there was no particular strategy in place to support children who had 'special educational needs'. In the comprehensive school's previous life, as grammar and secondary modern schools, the eleven-plus mathematics and English examinations were considered enough to identify the needs of children. For many people at that time, children with mental disability were not deemed educable at all.

As a new pastoral head, who somehow ended up *force majeure* as 'the expert' on those deemed ineducable, I felt very isolated. It sometimes appeared to me that no one really cared about these children. In fact, this was not wholly true, because many of the senior management and teachers of the more academic children did care. But what they cared about was that these children were disrupting the brighter children's learning.

Then, in 1973, something happened which gave me some hope. Rather surprisingly, the person who gave me a glimmer of hope was the 'Milk Snatcher'. In 1973, Margaret Thatcher, by then Education Secretary in Ted Heath's Conservative government, announced that she proposed to appoint a new Committee of Enquiry. Mary Warnock, an Oxford Fellow and headmistress of Oxford High School for Girls, was to be its

Chair. The Committee was to review the educational provision for children and young people who were:

Handicapped by disabilities of body or mind, taking account of the medical aspects of their needs, together with arrangements to prepare them for entry into employment; to consider the most effective use of resources for those purposes; and to make recommendations.

Mary Warnock: a breath of fresh air.

The Committee held its first meetings in September 1974, supported by four sub-committees. Later, in 1975, I was one of those called to attend one of these sub-committees. All of those who were there felt that we were part of a very significant and radical development. In due course, in 1977, the Committee of Inquiry published its report on the *Education of Handicapped Children and Young People*.

The report was to change the educational picture for children with disabilities very radically. Most of the recommendations were later enshrined in the Education Act of 1981. The report introduced the term 'Special Educational Need', which would be used to identify any child needing extra or different support. The report argued that 20 per cent of all children have special needs at least for some part of their educational career and recommended that segregated special schools should be provided for those with the most complex and long-term, multiple disabilities. The role of mainstream schools should be to develop their provision to meet the needs of all the other children.

Whether the child was placed in a special school or would remain within a mainstream school, there should always be an agreement with the parent. To help to facilitate the integration of children within the mainstream it was recommended that there should be an expansion in special needs advisory and support services. In order to ensure that the educational needs of the children with the most severe disability were protected and that they received appropriate resources to make progress, the report recommended the production of statements of special needs. These statements were to be issued by local authorities to individual children only after a five-stage assessment process had been worked through. However, once a statement had been issued, the local authority had a statutory duty to make the provisions listed on the statement.

In 1982 I was appointed as deputy head in another school. Here I found that the special needs children were not even integrated within the school itself. Accordingly, the first thing I did was to engineer the geographical move of the department right into the centre of the school. This was more than a simple symbolic statement; it also allowed these children to have easier access to the school library and the resource centre. Following my rather limited involvement in the Warnock Review, the school decided to take the concept of integration between mainstream education and specialist school provision a few steps further. We joined with the Northern Counties School for the Deaf in running a programme called 'Project Respond'.

The children with higher-level special needs joined classes within school and were required to follow a normal timetable. Most of these children had multiple disabilities, including being blind, deaf and confined to wheelchairs. Some were also autistic and many had other health issues.

One key element of the project was to take a group of children for a weekend experience in Keswick. None of the children involved had any defined special needs. They were then divided into groups. One group wore invisible earphones, which played white noise incessantly. Some children wore dark glasses, which reduced their vision by up to 100 per cent. Others were asked to use wheelchairs. All were required to apply these restrictions at key points during weekend.

Many of the children, when questioned about the experience, considered it was one of the most intense and valuable learning experiences they had ever taken part in. The difficulties and, sadly, the abuse they encountered were both shocking and salutary for these children.

At the end of the Project Respond we took a mixed party of our own pupils and children from the Northern Counties School for the Deaf to see the Moscow State Circus. The Russian clown, Oleg Popov, quickly noticed some of our children using sign language and 'signed' to them in British Sign Language. Our children then proceeded to communicate across the circus ring.

This was undoubtedly one of the most emotionally charged moments during my life in education. I realised just how much, as teachers, we learn from our pupils.

Many years later in 2008, Lady Warnock described the system she helped to create as:

Needlessly bureaucratic.

She called for the establishment of a new enquiry to ensure that children with special educational needs are not:

The victims of institutional pessimism.

This is a challenge none of us should ignore, or take too lightly.

CHAPTER 35

SCHOOL ASSEMBLIES AND NAPCE

The significant contribution made by a school's pastoral system on how well a student succeeds, both academically and personally, is beginning to be recognised. Many of us believe all children are important, not just the academically able. We also establish the National Association of Pastoral Care in Education (NAPCE), a forerunner of 'Every Child Matters'.

Be sensitive to the needs and views of individuals, providing for the physical and emotional welfare of all children and staff.

Hardly here, no progression indicators, always undermining authority ... still, enough of my problems, what can I do for you, Smith?

In the 1980s, the pastoral care of pupils was a prominent element in the establishment of the new comprehensive schools. One possible reason for this was a fear that these new large organisations might have the effect of reducing the concern shown for each individual child.

Consequently, the new pastoral heads were thrust into their roles without adequate training and without any substantial support. In addition, many of us were increasingly dissatisfied with the prevailing perception of our role. We felt we needed to 'professionalise' our role as pastoral carers, but there was no clear voice we could listen to. Thus, Her Majesty's Inspectors at the time were all very subject focused and local authorities often appointed as a link person someone who had no personal or practical experience of the role.

By 1980, I had just completed my Master's degree in Education. Naturally, my thesis was related to pastoral care. At this point, a local secondary school headteacher invited me to talk to his staff about this issue. I was also asked to address a meeting of pastoral heads across my local authority. The response was quite remarkable. We all had very similar feelings and overall felt isolated and without any significant professional support. I then decided that I would visit all of the pastoral heads within our local schools.

In 1981, as a result of everyone's efforts, we decided to create Gateshead Pastoral Care Association. This brought together educationalists, social workers, psychologists and other key professionals with an interest in pastoral care and the broader question of student welfare. A young committee member in this was Steve Munby, who eventually became a significant figure in education as the Chief Executive of the National College for School Leadership.

While the main focus of our new Pastoral Care Association was on all aspects of personal and social education, one of my particular interests was the contribution which school assemblies made to student development.

One especially memorable school assembly took place when a rather self-important headteacher complained to his head of music about his choice of music for assembly. The Head of Music always played a calming diet of Mendelssohn on his Dansette record player, when the head entered for the assembly. This calming set of musical choices didn't fit in with the headteacher's idea of 'leading the troops into battle'. Neither was it a good backdrop for his predilection for talking about how he 'bombed Germany during the war'. Later, following three weeks of the *633 Squadron* and the *Dambusters* theme music, the hall was packed and ready to hear the latest musical choice. When the head entered this time, it was to the strains of:

Jesus Christ Super Star ... who do you think you really are.

He was only human, so he finally cracked.

As a pastoral head, I spent a lot of time preparing whole school assemblies for the children.

One of my favourites was the 'Tie Assembly'. For this, the Head of Music would wear a tie tucked into his pullover. I would then rather theatrically insult him, pulling out his tie and cutting a bit off with a pair of scissors. I would then tuck it back in and apologise to him humbly and profusely. Following a few further insults, the tie was

eventually so short it could not be put back in without showing a gap. Clearly, my apologies could no longer mend the division and it was apparent to everyone.

Meanwhile, as all this was going on, P P Arnold's 'The First Cut is the Deepest' was being played on the Dansette. This Junior Assembly was in fact about bullying, thinking about *cutting* remarks, which cut very deeply and in the end cannot be easily forgiven. When used for older pupils, the assembly was really focused on the nature of bereavement and the *final cut*, which may or may not be the end. In 1988, this assembly was accompanied by Mike and the Mechanics and their song 'The Living Years'.

Another favourite we called the 'Egg Assembly'. I would ask a pupil to try to crush a fresh egg by pressing each end of the egg with their hands. It is in fact impossible to break the egg this way. The theme in this case was *inner strength*. In the background, the school choir sang Labi Siffre's 'Something Inside so Strong'.

Unfortunately, on one occasion, this assembly nearly had a sticky end. At the time I was being inspected and under some pressure. Partly because of the circumstances and complicated by sweaty hands, the egg slipped somehow and bespattered the inspectors who were sitting in the front row. Luckily, even inspectors have a sense of the ridiculous!

A pastoral head was a new invention at the time and so I often would visit other people who had a similar role to seek ideas for my assemblies. One of my favourite people and models was Bill, who worked in a neighbouring comprehensive. I asked to watch one of *his* assemblies. We met in his office, as the children were beginning to assemble and just as the children started to enter the hall, Bill lit up a fag. When his deputy put his head around the door and announced that all the pupils were seated and waiting for him, he slowly placed his half-smoked Woodbine in the ashtray. He walked to the front of the hall, made a brief announcement, said a prayer, and got back into his study in time to finish his cigarette. I suppose the Woodbine part of this story makes it perfectly clear that the health part of what we now term Personal, Social and Health Education – now usually abbreviated to PSHE – was still in its infancy.

I was then approached by Michael Marland, a nationally renowned headteacher, who together with a number of other leading educationalists wanted to establish a similar association across the UK. So it was that, in 1982, we established the National Association of Pastoral Care in Education – or NAPCE.

Just like the Gateshead Pastoral Care Association, NAPCE took off like a rocket. We soon established regular conferences in the North East, usually held at Beamish Hall. The whole focus of these weekend events was to agree on how we could ensure that the needs of individual children were placed at the forefront of our educational thinking.

Just before the first Beamish conference, I received a letter of complaint from the local Her Majesty's Inspectorate. They argued that, as teachers, we were not properly qualified to run training programmes and that we should abandon the conference. At this time we were a long way from a 'school-led training system'. Needless to say, we disagreed and the event went ahead.

Within a couple of years, we decided to hold our first national conference at Bede College, in Durham. While the conference was in the end a great success, there were teething problems evident even before it opened. For example, one group of female teachers from London complained to me regarding the way they were welcomed at Durham railway station. On arrival, they were greeted by Trevor and Steve, two pastoral heads from East Durham who said:

Welcome Hinnies.

When they were rebuked for calling them '*Hinnies*', Steve said: '*I apologise, pet.*'

This of course further enraged them all; they were very upset. '*We are not your pets*', they complained.

When Trevor tried to make amends, he offered to carry their bags 'because *they might be a bit too heavy*'.

At this point, relationships broke down entirely. However, I did, in the end, manage to patch things up and persuaded the group to stay on and continue with the conference.

Unfortunately, I had forgotten all about the brief I had given to the Conference President, who also came from London. He had asked me for advice on how he should open the conference. I recollected that, a few years before, in 1977, Jimmy Carter, the American President, visited Newcastle. Carter had a storming success when he uttered the words: '*Howay the lads*'.

Thinking this was a good idea, a marker for our President, I advised him to welcome the conference by saying: '*Howay, lads and lasses*'.

I was hoping this would make sure that our conference was fully inclusive of both men and women. My hopes were dashed, because as soon as our President mouthed the fatal words, our group from London walked out, never to return. Pastoral care requires sensitivity.

CHAPTER 36

RELIGION AND EDUCATION

The relationship between religion and education becomes intertwined with my daily attempts to be a teacher. Discussions about religious education, school assemblies, faith schools are often prickly and sometimes combative. I regularly join forces with my deputy head colleague in the neighbouring Catholic school to break up fights.

Be considerate of the views of others and seek to understand how best to integrate different perspectives and beliefs into their organisations.

I'm with the Catholic school during the day, my Council foster mother at night, and my Dad on a weekend. I'm the perfect example of the legal division between Church, state and family.

In 1982 I was approached by a senior education adviser in Gateshead, who suggested I should apply for a deputy head's post which had come up in a comprehensive school in North Shields. The post was dramatically different from the pastoral responsibilities I had undertaken in my present school. The post involved being responsible for the curriculum and the timetable. The school was also physically and socially very different from what I was used to; it was much smaller and also in an area of extreme poverty and disadvantage.

However, there was one thing that was exactly the same: the ongoing battles with the local Catholic kids. These battles had not been as prominent during the period when the tripartite system was operating. Like most schools, the local Catholic schools were easily defined, either as secondary modern or grammar schools. But, when all the schools became comprehensive, the competition between Catholic and non-Catholic schools rose to high intensity.

From the start of my teaching career the relationship between religion and education intertwined with my daily attempts to be a teacher.

I recall when in my first school, a secondary modern, I was given the task of supervising a small number of Jehovah's Witnesses, who were 'opted out' and did not attend the morning religious assembly. While this was the rightful choice of the parents, I always felt that this aspect of my job sat rather uncomfortably with my core belief in an all-inclusive comprehensive education. In addition to this, I was also required to take morning prayers, lead religious assemblies and teach religious education lessons.

In the 1960s and 1970s, new programmes were introduced into schools, which attempted to address religious and social divisions but, despite all such efforts, the faith divisions persisted.

Working as a deputy head in the 1980s, I was now regularly having to deal with the battles between our children and the Catholic children from another local school. After one of a number of pre-arranged fights on neutral ground between the schools, I confiscated an air rifle from one of my students: '*It's for shooting sparrows and Catholics*,' he admitted.

His defence was that the birds didn't seem to mind and he would only shoot the Catholics '*in the bum*'.

The problematic relationship between the Catholic and other secondary schools in my part of the North did not surprise me. Long before, when I was 18 and told my grandfather that I would like him to meet my girlfriend, he only asked one question. The question wasn't about her parents' background or where she lived or if she was black or white. The question was simply:

Is she a Catholic?

To a working-class man, brought up in a Pennine Dales village at that time, this was a very important consideration. The Catholic Church seemed alien, with its strange rituals and traditions. At the same time my grandmother, a committed Wesleyan Methodist, was also having issues with the Primitive Methodists within our own village.

For nearly two decades my grandad had supported the sweeping changes brought about by one of his heroes, Richard Austen Butler, in particular the Education Act of 1944. He could go along with RAB's main proposals, including all maintained schooling to be free and the three-tier selective secondary state schooling system. However, my grandad, whose professed atheism was met with a great deal of angst within my Methodist family, had grave concerns about Butler's introduction of the statutory requirement for collective worship. His simple view was that:

Religion doesn't belong in school.

When Butler was introducing the 1944 Act, the toughest problem of all was ensuring the support of the Churches. He knew that if he fell out with either the Anglicans or the Catholics, it would scupper everything. Butler's answer was to hoist the Churches 'by their own petard' by promising that religious education and worship would be at the very centre of state schooling and of the school day.

Accordingly, the Butler Act required all maintained schools in England and Wales to provide '*a daily act of collective worship for their pupils*'. In community schools, the law stated the worship must be:

wholly or mainly of a Christian character.

Within this framework, both Anglicans and Catholics would be able to determine the nature of the schools' daily act of worship. Religious education would be required in every school in the country. Nevertheless, the rights of parents were protected and they could choose to opt their child out of the daily act of worship if they so wished.

Butler then negotiated a deal with the Churches over capital funding. The State would pay for their schools, including helping to finance the repairs made necessary by thousands of inadequate buildings. Butler's formula had been that Churches would provide 50 per cent of the capital costs if they wished to acquire 'Assisted' status. If they could not undertake to do so, then the schools would become 'Controlled' and lose their managerial autonomy, which would be taken on by their own local education authorities.

In the decades following the Second World War, the clear trend was towards the incorporation of Catholic and Anglican schools into the new state system. Before the 1950 election, the Catholic and Anglican Churches requested that government funding for 'Aided' status be raised to 75 per cent. This fitted in well with the Conservative Party's drive for educational expansion at the time and, as a result, the Education Act of 1959 incorporated this provision.

After 1964, under a Labour Government, a policy was aimed at allowing the denominational schools to join the developing comprehensive school movement. The Education Act of 1967 increased the grant for any new 'Aided' schools to 80 per cent, while the Education Act of 1975, again under a Labour government, raised the grant once more to 85 per cent.

Today the concern about faith schools is no longer so strongly focused on Catholic and Anglican Church provision. The focus has shifted to that of other faith groups, including Muslim schools. The conspiracy theory once applied to the Catholic Church by my grandfather is again, and just as unreasonably, being applied to the Muslim community.

In 2014 Birmingham City Council commissioned my associate, Ian Kershaw, together with colleagues from Northern Education, to investigate the 'Trojan Horse Affair', investigating in particular, the governance and control of schools.

This was a debate strongly influenced by the tabloid press, which dealt with the matter in terms that could not be described as either measured or rational. Indeed, Ian found that there was no evidence of a conspiracy to impose an Islamist ethos within some schools.

Religion has always been one of the most controversial aspects of our national education system. Indeed, somewhat contentiously, in 2015, a former Education Secretary of State, Charles Clarke, argued that schools should end religious instruction altogether, abolishing mandatory worship and undertaking the teaching of morality instead.

Passing on the morals and beliefs of society from one generation to the next within schools is one of the most important duties of an education system. Most people nowadays would probably agree that there is still a place in our schools for the type of religious education that reflects the multi-cultural realities of modern Britain.

We have certainly come a long way from the time of my grandfather and his views of religious education. Today faith schools are a critical part of an inclusive education system. In my view, they enrich our education system, many being at the forefront of education advancement.

I am now a grandfather. My own grandfather would be surprised to know that all five of my grandchildren have been baptised as Catholics. If, one day, my granddaughter visits me and asks me to meet her new partner, I do not expect my first question to be:

Is your partner a Primitive Methodist?

CHAPTER 37

TECHNICAL AND VOCATIONAL EDUCATION

Technological and vocational education responds to the 'white heat' of the techno-logical revolution. The 'great debate' starts. Perhaps this is one of the few times that we achieve the 'Goldilocks Position', when we get the balance right between central direction, local decision making and individual creativity.

Seek dynamic decision-making, combining 'top-down, bottom-up, inside-out and outside-in' influences to create a cohesive whole.

Once I learn how to access Wikipedia, is that all the education I need?

In 1967, my school took a giant leap forward in the use of educational technology by introducing the overhead projector. The chalk dust and blackboard rubbers would be a thing of the past. The sales pitch was powerful:

No more tired arms writing on the chalkboard, you can clean it easily with a tissue or paper towel and, best of all, you can keep an eye on the class as you write!

Vocational and technological education was certainly *not* at the forefront of every headteacher's mind when they designed their school curriculum in the 1960s and 1970s.

In 1963, Prime Minister Harold Wilson warned that, if the UK was to prosper, a 'new Britain' would need to be forged in the:

white heat of this scientific revolution.

Two years later, the Brynmor Jones Report made some highly influential recommendations about vocational training and also supported the use of technology. The report, for the first time, categorised audio-visual education, programmed learning, distance learning and early work with computers under one name – Educational Technology.

A decade or so later, in 1976, Jim Callaghan, who was then Prime Minister, made a famous speech at Ruskin College. This started the 'Great Debate' about adapting the curriculum to make best use of all the new technologies.

However, it was left to Margaret Thatcher, who became Prime Minister in 1979, to advocate more directly a clearer focus on computers and their technological applications in the science, mathematics and English curricula in schools, and to highlight the importance of this technological awareness to the country's economic prosperity.

However, in fact, information technology was developing only slowly in education. It was not until 1982 that the BBC launched a major programme to support computer literacy.

Then, in 1983, there came a dramatic shift in the central government approach to the vocational curriculum. The Technical and Vocational Education Initiative had arrived.

TVEI was eventually to become one of the UK's largest-ever curriculum development programmes, costing around £900 million. In 1983, high-level youth unemployment was becoming a major concern and employers were arguing forcefully that the school curriculum should be strategically redirected. It was argued that the school curriculum should be more relevant to employability and preparing young people for work.

With the TVEI programme, the government had clearly decided to achieve this objective very directly through funding policy. Before TVEI arrived, most education monies for schools went directly to local education authorities, who spent it on their own priorities. Margaret Thatcher turned to the Manpower Services Commission to fund TVEI, thereby excluding officials and educational professionals both in central government and in the LEAs. This fresh focus on 'new technology' and, in particular, information technology, was linked to the emphasis on high-tech industry in the 1980s.

LEAs were, of course, involved as the direct line managers and designers of TVEI schemes but they had to conform to centrally devised and quite specific guidelines. All the plans and designs put forward would have to:

- be linked to subsequent training or vocational opportunities;

- include work experience;

- be responsive to local and national shifts in 'employment opportunities';

- combine both general, technical and vocational education;

- include 100 students at a time, primarily within the 14–19 age range, within each separate scheme; and

- be properly coordinated. It was recommended that each LEA and each participating school should appoint a coordinator.

TVEI was at its peak between 1983 and 1987 when it most certainly drove the 14–19 curriculum agenda but, from around 1988, its influence waned as the Department of Education and Science reasserted itself. Eventually, the TVEI programme would be killed off by the emerging National Curriculum in 1997. However, its influence remained in many areas and in many minds: for example, the National Curriculum established a statutory framework of ten subjects, within which information technology survived as an important strand of design and technology.

Increasingly, throughout the 1980s, computer studies was available as an examination subject in almost all secondary schools. The new emphasis was on problem-solving and using computer applications in a variety of practical situations. This emphasis resulted from the over-concentration, in the early days, on programming skills as the route to overall technical competence.

Today, the wheel has turned again and the guidance in National Curriculum Computing programmes of study stresses that pupils should be taught:

- the principles of information technology and computation;

- how digital systems work; and

- how to put this knowledge to use through programming.

The TVEI initiative certainly showed up the deep divisions that existed about different political and ideological beliefs within education and training. These differences are still there, gently simmering below the surface, particularly about the need to introduce technical and vocational elements into the school curriculum. These fundamental differences in ways of thinking have continued to plague British education and training policies right up to the present day.

We are still arguing about the power of technology to transform how people learn. Prior to the COVID-19 pandemic, while we had whiteboards in virtually all classrooms and children habitually used laptops and tablets, there were still plenty of textbooks, pens and photocopied sheets to be seen in classrooms. The desks in classrooms in the main still faced forward, with the teacher at the front.

Because of its far-reaching impact, the pandemic has given us massive insights into how the role of technology can radically shift to reach students and how to adapt learning processes in challenging times. We are now asking how we can ensure continued access to education and how we can support students that are physically displaced from schools.

Even before the pandemic, radical ideas were still being put forward, ideas like the 'flipped classroom'. This idea has gained popularity in American schools and involves inverting some traditional teaching methods, for example, by delivering instructions online from outside the classroom and then using the time in school as the place to do individual work.

The tragedy of the eventual demise of TVEI is that it was one of the few times in education when we got the balance about right between central direction, local decision making and individual creativity. It was certainly one of the most stimulating and fulfilling times in teaching. It encouraged curriculum construction as a practical, multi-faceted, multi-level activity involving constant adaptation, modification and re-thinking. It occupied the middle ground between central prescription and decentralised, school-based approaches. Perhaps this was the real lesson that TVEI taught us? It will be interesting to see whether we learn the same lesson from COVID-19.

CHAPTER 38

CORPORAL PUNISHMENT

The era of state-sanctioned corporal punishment comes to an end in the 80s. For some, to institutionalise this form of punishment is a shame on our education system. For others, it couldn't come back soon enough. We are the last country in Western Europe to ban this practice in our schools.

Our treatment of children and staff reflects the respect and value we place on our fellow human beings.

Tell me again how this hurts the teacher more than it hurts me?

Spanking, caning, whacking, beating and the corporal punishment of children seemed to have been around in schools for an embarrassingly long time during the very early days of my career in teaching. In school, corporal punishment was defined as:

causing deliberate pain or discomfort in response to undesired behaviour by students in schools.

As a pupil and a young teacher, I considered it was just part of the everyday life of the school.

Then, something quite remarkable happened. In 1986, two years before I became a headteacher, corporal punishment in all state schools was outlawed altogether.

In my first school, the senior staff all carried the same type of tawse and this was certainly used on me when I was at my infant school. The last headteacher I worked for in my first comprehensive school already had a record in this field! Ironically, he had been in all the newspapers for mass caning girls who were involved in a pupil strike. I remember that the headteacher I worked for as a deputy head would often use the words:

Caning is useful when you haven't time for psychology.

In May 1947, the Foundation for Educational Research was invited to investigate the effects on children of various forms of punishment and reward. David Rennie Hardman, the Parliamentary Secretary to the Minister of Education and the former MP for Darlington, had instigated this study. Interestingly, Darlington is still a well-known Quaker town and this may have some bearing on the matter. In Harman's opinion, corporal punishment was completely indefensible:

It was bad for the child, and it was very bad for the adult who administered it.

He also argued that it was important for the Ministry to move carefully at a time when public opinion still had to be convinced that, without corporal punishment, discipline would be maintained.

Legal disputes about corporal punishment were not uncommon at this time. Only two years earlier, in 1945, 'bare-bottomed slippering' at a preparatory school was held to be neither excessive nor unreasonable. Even 15 years later, in a 1959 case, a six-stroke slippering for a 12 year-old was deemed reasonable by magistrates.

In 1947, I was a sensitive and normal two year-old living in England. Unfortunately, I had not been born in Poland, where corporal punishment had been outlawed since 1783. Nor was I French, where such beatings had been banned since the First World War. It was just my luck to be born in the UK, where this summary of physical justice would not be abolished until almost 40 years later.

For many years I suffered the tawse treatment. The tawse was a leather strap used in infant school and later in primary school came the cane. In secondary school corporal punishment might involve any implement teachers could get their hands on, including the rattan cane, the leather strap, a wooden yardstick, blackboard rubbers, gym shoes, or Bunsen burner tubes and, of course, more routinely, the odd slap around the ears.

In fact, the rattan cane was the favoured instrument. In length it varied between 90 and 100cms. If administered vigorously, its use would leave painful wheals or 'tramlines' across the posterior, often lasting for several days.

Gordon Brown once admitted with a wry grin, when he was Prime Minister, that he had been punished with a tawse in school. That belt would probably have been a Lochgelly tawse, a strip of leather, one end of which was split into a number of tails. They were specially made in the Fife town of Lochgelly and were widely used in Scottish schools at the time.

Unlike Scotland, the leather tawse was used only in relatively few places in England. Again, it was just my luck, because two of these 'relatively few places' were Gateshead and Newcastle. On my appointment to the staff of my first school I discovered that, because it was in Gateshead, the leather tawse was in regular use for disciplinary purposes at the school. Senior teachers would carry the carefully folded tawse in their jacket pockets. I have to admit that, at the beginning of my career, I rarely questioned either the effectiveness or the morality of corporal punishment.

For many pupils, particularly the academically gifted, those good at games and, of course, the girls, this violent aspect of schools was rarely seen. However, I can remember clearly that, when the new Sex Discrimination Act came into being in 1975, there were – perhaps tongue in cheek – suggestions that girls would henceforth have to be caned as much as boys.

But, undoubtedly, attitudes to corporal punishment were beginning to change. In primary schools, where corporal punishment was common in the 1950s, it tailed off quite quickly. Indeed, by 1982 a third of Britain's 35,000 schools had already banned corporal punishment altogether. But, it is a fact that no LEA had banned corporal punishment completely before 1979/80.

In 1982, corporal punishment in Britain's schools was dealt a death blow by the European Court of Human Rights. It ruled that the beating of school children against their parents' wishes was a violation of the Human Rights Convention because parents should have their children taught in a legal way:

In conformity with their own religious and philosophical convictions.

Britain was now isolated on this matter, being the only country left in Western Europe that still allowed corporal punishment in schools. A couple of years earlier, in 1979, Sweden went even further by prohibiting corporal punishment in all spheres of life – including parental homes, schools, the penal system and other alternative care settings.

Tom Scott of the Society of Teachers Opposed to Physical Punishment (STOPP) responded positively, hailing it as a:

Tremendous day for children, parents, teachers and society as a whole.

The advice from David Hart, General Secretary of the National Association of Headteachers was to 'carry on caning'. He said that the judgement, which did not actually ban caning, would only cause confusion in schools. Schools will, he said, have to distinguish between children who are allowed to be beaten and those who are not.

The outlawing of corporal punishment in state-run schools and in private schools, which received partial funding from the government, became law in 1986. The Act was passed through Parliament by a very narrow majority; some of the pro-corporal punishment MPs did not manage to vote because they were stuck in traffic jams caused by the wedding of Prince Andrew and Sarah Ferguson.

Today the argument about corporal punishment still continues, with many parents and commentators, some teachers and community leaders, and even young people maintaining the belief that moderate and properly regulated caning helps to maintain order.

In 2008, a survey in the *Times Education Supplement* found that one teacher in five and almost a quarter of all secondary school teachers would like to see corporal punishment reinstated. A similar survey in 2011 found that half of all parents and 19 per cent of students also wanted to bring back the cane.

Support remained high for almost all traditional forms of punishment including:

- **sending children out of class (89 per cent);**
- **after-school detentions (88 per cent);**
- **lunchtime detentions (87 per cent);**
- **expelling or suspending children (84 per cent); and**
- **making them write lines (77 per cent).**

Much less popular were:

- **shouting at children (55 per cent); and**
- **embarrassing children (21 per cent) – this was frowned upon.**

In 2013, I was talking to an MP who happened to be on the threshold of knighthood, while he was bemoaning the loss of corporal punishment in schools:

It never did me any harm, he spouted.

Neither did those leeches doctors used in medicine in times gone by, I thought glumly.

CHAPTER 39

VISION AND THE LEAD PIPE

I am now a headteacher. I now have no excuses. The type of school I want to run *must* be better than the ones I attended as a child. I understand that vision should always precede strategy. Even so, after all the lessons I have learned as a pupil and a teacher, I start with a 'half-baked' vision. I am also taught by a parent how to 'twoc' cars.

The only vision worth having for education is one that is shared and which unifies and excites those we serve.

The new mission statement:
'Empower cross curricular child-centred thematic outcome-based programmes, by advocating assessment and data- driven collaborative thematic processes. We will drive, embrace, expedite and facilitate interdisciplinary and mission-critical multi-disciplinary curricula by optimising, recontextualising and unpacking our interdisciplinary approach.'

Not happy about the new mission statement ... Ofsted may still understand part of it.

I must admit that, on the day of my appointment as a young headteacher in the late 1980s, I did *not* have a vision for the school. However, as a deputy head, I had formerly been taking part in a training programme on 'visionary leadership' and, more than 20 years before that, my first year as a student coincided with Martin Luther King's '*I have a dream*' speech. In addition, I understood the necessity of having a clear and compelling vision of what success would look like. So I was certainly up for having my own dream.

The greatest job in the world.

I remember standing in front of what appeared to be an enormous school building, extremely worried that I did not have a mission or vision for the school. I couldn't see, or even visualise, what I wanted to achieve. I definitely lacked that authoritative vision that was often so eloquently described to me by my set of 'hero heads'. At the time a 'mission' was what the American astronauts went on and 'vision' was some-thing to do with either religion or smoking dope.

Instead, what I seemed to have in my head was a partial picture of what the school could be or might be in the future. Right from the start of this new challenge I tried to develop a shared vision of transformation, continually testing it out on my unfortunate staff and our pupils.

I saw my key role as the person who would work *with* staff, students, parents and the community to develop a sense of direction and, indeed, hope for the school. Having experienced having things done *to* me during my time as a pupil, a young teacher and a senior member of staff, here was my chance to apply my own thinking. If any of the staff in the school had known anything about my personal background and professional experiences, they could probably have spotted the origins of my approach.

At this time my vision was of a school that was clearly at the centre of the community and yet a *safe haven* from the often dysfunctional experiences the children faced. I wanted the inside of the school to be accessible, while, at the same time, making it very different from the external environment. It was to be a calm place of safety and, most of all, learning. To put it another way, I didn't want a school that treated children and parents the way I and my own family had been treated.

I promoted a vision of a school that was filled with: *'Caring, confident and capable children'.*

I have tried to apply this to my own children. Although I didn't know then that my children would eventually work in the fields of accountancy, human rights, law, medicine and international development, I would have wanted them all to be confident in what they did, capable of high achievement in their chosen profession and certainly caring about those they serve.

We introduced a strap-line for the school, emphasising our wish to:

Develop pupils' potential and improve their prospects by working in partnership with the community.

All good stuff, of course. And, indeed, we worked very hard to involve pupils and parents in the development of the school vision – unfortunately, we were not always successful in doing this.

One day one of my more interesting pupils was caught walking out of the school with a metal pipe stuck down his trousers. He was sent to me. Subsequently, he explained that the pipe had '*fallen into his trousers'*.

I met his father and explained that my vision for the school was a place where property could be left in the expectation that it would be respected by other people. The father, who was six feet tall with a Mohican and a 'cut me' tattoo across his throat, looked at me in disbelief. He then called me a 'naive nugget' and then, to my increasing despair, agreed with his son that the pipe must have fallen down his son's trousers.

Having tried to demonstrate the impossibility of a pipe 'falling' into someone's trousers, I decided to try another tack. I leaned forward at 45 degrees. This was an approach I had picked up from my pastoral care days. I then oozed a ton of empathy and said I was more worried that the pipe might be used to 'twoc' cars by breaking the windows and forcing the ignition. The father then also leaned forward at 45 degrees, oozing pity and said I was completely wrong:

That pipe's the wrang size for twocking cars.

You will understand from this that my vision was certainly not shared by all my parents. In the future I realised that a vision must always be a shared one; however, in the childhood of headship, dreams are a reality.

The only vision worth having is a 'shared vision', one that everyone will sign up for and be motivated to achieve.

In the late 1980s, headteachers were very much focused on their own school's unique vision, looking at life through their individual and different approaches to the curriculum. At meetings of headteachers, we would often express and promote very different views on the purpose of schooling. Some, like me, would emphasise the community side of a school; others would place more value on academic aspects, while others might stress the performing arts. The one uniting factor for all these opinions was that headteachers saw themselves as curriculum designers and, consequently, their varied visions were delivered through a wide range of different curricula.

Today a school developing its own unique vision is very much subservient to the vision for education espoused by different political parties. The headteacher's ability to design a unique curriculum has been increasingly constrained by various governments since my time as a young headteacher.

During the 1990s each political party had a particular vision for education.

The Conservative vision for education seems to be thousands of independent schools or groups of schools, that will spend their time competitively vying for parental approval – and yet operating with a common curriculum.

The Labour vision would be one of 'relatively autonomous schools' working within a local democratic framework – but also operating a common curriculum.

The Liberal vision would place schools much more under the direction of local authorities – but again with a common curriculum.

UKIP would apparently want grammar schools back – complete with a 1950s curriculum.

How visions and missions are implemented also changes on a regular basis. Under the last New Labour government, there was a great emphasis on national, regional and local education planning. Under the Coalition government, there was a great emphasis on the reduction of planning and bureaucracy. Under the most recent Conservative government, the official emphasis is supposedly on a school-led system rather than one led from either the centre or by local authorities. However the centre seems to be gaining ground.

We often hear politicians talk grandly of their vision for education. We all listen carefully as the *vision* word is bandied about before an election. But, in my experience, senior politicians rarely declare a really personal vision for education. Usually they are describing policy, pet projects or delivery mechanisms. Remember that visions can often be myopic or astigmatic!

CHAPTER 40

LEAVE SOME ROOM FOR THE DANCE

In 1988 the National Curriculum is introduced, just as I become a headteacher. The 'Great Debaters' come to the conclusion that the design of a school curriculum fit for a modern economy is too important to be left in the hands of headteachers and school governors. Many headteachers are angry that their professional responsibility for curriculum design is being undermined. Others are excited by the prospect.

A key focus of the curriculum is to assist all children to learn and achieve.

I have a plan for my next forged absence note, I'm joining the creative writing class.

One of my favourite films of the early 1990s was *Strictly Ballroom*, which told the story of a truly original dancer, who wished to express himself and be more creative while taking part in an Australian ballroom dancing competition. The judges wanted to apply the rules and standards, using fixed guidelines about 'what makes an outstanding dancer' that were clearly based on a view of dancing that held sway during their childhood.

The judges were much more concerned about ensuring that judgements could be made about the comparative merits of the dancers, rather than about developing a love of dancing. The creativity and innovation exemplified by the young dancers were to be crushed.

In 1988, when the National Curriculum was introduced into England, Wales and Northern Ireland, the discussion about state control over curriculum design issues and professional autonomy and creativity was very intense, indeed. There were two principal aims set out in the document.

The *first aim* was that:

The school curriculum should aim to provide opportunities for all pupils to learn and to achieve.

So, 'core and foundation subjects', 'attainment targets', 'programmes of study' and arrangements for assessing pupils' knowledge, skills and understanding were all introduced.

Department of Education and Science

Personal and social education from 5 to 16

Curriculum Matters 14

AN HMI SERIES

HER MAJESTY'S STATIONERY OFFICE

One of the HMI discussion documents, warmly welcomed by headteachers.

The *second aim* was to:

Promote pupils' spiritual, moral, social and cultural development and prepare all pupils for the opportunities, responsibilities and experiences of life.

Many headteachers and governing bodies had, for a number of years, accepted the need for the school curriculum to be revised. This was considered to be the logical consequence of the 'Great Debate', which had been called for in 1976 by the Labour Prime Minister James Callaghan and supported by the 15 discussion documents that were subsequently produced by Her Majesty's Inspectors between 1977 and 1982.

As a result, teachers welcomed developing a national consensus on what should be taught in schools. They also fully supported the argument that, by providing a common curriculum, parents would be able to make better comparisons between schools.

However, most headteachers at the time were proud of their record as curriculum innovators. Indeed, heads had seen their primary role as developing the curriculum in schools in response to the needs of individual children *and* local and national economic and social changes. We were now becoming concerned that we were to be simply 'curriculum deliverers'. Our prime concern was that the state was increasingly seen to be taking direct control of the curriculum. In a speech at this time I noted that, just at the point when we had denationalised many of our major industries, we were starting out on a process to nationalise knowledge.

Because at the point of introduction only certain subjects were included in the national plans, we front-line deliverers in the schools and communities were able to retain some flexibility and opportunity to promote our own curriculum philosophies.

Like many school leaders at the time, I considered that the second aim of the National Curriculum, *'to promote pupils' spiritual, moral, social and cultural development and prepare all pupils for the opportunities, responsibilities and experiences of life'* to be particularly important. In fact, one of my own school's stated key aims was:

To enhance children's love of learning, encourage creativity and develop personal and social skills.

This was, of course, in addition to delivering the nationally prescribed curriculum. Our school plumped for a core curriculum that comprised community and social education, art, music and drama. All our children were involved in community and work experience programmes that we considered fundamental. We earnestly believed that the community we served would significantly benefit from this approach and that it would be an important means by which we could engage young people in developing a love of learning.

Since 1988 numerous Secretaries of State have focused their attention on their notion of core curriculum subjects, mathematics, English and science, and later tampered with policy regarding the wider curriculum.

This approach to policy-making is a bit like adjusting to the wind when sailing; when there is an AIDS epidemic, there is a call for increased sex education; when there is a short-fall of employable young people for industry or other sectors, there are moves to provide compulsory careers education; when health-care

Secretary of State, Kenneth Baker. The 1988 Act was referred to as the Baker Act.

provision becomes increasingly expensive, there are moves to provide more health education; and when the numbers of obese young people are seen as a problem, then timetabled cooking and nutrition education are demanded.

Similarly, concerns about religious fundamentalism have more recently led to the modification of citizenship education. It's debatable whether this is good policy reacting to emerging needs, or simply a set of knee-jerk reactions to the prevailing headlines. What this approach does not deliver is a stable system with clear underpinning principles.

A quarter of a century later a wide-scale review of the National Curriculum became really necessary and it was undertaken by Michael Gove. This review, in 2013, was set against numerous concerns about the impact of having a national measurable system that would improve choice and raise standards. Central government control over the subjects being taught in our state schools was to be extended.

The review specified that the National Curriculum should have the following aims at its heart.

- *First, to embody rigour and high standards and create coherence in what is taught in schools.*

- *Second, to ensure that all children have the opportunity to acquire a core of essential knowledge in the key subject disciplines.*

The underlying message enshrined in these aims was that the 'key subject disciplines' contained the 'essential knowledge' that would allow progress. In stark contrast, the 'wider curriculum' received much less focus.

Meanwhile, Michael Gove appeared on TV at the time, extolling the importance of encouraging creativity in schools. I guess that my reaction was very similar to lots of BBC educationalists, by which I mean 'baby boomer creative' educationalists:

Of course, creativity is essential; it is essential if young people are to fulfil their potential and be successful; it is also essential if our communities are to flourish; it is undeniably essential in order for our economy to thrive.

Unfortunately, Michael Gove insisted that we must *delay* focusing education on creativity until our children had learned the basics. To put it another way, we were receiving the same message that I had been given when I was learning to play the piano. When, as a 6 year-old, I wanted to 'tinkle' and 'play about' on the ivories, my piano teacher would rap me on the knuckles with her ruler.

She insisted that:

We must learn the scales before we can improvise.

Similarly, Michael Gove takes the view, which he has often repeated, that:

You cannot be creative in English, unless you learn how to use grammar.

There is certainly truth in the argument that children, like footballers, painters and piano players, need to develop their skills and understanding in order to be *optimally* creative. The big danger in a linear and prescriptive curriculum is that some forms of creativity, like jazz, do not fit neatly into a step-by-step approach to learning. It remains true that too much curriculum prescription will squash creativity in both children and their teachers.

CHAPTER 41

OUR CHILDREN ARE PRICELESS

The 1988 Education Reform Act is overwhelming in its impact and implications. We are now to have control over spending the money and paying the bills. Many of the more experienced headteachers are concerned that they have given up control of the curriculum in turn for the ability to manage the finances.

We all have a responsibility to understand the implications of major policy changes before they are introduced.

Bringing in 90 year-olds will not increase our age-weighted funding total.

Up to 1988 the Butler Education Act of 1944 was regarded as the most important single piece of education legislation in England, Wales and Northern Ireland. Then, in the late 1980s, another 'big beast' came along.

The 1988 Education Reform Act was bringing changes and implications that I, as a young and inexperienced headteacher, didn't fully comprehend. While I was enthusiastic about the changes and the immediate repercussions on my own school, I didn't really cotton on to the implications for the whole education system.

There was a mixed reaction from my fellow heads. Some were for and some were against the proposed changes. The main concern, for most headteachers, was:

What will this mean for my school?

So, if my own school was going to be better off, why should I have to worry about the whole system of education in the UK? Perhaps this was the beginning of the disintegration of the solidarity of the education community?

One of the key changes that the 1988 Act would bring about was the introduction of Local Financial Management, later to be known as Local Management of Schools – LMS for short.

Before 1988, schools only had control over 'capitation'. Every year we would receive our capitation allowance, based on a headcount. For my school at the time, this was around £25,000 in total. Essentially, this covered the cost of books and materials. But in any modern school the greatest part of the budget is in fact needed to cover staff costs, with a rather smaller proportion covering building costs. Up to this point, all the staff were employed and the buildings maintained by the local authority.

Before LMS took hold, I would have an annual meeting – really a structured argument – with the local authority and we would haggle about the number of staff I was entitled to. I would argue that the numbers coming in would justify, say, 60 teachers, and the LEA Director would pitch in with an offer of 59. On the whole, we would then come to a civilised compromise of 59½.

Now things would be different because my new responsibility for the school buildings introduced new areas for discussion. At one meeting I wanted a new form of roof covering for a part of the building, rather than the type proposed by the local authority. I lost this argument, as the 'tarmac team' within the local authority were the only people who could fix the roof.

When local management of schools was introduced, headteachers were given far greater control and we found ourselves managing almost the whole budget. It then became the responsibility of the local authority to transfer the school's budget to the governing body.

School budgets would be determined on the basis of an 'allocation formula', calculated through the number and ages of the pupils in the school and the number of pupils with special needs.

Miraculously, a new phrase now entered general school management parlance:

The age-weighted pupil unit.

My governing body would also now take on responsibility for the appointment and dismissal of staff. Before 1988, only the local authority had been able to do this.

These shocks to the system occurred in my first years of headship. However, to be honest, as a young head I was more excited than nervous about this innovation. The longer-serving heads were concerned about the change altering the focus of their role from that of a traditional headteacher to a 'head manager'. Nevertheless, while I welcomed the greater control given to me as a headteacher, I did have some reservations. In particular, my personal issue was the implicit dangers involved in treating the school as a business, rather than focusing on the needs of individual children.

I remember, at this time, giving a talk to the National Association of Pastoral Care, entitled:

Suffer the Age-Weighted Unit to come unto me.

My point was that there was a danger that we would start viewing children less as individuals and more as potential sources of income.

Many heads at the time were concerned that the local management of schools would make them institutional managers rather than educationalists. There was some substance in this view, as the headteacher role changed and was now focused sharply on employment law, health and safety legislation, buildings maintenance, the budget and the appointment and dismissal of staff.

In fact, the apparent new freedom that was on offer, the freedom to manage a budget, was considered by many headteachers to be largely illusory. As the staffing took up the bulk of their budget, the ability to be creative and introduce their own financial priorities was distinctly limited. As events unfolded I began to wonder whether the year-on-year reduction in the school budget that occurred after LMS was introduced was just a pure coincidence.

Eight years after these crucial changes I would be appointed Director of Education for the LEA in which I worked as a headteacher. At one point during my tenure as Director, I was presented with a toy baby polar bear. This was to celebrate the polar bear joke that I had retold ad nauseam during the 1990s. To satisfy your curiosity I will tell it again now:

One day a baby polar bear confided to his mam that he did not feel he was a polar bear:

Have you white fur? his mam asked.

Yes, replied the baby bear.

Well then, you are a polar bear, said his mam.

The baby bear was not satisfied and repeated his concern that he did not feel at all like a polar bear:

Have you big padded feet to protect you from the cold snow and long eyelashes to protect you from the snowy glare? said his mam patiently.

Yes, *answered the little bear.*

Then you are a polar bear, *said his mam.*

As the little bear continued to express his anxieties, his mother said:

Do you like fish?

When the little bear admitted he liked fish, the exasperated mother bear finally cracked, saying:

You have white fur, pads on your feet, long eyelashes and you have fish every Friday night. So why do you still think you are not a polar bear?

Because I'm bloody freezing, *cried the baby bear.*

For a number of years after the introduction of Local Financial Management and Local Management of Schools in the early 1990s, headteachers would continue to express concerns about this substantial change in their role. My answer was always to tell the polar bear joke.

When the headteachers I worked with continued to question their dual role as headteachers and institutional managers I would again tell the polar bear joke and then say:

Do you manage a budget? Do you appoint staff?

Are you concerned about staffing appointments and legal issues?

Did you not always have an involvement in these issues before and after LMS was introduced?

I know that all these responsibilities seem a long way from being a teacher and can leave you 'cold', but the bottom line is that you are a manager as well as a headteacher, and you always have been.

It is an interesting irony that, prior to LMS, headteachers had much more control over what was taught in their schools but very little control over the money. Today, it is the other way round.

Of course, I then had to explain to governors, who are unpaid volunteers, that they had significantly increased responsibilities for all aspects of the management of the school. They, too, then had to suffer the polar bear joke!

When I became Director of Education I did think momentarily and wistfully about asking all the school crossing wardens to put on their 'lollipops':

Caution! Age-Weighted Unit Crossing – Value £2300.

I didn't, of course. But, despite all these questions about resource management in schools, I still continue to believe that all our children are utterly priceless.

CHAPTER 42

THE OFSTED PHENOMENON

The Office for Standards in Education (Ofsted) is set up following a period of sustained criticism of English state education. Between March and September 1992 an inspection framework and handbook are written, and thousands of inspectors are trained before the first inspections begin in 1993. During a discussion about Ofsted with Prime Minister John Major, I nip out of Number 10 to have a pint.

Never place external inspection as the main focus of any organisation.

Keep quiet about the hellfire. Ofsted are here.

In 1993, all the things in my educational universe changed radically. I was standing among a group of secondary headteachers, talking about a new inspection regime called Ofsted. The joke, that there is only one 'f' in Ofsted, was invented there and then.

At the end of the meeting, the Director of Education sidled up to me and passed me a brown envelope. *'You've just won the first prize',* he said.

It transpired that my school would be one of the first to be subjected to the new Ofsted inspection process. My mind was racing, fuelled by anxiety. I asked:

What will it be like?

What will they do?

Who will they be?

I haven't a bloody clue, *came the Director's response.*

There is a story, which went the rounds at the time, about a headteacher who died and was given the choice either to go to heaven or to hell. Out of curiosity, he asked if he could have a look at hell before deciding. When he arrived, the Devil showed him a beautiful beach beside a bright blue sea and lots of people enjoying themselves in the sunshine. He immediately decided to pick hell. On the following day, he was taken back to hell and the Devil showed him a dirty, oil-covered beach, a stormy sea and dark thunder clouds. All the people were cowering under tarpaulins.

Why the difference? *asked the shocked headteacher.*

We had the Ofsted team in last week, *came the reply.*

Because we had lots of notice, we worked hard to make our school look good, or at least as good as possible, for when the inspectors arrived. The questioning about whether Ofsted will ever manage to get a true picture of schools had begun. In the future, they would introduce 'short-notice inspections' to reduce the ability of schools to make special preparations for the Ofsted visit. But, to be frank, what school wouldn't want to look its best for the big occasion?

Happily, my school did well in this first inspection and we felt the enormous relief that so many schools have experienced since, the relief of 'surviving' the inspection.

The Education Reform Act of 1988 brought radical changes for the Inspectorate. The new National Curriculum would now have to be policed by a new system of monitorial inspections, taking place every six years. Of course, school inspections had been around for a long time.

In 1837, Seymour Tremenheere and the Reverend John Allen were both appointed as school inspectors to monitor the effectiveness of the Annual Grant to the Societies, which was provided to Church of England and non-denominational elementary schools for poor children.

Following the Education Act of 1902, inspections were expanded to state-funded secondary schools. Nevertheless, after the Second World War, there were still only 500 or so 'general inspectors' every year. Each inspector was expected to cover between 150 and 200 schools, so it was not possible to operate a regular cycle of inspections with the available resources. Over time a larger number of inspections were undertaken by inspectors based in local education authorities. In this situation Her Majesty's Inspectors (HMI) operated as the eyes and ears of the Secretary of State, reporting on the condition of education across the country.

During the 1950s formal etiquette had to be observed in the Inspectorate. For example, the following generally applied:

- **all male HMIs addressed one another by their surnames;**

- **female HMIs wore hats;**

- **grammar school heads received a warning of a visit;**

- **primary school heads did not require any warning;**

- **letters to grammar school heads would begin 'Dear Smith', while those to secondary modern heads would open with 'Dear Mr Smith'.**

Prime Minister John Major had been concerned about the variability of local inspection regimes and decided to introduce a national scheme of inspections through a reconstituted HMI. The result was the birth of Ofsted when the Office for Standards in Education was established.

Under the Education (Schools) Act in 1992, Her Majesty's Inspectors would supervise the inspection of each state-funded school, and then publish the reports for the benefit of schools, parents and government. This was instituted to supersede the system by which the results were reported directly to the Secretary of State.

Later on, John Major asked me and another couple of headteachers to meet him at 10 Downing Street to give our views on the changes that were being implemented. During the meeting, John Major was forced to attend a session in Parliament. At this point, tiring of the gin and tonics and vol-au-vents, I persuaded the Bishop of London and another headteacher, Ian Kershaw, to pop across to the Red Lion for a pint.

An hour later two policemen arrived to inform us that the Prime Minister was now waiting to hear our views. I never quite persuaded the Prime Minister to continue the meeting in the pub.

Prime Minister John Major was worried about local inspectors.

We reported our view that while the new inspections were very disruptive, they were much more effective than local authority inspections, which tended to vary enormously both in quality and approach.

In 1999 I made a speech at the Annual Chief Education Officers' Conference. Her Majesty's Chief Inspector, Chris Woodhead, was present. During my speech I told the story about a headteacher who had unfortunately died:

On entering heaven, he said that all he wanted was a harp, a cloud and never to see an Ofsted inspector again.

A couple of hours later, a person dressed in a suit and carrying a clipboard arrived.

Aghast, the head jumped off his cloud, crying, 'I've just seen an Ofsted inspector'.

'That's not an Ofsted inspector', said his accompanying angel. 'It's God. He just thinks he's an Ofsted inspector.'

The Chief Inspector didn't laugh.

In 2005 short-notice inspections arrived. We were strongly encouraged to complete a self-evaluation form before the visit. The inspections then generally involved two or three days of attendance every three years, with two days' notice. Ofsted was also now beginning to inspect our ability to inspect ourselves.

This massive expansion meant that, as we neared 2010, there were more than 2000 additional inspectors employed by external companies.

In 2012 Ofsted admitted they needed to improve the quality assurance of this group of inspectors. During this period the HMIs were mainly focused on leading more complex inspections and supporting schools in 'special measures'. In the quest for better inspection, Ofsted directly employed HMIs and all part-time inspectors to ensure quality. The latter group were recruited mainly from the ranks of respected serving school leaders.

Ofsted has since further expanded its role. Today, Ofsted is known as the Office for Standards in Education, Children's Services and Skills. It inspects and regulates services that care for children and young people and services providing education and skills for learners of all ages. It also covers childminding, child day-care and teacher training providers. Every week, it carries out hundreds of inspections and regulatory visits throughout the country and then publishes the results online.

Ofsted reports to Parliament while stressing its independence and impartiality. The problem has always been that the organisation has had to respond to constantly changing political views of what a 'good standard' is, and exactly what it is that schools are trying to improve.

As you might expect, Ofsted has increasingly been criticised for having:

- **too big a span;**
- **a lack of focus on its core mission;**
- **an over-reliance on number crunching; and**
- **a negative impact on teacher workload and morale.**

While I accept that an inspection is essentially a 'photograph' of a point in time, we continue to place great reliance on Ofsted judgements, perhaps too great a reliance.

As my joke to the other chief education officers hinted, Ofsted inspectors are not all-seeing and all-knowing 'God-like' creatures. 'Who inspects the inspectors?' therefore, becomes a crucial question. As they scrutinise schools, we must, through Parliament, scrutinise the Ofsted team. Inspection has its place but a favourable Ofsted report judgement will never be the main outcome achieved by any school. *Successful learners, who continue to learn and achieve* in life is, surely, and must remain our main ambition.

CHAPTER 43

THE MORNING AFTER A TERRIBLE NIGHT

In 1991 my school is caught up in an urban riot, which causes £9m of damage in one night. The 1988 Education Act ignored the community leadership role of schools, as well as the personal and social development of young people. Headteachers are asking whether their role as 'community leaders' is still important in a centralised education system. I learn what a 'low empathy response' means.

Build good relationships between schools and their communities, understanding it is complex, demanding and incredibly important.

That'll take their minds off their regional problems.

In the 1990s there were a number of urban riots across the UK. One of the most serious was in the Meadow Well estate on Tyneside. It was my home turf. My own school, Norham Community High School, was on the edge of the estate.

For a number of years, the school had not had a boundary fence. It was thought that such a fence would separate us from the community. However, we maintained an 'aggressive daffodil-planting policy'. This meant that daffodils and other flowers were planted strategically around the front of the school. When we had first planted the flowers, they were regularly pulled up. Faced with this we would immediately replace them. After a time and a battle of wills they were left alone and became a source of pride for the school and community.

We also had installed a classic ha-ha, a sort of invisible ditch which ran down the side of the playing field. We'd designed this to protect the school fields without defacing the landscape and encourage our neighbours to see the school as part of the community.

On the afternoon of Monday 9 September 1991, the headteacher of Meadow Well Primary School rang me. She was very concerned about what was happening on the estate. We agreed to have a walk around the whole area and were soon aware that mini-barricades were being constructed at strategic spots.

Riot police protecting the firefighters during the 1991 Meadow Well riots. Permission of Ian Horrocks.

At 2am on 10 September 1991, I received a phone call from the police, who suggested that I come to the school immediately. As I arrived, there were police cars everywhere. The youth centre, a fish and chip shop, and an electricity sub-station were all on fire and there was extensive vandalism to many local buildings and vehicles on the streets.

The riots themselves had been triggered initially by the deaths of two local youths, who were killed when the stolen car, in which they were fleeing from police, crashed with fatal results. The police and fire crews that attended the scene had then been pelted with bricks. It was estimated that, at its height, 400 people were involved. Of these, 37 were arrested, including one individual who was jailed for four and a half years.

In the school, at a hastily convened meeting with the senior staff, we discussed how we should deal with the situation. Should we address the situation head-on or try to calm things by focusing on 'business as usual'? We agreed jointly on a way forward. The deputy head would take a 'normal' school assembly and then the children would go straight to their lessons. By doing this we hoped to demonstrate the importance we attached to the learning of our children.

As a headteacher, I had always been very clear in my own head that the conversations children have with their teachers should focus on learning. This was not easy to achieve, and in the early days of my headship, I frequently had to challenge children who would want to disrupt lessons and talk about anything other than what they were there to learn. In addition, I had to deal with staff doing much the same thing. Of course, I recognised that our children also had personal and social issues, which required support. So, we needed to provide opportunities for children to address these issues. Our response to the riot in a sense highlighted the necessity of achieving this balance in approach.

The next morning, children arrived in school and I had little doubt that many of them were there mainly to talk about the riots, certainly not to talk about the mathematics or science they were faced with.

The morning after the night before.

At the end of the morning assembly, the deputy head briefly referred to the fact that we were all aware of what had happened the previous night, but she emphasised that we were all in school now and had to concentrate on our school work and lessons. It was then announced that all pupils were to attend their tutorial groups mid-morning. This would provide a structured opportunity to discuss the previous evening's events and begin to address the impact of the situation on us all.

During the next two or three days, visitors who came to the school commented on the ethos in which the school was acting as a 'haven' and an 'oasis' when compared to the chaos reigning outside.

The following September, I was asked to speak at a conference in Brighton about the role of education within 'troubled' urban areas. The main reason I agreed to do this was that there were to be speakers from Los Angeles in California, who would be talking about how *they* had responded to the riots in their area. I had prepared a hand-written overhead projector presentation, in which I described the work we had done in engaging with the community both before and after the Meadow Well riots. Next on came an American psychologist, who wowed us all with his new-fangled PowerPoint presentation. Following our respective presentations was a question and answer session.

When I was asked what caused the riots in Meadow Well and the East End of Newcastle, I had to admit that the reasons were not necessarily the same in the different areas of North East England. The death of the two boys was a *trigger* event.

In Los Angeles, it was the acquittal of police officers accused of the beating up of Rodney King that was generally considered to have triggered the 1992 riots. My new American friend, when asked to comment on the police attack on Rodney King, said that the police had shown a:

temporary low-empathy response.

Unfortunately, the laughter from the audience at this Americanism drowned out his subsequent pearls of wisdom. However, I understood what he was trying to say.

All this is a really big challenge for community schools in fulfilling their role. How do they maintain their focus on upholding the school's values and the learning needs of all their children, while avoiding those damaging 'low-empathy responses', when faced by those whom we do not understand or who have very different values and beliefs from those we advocate?

Without a doubt, the relationship between schools and their communities is a complex one. Moreover, the role of schools in helping to achieve urban regeneration remains unclear. However, we need to admit that, in many communities, schools are now the only stable and constant organisations within the area. They are also places in which transformational learning takes place and, if we ignore the learning needs of children, we do them a great disservice. Similarly, if we ignore the well-being of the community in which the children live, we will be guilty of systematically limiting their ability to learn.

We need to remind ourselves of the critical role that schools can play as community leaders. The Meadow Well riots were a long time after Rab Butler's Education Act of 1944, which sought to encourage the spiritual, mental and physical well-being of the community. The Education Act of 1988, which preceded the riots, and succeeding legislation have ignored the vital role that education can play in community regeneration and cohesion. When a community is in turmoil, schools must ensure that no child is left behind and no child is lonely.

As a headteacher, surrounded by incredibly supportive staff, pupils and parents, I was fortunate and I never felt alone.

As Kurt Vonnegut, one of my favourite authors from the 1950s, said:

What should young people do with their lives today? Many things, obviously. But the most daring thing is to create stable communities in which the terrible disease of loneliness can be cured.

CHAPTER 44

STAR SINGER

The National Curriculum guides most of what now happens in schools – but not everything. Schools have the flexibility to develop their own unique offer. For many headteachers, this is an opportunity to focus on personal and social education and the creative arts. In the same year as the riots, our children perform at Buxton Opera House.

Creativity, more than data analysis, is the key to transformation.

His music teacher says he has Van Gogh's ear for music and his art teacher reckons he wouldn't let him paint a fence.

The most serious drawback with running a school that had just been almost overpowered by one of the biggest riots the region had ever seen was that, whatever was said face to face, the school would come to be identified by this single event. On the educational circuit, I would be greeted with:

So, you're the head of the school in Meadow Well, where the riots took place?

I would then get faux sympathetic, patronising and unpleasant comments like:

How are you coping? ... I guess it must be tough! ... I bet you spend most of your time controlling the little bastards, eh?

Yet, it is a fact that, in the same year as the Meadow Well riots occurred, our wonderful children – children from a 'riot-torn' community – were also to be seen performing at Buxton Opera House.

I have always had a belief in the importance of the creative arts as a basis and mechanism for rejuvenating organisations. In the first school I taught in during the 1960s we held an annual play week, which provided a platform in which every child in the school could perform on stage during a whole week of plays. A decade later, by which time I had become the Chief Executive and principal of Tyne Metropolitan Further Education College, I used the same approach to initiate a whole day at the College dedicated to wonderful performances presented by the students. It formed the basis for helping us to transmit an enhanced and optimistic vision for a very different kind of organisation.

On the Meadow Well estate at Norham High School, we decided to introduce an annual staff–student event. The first of these events was a medieval banquet. On the day we all sang traditional folk songs, while the PE staff and pupils became a troupe of tumbling acrobats. In addition, specialists in Japanese sword fencing displayed their art. The home economics department prepared a feast of medieval dishes and the school hall was transformed by the art department into a baronial hall. All the staff and pupils dressed in medieval clothes for the day.

One of the event's high points was the senior leadership team's 'Rapper Sword Dance'. There is a lot written about leadership and team-building. There is, perhaps understandably, very little written about using a rapper dance to build leadership commitment. To achieve the necessary standard, the leadership team had practised the traditional 'Winlaton Rapper Sword Dance' every Monday evening for a number of weeks. This was no idle caprice, as the Winlaton Sword Dancers were probably the first sword dance team on Tyneside, having been founded in 1850. It involved five dancers, a 'Betty' and a musician who plays a tin whistle.

This dance involves a very complicated and exact routine, conducted at breathtaking speed. There is no pause and it is executed at the rate of 160 steps per minute. The dance ends with all the swords intertwined to form a star, which is held aloft by one of the dancers.

The pupils and staff could not quite believe it when this quite serious bunch of senior staff piled into the school hall and completed the dance. We all left the hall elated that the dance had gone so well. My natural instinct was to stop while the going was good but, after a few shouts of 'encore', we foolishly decided to do the dance again.

Within one minute the intricate manoeuvres involved broke down and we nearly ended up garrotting each other. Luckily we managed a quick exit.

Strangely, the fortunes of the school began to turn around at about the same time as our dance ran into the sand. I often find myself wondering whether it was data analysis or the dance that provided the real keys to transformation.

The following year we held a 'Cowboy Night', complete with western outfits, music and a group from South Tyneside, who provided us with a wild west shoot-out.

In 1988 Mike Waller, our Head of Music, and Raymond Anderson, an English teacher, wrote a theatrical entertainment to celebrate the retirement of a member of the staff. New music was specially composed for the event and the staff had a great time putting it all together and our colleague left with happy memories of the school.

It was then decided to cement the Anderson and Waller collaboration with the production of a new musical for staff and pupils. The idea was highly risky and at that time quite revolutionary. First, pupils and staff were asked if they wished to take part and, if they did, then everyone was guaranteed a part in some capacity. I was asked, as the headteacher holding the purse strings, to support the show financially and to accept that I would have no editing rights. I somewhat nervously agreed to both these terms. I knew that this was important: Mike and Raymond wanted to feel in control of what they were doing and did not want to be subjected to 'central tampering'. In 1990 came the first production of *Mr Marvel's Music*. It was, naturally, set in a school and was highly successful.

The second musical was called *Star Singer* and it ran for three nights from 25 to 27 March 1991. *Star Singer* was a more ambitious venture than our first effort. There was a larger cast, with more staff involved, and I was presented with a request for a budget to build a substantial set. Impressive costumes were made for each of the three alien tribes that inhabited the Star Singer planet. The sell-out show prompted the need for new bleacher seating and an impressive speaker system was installed in the hall ceiling.

At around this same time, a national competition, a 'Quest for New Musicals' was announced by Richard Stilgoe. He had an impressive track record, having helped Andrew Lloyd Webber to write his musicals, including *Phantom of the Opera*, *Cats* and *Starlight Express*. Six new musicals were identified and an abridged version of *Star Singer* was then performed at Buxton Opera House. *Star Singer* was the only one of the six new musicals from across the UK to be performed by a school. So, here they were, our children, in the year of the Meadow Well riots, performing on a full stage at Buxton in the full glare of publicity!

The momentum we gained produced further success with *Sylvan*, set in Albion Wood, and *Charlie's Garden*, with our colleague Dave Gill excelling as the Seaton Sluice hermit. The underwater scenes in this production were spectacular and the plot lines full of genuine emotion, as well as the expected slapstick humour.

A touring production of *Titanic the Musical*, produced for our local primary schools, was a great success as they say, 'It went down well'. Raymond narrated and Mike accompanied the four actors, while the primary pupils wore lifejackets they had made at school. Our final production in this memorable series was *Run out of Time*, which was ambitiously set in the after-life with probably the strongest musical score of all.

With all these shows the Norham High School children had something to call their own, something that was both unique and a source of pride. Above all, they had fun taking part and would probably carry forward memories that would last them a lifetime. Within a year of this, our school was identified as one of the most successful urban schools in the UK. Maybe fun is the one card that is significantly missing from the school improvement pack?

A couple of years later I worked with some headteachers in Northern Ireland. The schools were continuing to provide the very best learning environment they possibly could in the midst of the large-scale political violence of the Troubles. Every school I visited was proud to show off their pupils performing traditional Irish dances and songs. As one headteacher perceptively said to me:

If we ever stop dancing, the Troubles have won.

CHAPTER 45

DEMING, THE QUALITY GURU

I meet E J Deming, who absolutely transforms my whole approach to leadership. All the learning and building blocks I have been putting in place over the years are cemented by the 'Einstein of Quality'. I now have a leadership philosophy that reflects my own deeply held values and beliefs.

Address the underlying causes of failure in our education system, drive out fear, cease reliance on inspection, and remove the barriers to our children's natural desire to learn.

After checking, monitoring, scrutinising and examining input, progress and achievement data, I have decided to go to the pub and get ratted. Fancy coming?

The introduction of Ofsted in 1992 started the increasing trend and focus on analysing electronic data in order to judge schools. By 1995, Microsoft Excel had become the market leader in electronic spreadsheets. This passion for analysing electronic data was not, of course, restricted to schools. Indeed, my other major interest, football, was also going to suffer the scrutiny of electronic analysis.

The worry with the introduction of Ofsted approaches was that schools would become reliant on external inspection, rather than developing their own critical abilities in evaluating their strengths and weaknesses.

Edward Deming is one of the biggest influences on managerial theory and, through him, I discovered a whole world of managerial thinking that had rarely entered the consciousness of headteachers before this time.

Deming, although an American, was awarded Japan's highest honour for transforming Japanese industry after the War. In 1982, he had published a book with a really snappy title: *Quality, Productivity and Competitive Position*. It was eventually to have a new title: *Out of the Crisis*. At first sight, many of Deming's ideas seemed a long way from the world of education. Total quality management approaches, while prevalent in industry, were not in evidence in schools.

Just when Ofsted began, Deming published his final book, *The New Economics*.

In this book, Deming argued that we tended to *tamper* with organisational improvement, rather than addressing the real underlying causes of poor performance. One powerful statement by Deming stood out in his argument that we should:

Cease dependence on inspection to achieve quality. Eliminate the need for inspection on a mass basis by building quality into the product in the first place.

Deming considered inspection is too late and inefficient, and costly. It is too late to react to the quality of a product when the product leaves the door. Quality comes not from inspection but from improving the production process. He contended that:

Corrective actions are not inspection.

In 1992, I had been assured that the introduction of mass inspection was absolutely necessary if we were to improve our schools. Now I was being told by Deming that this is the wrong way to go about improving schools or, indeed, football clubs or any organisations you care to think about.

Deming claimed that 94 per cent of all the problems faced in education or at my favourite football club, Newcastle United, were due to the underlying systems adopted in these organisations. The 'special causes' approach, actions such as the recruitment of a world-class manager or headteacher, will, he indicated, have only a limited influence on results. The trouble is that we tend to focus on the special causes, whenever football clubs and schools go up and down the league in a particular season. We contend that:

It's the board, the boss, the referee ... or Ofsted ... that's the problem.

Of course, special causes, such as the recruitment of a world-class manager, may influence the league position, but essentially variations in performance are inherently part of the *total* system, which in the end will lead to mid-table obscurity.

We examine minutely and comment upon all variations in the performance – up or down. This is generally a waste of valuable time and effort. All we are actually observing is the normal variation over time. If we were to plot the club or school league positions over the last ten years, there would be only a couple of times when we should get really excited, which is when we enter the top four or get relegated.

Increasingly in the 1990s, education and football appeared to be running along the same lines: the constant analysis of performance and the basing of judgements on year-to-year indicators or even on last week's results! Whenever there is a dip, we tend to react less than rationally – usually by changing the leadership.

The reality with Newcastle United is that the statistical average, mid-table obscurity, has remained generally constant over the last 20 years.

So, if this year our own clubs and schools end up in the bottom half of the table – in mid-table obscurity – we will put this down to a special cause. For example, we will blame the management or staff or the player recruitment policy. If we end up a little higher, we will still ascribe this to the same special causes.

This misperception is because we fail to address the underlying cause, which is the total system on which football and education are based – things like governance, finance, staffing policy and customer relations. As a result, we tend to tamper rather arbitrarily with the system.

Imagine for a moment that you are firing at a local rifle range. Your shot just misses the centre of the bull. What do you do about it? There are a number of possible responses, although I guess that you would keep moving the rifle, reacting to where the last bullet landed, perhaps like this.

Answer 1: Your bullet is one inch to the right. Aim one inch to the left of your first shooting position to compensate. In other words, we do the opposite of what we have been doing for many years;

Answer 2: Your bullet is one inch to the right. Aim one inch to the left from the last bullet hole. We keep the policy but make some adjustments;

Answer 3: Your bullet is one inch to the right. You are reasonably pleased, so you aim for that particular position again. Here, we base our strategy on 'what worked the last time'.

This is classic *tampering*. These responses are common at Newcastle United and also in the world of education. The simple conclusion is that we would have been more likely to hit the target if we hadn't moved the position of the gun at all.

Quite simply, in many circumstances, doing nothing may be more effective than quick-fix tampering, whenever you've failed to take the time to find the root cause of the problem.

I have heard football clubs, and schools, say one of the reasons for their poor performance is the inability to recruit good enough players or teachers. This *may* be true, but, here we go again, blaming the whole of the problem on some isolated 'special cause'.

The problem with this solution is that it diverts us from examining the underlying problems and it prevents us from asking critical questions about the total system.

So, the football club might ask.

1. **Do our values and principles attract players?**

2. **How effective is our scouting system?**

3. **How attractive are our salaries?**

4. **How effective is the medical screening and physiotherapy system?**

5. **How effectively have we implemented systems to cover for the possible loss of our best players?**

6. **What is our youth system and how effectively will it be in providing a constant feed of new, young players?**

We can apply this sort of thinking to education, too. If a school has poor mathematics results, the blame will clearly be placed on the management of the individual school and it will be assumed and stressed that this is a problem unique to the school. This then allows all of us to avoid questioning the underlying problems in the education management system that have led to this situation.

So the following questions need to be asked.

- **Are the values and principles inherent within the UK education system attractive to potential teachers?**

- **How effective is the national recruitment policy for mathematics teachers?**

- **Do the salaries compare well with industry?**

- **How effectively does the UK screen potential mathematics teachers and induct them to ensure they are fit for purpose?**

- **How effective is the inspection regime in encouraging the growth of mathematics teaching?**

- **How good is the education of mathematics graduates at university?**

For too long we have simply been tampering with education, rather than assuring its quality. In fact, I would describe it as 'kludging', or tampering on a mass scale. Addressing the limitations of the whole system will take time and effort, backed by serious research. Difficult, yes, but it must be done.

CHAPTER 46

DEMING MEETS ELSIE

The quality control of what schools teach and how schools deliver the curriculum is now clearly in the hands of the central government. While many in business and commerce are concentrating on improving the quality of their products, schools are increasingly focused on what the external inspectors think.

Listen to the voice of children and the voice of the process of learning in order to continuously improve our schools.

As a young headteacher in the 1990s, I became particularly interested in applying the Deming philosophy to schools, and in due course, I joined the Board of the British Deming Association.

The role of the headteacher was changing. We were being told that we were business managers, as well as being in charge of the teachers in our schools. But this was happening more than a decade before the National College of School Leadership was established. In the 1990s we were rarely described as school leaders. I was the *headteacher* and my deputies and senior staff were referred to as the Senior *Management* Team. Yet, here we were faced with Edward Deming saying that we should introduce 'leadership' into our organisations.

I then took the plunge and immersed myself and my staff in the Total Quality Management approach. We began to consider seriously the impact of the leadership we provided on the systems within the school. Prior to this, the emphasis was always focused on the main role of leaders, which was to develop a compelling vision that would motivate staff and students to move with a passion.

This new Quality Management approach very much focused on management and improving the ability to develop the systems in our school, so that we could reach our goals in a timely and cost-effective manner. The need to be cost-effective was particularly relevant, as we were facing a year-on-year reduction in the available resources. We saw the systems in our school as a means by which children could achieve their objectives. This was so, whether the objective was good exam results or an improved impact on economic and personal well-being.

In this quality quest, one system we introduced was curriculum-led staffing.

At the time many headteachers were attending a programme in Llandudno, which provided a system by which we could analyse our curriculum and staffing needs. This approach led to significant gains in how we deployed our staff. This meant we used staff resources in a more coherent and cost-effective way.

In addition, we strengthened the influence of outside voices – particularly exploring the voices of students and parents to provide feedback on how we could improve our school. In doing this we applied quality improvement tools such as *Ishikawa*. This was a cause and effect analysis that allowed us to categorise the possible causes of a particular problem so that we could identify its roots.

At the same time, we took on board a belief that our children and staff wanted to learn and develop. This required a 'no-blame culture' to be a central pillar of our thinking about the school.

We worked hard on these changes and it was considered a great plus that, when the Deming UK Board visited the school in 1992, they described it as:

One of the best examples of total quality management in the UK.

This accolade was earned partly because of the attention we paid to two elements of the Deming approach, which had particularly struck a chord:

● *Listen to the voice of the customer; and*

● *Listen to the voice of the process.*

Deming had a very positive view of human nature, emphasising people's fundamental desire to learn and to challenge themselves to achieve more.

At the British Deming Association Annual Conference in Birmingham in 1993, Dr Myron Tribus, one of the most powerful advocates of the Deming approach, argued that any of the extrinsic motivation strategies we use – rewards, prizes and examination certificates – would have only a limited impact. He suggested that, if we assumed that children by their very nature loved learning, then it became our job to remove barriers within the system that reduced their access to learning.

He then told a thought-provoking story about a group of boys who had smashed the windows of a house on the corner of an ordinary street. It was occupied by an old man. Each week the windows were broken again. Each week the old man repaired the damage. Eventually, the old man decided to go outside to confront the boys. Instead of simply telling the boys off, he made a point of saying that he was usually rather lonely and he quite enjoyed the excitement of the windows being broken. He ended up by offering the boys £1 a week if they would continue breaking his windows. They agreed, but after another couple of months, he told the boys he was a little short of cash and asked if they would accept 50p. They somewhat reluctantly agreed to this.

Two months after this, he owned up that he could no longer pay them. They deliberated and then told the old man that they would refuse to break his windows in future because the external rewards he was offering were not enough.

As a new and trendy headteacher in the 1990s, I began to consider using any means possible to motivate my students.

This certainly fitted in, because I was constantly being told that leadership is about motivating people. For example, in the foyer of our school, we once mounted giant posters of Brad Pitt and Julia Roberts. The posters told students that, if they improved their attendance, they would get free tickets to the cinema.

This is where Elsie gets to meet Deming. One morning I met Elsie Spotham in the corridor. She was one of my most persistent absentees. Our offer in the foyer made no difference to her and the delights of free cinema tickets had no effect on her.

I recalled one of the key points made by Deming:

If the system is obstructive, then any form of encouragement or even threat will not make any difference.

What I needed was for Elsie to describe the obstructions in the system. In effect, she became my in-house management consultant on this issue.

As a result, I discovered that Elsie was essentially the lead carer for her younger brothers and sisters. She took them to our neighbouring primary school in the morning but, because the primary school didn't open its doors until 8.45am, she was never able to get to our school in time for morning registration.

When she arrived late, the *system* dictated that she should be placed in detention. This meant that she would be unable to collect her siblings after school. So Elsie simply stayed away. The staggering truth was that it was the blind systems that my primary colleagues and I had designed, with the best of intentions, that obstructed her opportunity to attend.

Shortly after this came to light the primary school agreed to open earlier and Elsie was able to get to my school on time in the morning:

I had listened to the voice of the customer and listened to the voice of the system.

A few weeks later I noticed that Elsie was continuing to be absent. When I enquired why this was, she answered:

The lessons are crap.

I had forgotten about that part of the system!

Recently, I saw a series of photographs of children living in a mountainous village in China having to cross a valley hundreds of metres deep on a rickety homemade cable car in order to get to school. They also climbed wooden ladders, crossed rope bridges, rode on horses and walked along narrow ledges. They did all this because of the love they had for learning at school. They did not do it for fear of punishment or for some external reward.

The village elders viewed their role in the matter to be removing the barriers to school by providing the ladders and bridges.

While we may not have to deal with physical barriers like this in the UK, we still have very real barriers to learning, often as a result of the systems we have designed. How many of us find shopping in a new supermarket very hard indeed, just because the goods are organised in a different way to our local shop? Imagine how the systems within secondary schools might appear to an 11 year-old entering a much larger school for the first time.

My concern with regard to our modern education system is that we are probably too focused on extrinsic rewards – particularly passing examinations and satisfying Ofsted. If we are really serious about improving education in the UK, then we must not ignore the role we all share in making learning accessible. Teachers, parents, employers must remove the barriers that frustrate our love of learning *and* our love of teaching.

Perhaps most crucially of all, we must listen to the voices of children. Don't just walk a mile in their shoes; try a day thinking yourself into their heads. They may have a lot to teach us.

CHAPTER 47

THE SPECIALIST SCHOOLS MOVEMENT

In the 1990s, the 'bog standard' comprehensive school is being challenged and schools are encouraged to leave LEAs. With the backing of Rolls Royce and other major employers, and in the presence of the Secretary of State, I announce that I wish my school to become a Community Technology College, *within* a local authority. The national policy is changed to allow this to happen.

School 'self-management' must have a relationship with democratic oversight.

We are about to launch a new, exciting and innovative type of school. We'll be using books.

ncreasingly, I was beginning to understand the sort of political forces that were having an impact on my school. The comprehensive system I had joined in the 1970s was being challenged on many fronts.

Most of the headteachers I met in our regular meetings were committed to implementing the 'comprehensive ideal'. We had mostly been involved at the beginning of the comprehensive movement. We well remembered the divisions that the tripartite system inflicted on us. It was only natural that we would fight against the challenge to the comprehensive ideal.

One major challenge at this time was the economically driven need to promote subject specialisms within schools. Later on in the decade, Tony Blair – that famous product of Fettes Public School – would notoriously reinforce the need to confront and challenge:

the 'bog standard' comprehensive.

Many on the political left considered that John Patten, the Secretary of State for Education at the time, and the Prime Minister, John Major, were keen to undermine the comprehensive system itself. Perhaps they were intentionally aiming to break up the comprehensive system by opening up the route to specialisation.

John Patten argued that subject specialisms in UK schools were already emerging and that we should on no account treat children like identical vegetables.

John 'Patter' Patten served as Secretary of State for Education 1992–94.

The 1993 report, *Learning to Succeed,* produced by the independent National Commission on Education, chaired by Lord Walton of Detchant, considered that the aim of creating greater choice and diversity was not truly compatible with the other more democratic aim of giving all children equal access to 'high-quality' schooling.

Patten disagreed with Lord Walton and his 1992 White Paper, *Choice and Diversity: A New Framework for Schools,* would form the basis of the 1993 Education Act. He argued that the provision of education should be geared to individual needs. He was a man with strong opinions and while he was Education Secretary, Patten described my hero, the Birmingham Education Chief, Tim Brighouse as:

A madman ... wandering the streets, frightening the children.

Brighouse sued for this less than endearing description and won substantial damages, which he then donated to educational charities.

In 1994 Patten went even further and announced that the government would encourage the setting up of new grammar schools and would allow grant-maintained schools to select a greater proportion of their intake. The opposition to the move towards specialist schools argued that Patten's strategy was to achieve selection indirectly through the back-door mechanism of specialisation.

The Specialist School and Colleges programme of the 1980s and 1990s was to highlight many of these dilemmas.

The City Technology Colleges initiative, which had been established in 1988, had attracted a disappointing level of business sponsorship and, in the five years following its introduction, just 15 new schools had opened. Consequently, the initiative was transformed into the Technology College programme in 1993.

The years from 1993 to 1995 saw the launch and development of the Specialist Schools programme. This brought about a dramatic widening of scope to include schools specialising in modern foreign languages from 1994, and sports and arts from 1996.

Rather than aiming to establish new schools, the programme for specialist schools was aimed at high-performing existing schools.

It was originally restricted to grant-maintained and voluntary aided schools and excluded local authority maintained schools. The programme was later characterised by a House of Commons Select Committee as an embodiment of Conservative aspirations for secondary education. These aspirations were combined and included:

Promises of raised achievement with significant investment from business, institutional autonomy, competition between providers and choice for consumers.

It was certainly supported by leading employers, including Rolls Royce. Significantly, a number of headteachers immediately began to advance the case for extending the programme more widely to include local authority maintained schools.

During this period I was invited to speak at a conference in Brighton, which was to be attended by the new Secretary of State, Gillian Shepherd. In the months before the conference, I had held meetings with major employers in the North East, including Rolls Royce, Procter and Gamble and Swan Hunter. As a result, I had managed to pull together a substantial amount of funding for my school. I announced at the Conference that I was intending to establish a specialist school and yet continue to operate within our local authority. We proposed to call the school a community technology college. At the conclusion, there was a resounding cheer from the headteachers in the hall. I had clearly touched a nerve and I was a little shaken. This was, in fact, the first time in my education career that I had popped my head above the political parapet.

In 1995 the opportunity to become a specialist school was opened up to all maintained secondary schools. By July 1995 Robin Squire, Conservative

Under-Secretary of State for Education, announced the first schools had been designated to operate as technology colleges from September 1994. Following this announcement Squire visited my school. Little did I know then that he would eventually lose his seat in Parliament and sign on for the Job Seeker's Allowance.

DfE booklet on Schools for the Future.

Then, in the 1990s, my school became one of the first local authority based technology colleges. As a result, we were allocated funds to improve our technical facilities. The *Yorkshire Post* described Norham as the 'School for the Future'. We decided, as part of our upgrading programme, to introduce 'the information superhighway', as it was known at the time. While doing this, I never envisaged the extent of wireless technology that we have in place today. If someone had told me then that a future headteacher would be concerned about children bringing their mobile phones into classrooms, I would have simply been incredulous.

Each school designated would receive a one-off capital grant of £100,000 plus additional recurrent annual funding of £100 per pupil to help implement its development plans. A total of 85 schools across the UK were identified, including my own school, Norham Community High School, North Tyneside. Others designated within our region were Prudhoe County High School in Northumberland, the St Thomas More School in Gateshead and Walbottle High School in Newcastle.

A key priority of the newly named Norham Community Technology College was to change the learning environment we provided. This would now be founded on the National Curriculum but would develop a strong technological and vocational focus. This new focus was supported by the new facilities we had acquired in technology and science. Our sponsors included the Rolls Royce Power Group and Procter and Gamble, as well as a long list of local companies. This would in turn further the skills, employability and life chances of our children and it formed a central plank of whatever we did.

Information Superhighway

input

The Internet: Every computer plugged into the world's cable network - including thousands acting as libraries or noticeboards.

Cable TV

input

Typical 50-channel package includes eight in foreign languages, one specialising in science and one in history, plus 24-hour news, sport and entertainment.

Cyber cafe

Pupils research homework or talk to friends worldwide.

Electronic libraries

Satellite pictures, film archives, encyclopaedias, music, talk, all cross-referenced, so a geography lesson can move on button-clicks from a map of S.America to a satellite view of the Andes.

School networks

input

Links to other schools locally and abroad. Older pupils help younger ones. Teachers swap lesson files and check on absentees. Sick or excluded children, plus adult learners, take lessons at home.

Language lab

Children work at their own pace on audio-visual lessons chosen for their known effectiveness

History

Computer, with projector, runs pre-programmed sequence of maps, cartoons, film and reminiscence, to help explain battle of Passchaendale.

Fitness Centre

Cameras record techniques for analysis. Output measured against heart rate, etc, on running and weights machines. Sporting heros glue lessons via video link.

Food Technology

Cabbage boils by molecular disturbance on a cool hob. Computers make quantity and nutrition calculations for mass catering and run market research info.

CADCAM workshop

Computer-aided design and manufacturing have replaced woodwork, etc. Pupils might be asked, for example, to design and furnish a house in three-dimensional drawings and then set up machines to make a metal door-knocker suitable for mass production.

Welcome to Norham Community Technology College

Administration

Classroom computers send in lesson-by-lesson registration. Technicians trawl the networks for useful information for memory banks.

Yorkshire Post depection of Norham High School, 'The 21st Century School', 1996

YORKSHIRE POST Graphic:Graeme Park

In 1997, the incoming New Labour Government announced that it would maintain and expand the specialist schools programme but expand the 'community role' of these schools. New Labour also introduced a new provision, giving schools the power to select 10 per cent of pupils on the basis of aptitude.

I always considered the specialist college programme to be an opportunity to redress the inequality between vocational and academic qualifications. Accordingly, our curriculum was designed in partnership with local employers. Our new Technology College would also have a clear focus on community regeneration, including an employability strategy involving local parents. The community comprehensive principle was to be fully maintained and our new name said it all: Norham *Community* Technology College.

When the school in due course became oversubscribed, we took care to ensure that our first choice was to take children from our local community – we rejected our right to select up to 10 per cent of our pupils based simply on aptitude.

Surprisingly, even in the white heat of change at this time, the idea of a specialist school was never central to our parents' view of the school. When we commissioned independent research, asking why parents put our school at the top of their list, they emphasised:

Academically well-qualified staff and the standards of work achieved.

Technology, ostensibly at the heart of these changes, hardly got a mention.

By October 2010, over 95 per cent of secondary schools had become specialist schools. Unsurprisingly, the direct government funding for specialism was then removed by the Coalition Government. Apparently, specialism was no longer special. *Plus ça change.*

Today the debate about comprehensive provision versus specialisation has become less heated. There is now more focus on autonomous schools delivering within the limits of a nationally prescribed 'academic' curriculum.

But still there remain a number of dilemmas within the UK education system that we have yet to resolve. Consider the following.

1. **Providing specialist provision for children and, at the same time, maintaining equal access for all children to a broad and balanced curriculum.**

2. **Supporting the 'comprehensive ideal', while also ensuring choice and diversity.**

3. **Ensuring equality of esteem between vocational and academic qualifications.**

4. **Properly and fully engaging business with education.**

So, many issues remain with us. We will, of course, continue to fight for equality of esteem between vocational and academic qualifications by properly engaging with the business world. But governing boards and headteachers are probably right to persist in maintaining their pupil- and community-centred comprehensive principles, while carving out unique and special identities.

CHAPTER 48

TRANSFORMING OUR SCHOOL

I am now an experienced head. My school is being celebrated as 'achieving against the odds'. I am given the opportunity by Her Majesty's Inspectorate to reflect on my school's practice and explain why my school has been so successful. I meet other headteachers who are as passionate as me about improving the lives of children.

The important criterion for success is that a child's desire to learn continues after they leave, and that a school continues to improve after the leader departs.

Supposing we all close our eyes and wish for a new school.

It was now nearly eight years since I became a headteacher in 1988. Like many of those in this position, I had been trying to balance the need to deliver nationally prescribed programmes and at the same time develop a school that was unique in its nature and secure in its reputation. But I have to admit that I never properly reflected on what I had been doing – I was too busy.

It was at this point I was given an opportunity to look back. Together with 11 other headteachers across England, I had been involved in a research programme called 'Schools Against the Odds'.

For a period of more than two years, Her Majesty's Inspectors had been analysing why certain schools had been able to buck the trend in performance for schools within socially and economically challenging areas. The headteachers in the programme, myself included, received no information about the other headteachers and schools in the group.

In 1996, the group met for the first time in London. We were all signed up to the Andy Hargreaves' view that high-performing organisations have a culture of creativity and risk. At the beginning of the meeting, we were all asked to state the single most important thing we had done in order to improve our schools. We provided a wide variety of answers.

One headteacher described the day after her appointment, when she had discovered that the ceiling in the school hall contained a mural that had been painted over. In one weekend she and her husband had cleaned the ceiling, revealing, to the astonishment of the children on the following Monday morning, a Sistine Chapel-style painting.

Another headteacher had bought a couple of hundred bicycles for her school and every break children would cycle round and round the school grounds.

I proudly told them about my 'aggressive daffodil planting policy'.

A school without a fence.

And what was the one thing that united us all in what we picked out? It was quite simple: we all shared a passionate drive to make the lives of our children substantially better. During the meeting, I was thinking privately and silently that *some* of the passions being displayed verged on madness! They were indeed the quirkiest bunch of headteachers I've had the privilege to know.

I described how, towards the end of the 1980s, my school, Norham High School, had been sliding slowly but steadily into decline. For example, the school was designed for an intake of 180, but in 1988 only 77 pupils turned up. My school was one of the most unpopular schools in the area. It was perceived as a 'rough' school. It was indeed on the edge of North Shields and was serving a working-class catchment, including a very run-down housing estate. The GCSE results were abysmal – in 1988 only 5 per cent of pupils gained 5 or more A* to Cs. Only 56 per cent of our pupils gained 5 or more A* to Gs.

Part of this could be accounted for by the 81 per cent attendance rate – but only *part*. It was not surprising that only 20 per cent of our pupils stayed in education after GCSE. With the school roll falling faster than the lead off our roof, we soon found ourselves overstaffed by a terrifying 50 per cent. At this time the local authority began talking about closure – again a terrifying prospect. Nothing short of resurrection was required.

As part of the 'bucking the trend group' process for HMI, we were asked to outline the eight key elements in our own personal journey towards improvement. Not surprisingly, there was a great deal of commonality between our approaches.

For what it is worth, this is what I shared with my colleagues. It may reflect some of the reality of the journey taken by Norham High School.

1. **First, identify the causes of low self-esteem.**

    The first move we made confronted our low morale, low expectations and low standards. Teachers and pupils were suffering from chronic low self-esteem. We did not concentrate on encouraging and motivating the poor school attenders or the low achievers. Instead, we asked what it was that was preventing the child from attending school and the teacher from being successful in teaching them. We felt that:

    To impose high expectations without dealing with poor self-image risks anxiety and hopelessness.

    This is probably something that government inspectors should take note of.

2. **Next, start with the easiest things first – attend to the bricks.**

    The management team began a rolling programme of refurbishment of classrooms and corridors. So, the graffiti seen around the school was effectively eradicated. Then, our new security measures dramatically cut the losses from break-ins and vandalism. The pupils were fully involved in our refurbishment decisions.

    School buildings should reflect our love of children, just as shopping malls reflect our love of consumerism.

3. **Then, build a positive culture, offering a lot of security and a little challenge.**

    Loyalty is contagious. The new management style opened up issues that had never before been shared with staff. Over the first year, the overstaffing was resolved by applying curriculum-led financial planning, unprecedented levels of consultation and sharing problems with colleagues. Any departing teachers were not abandoned; they left to go to attractive positions negotiated by management.

    If Dunkirk could be identified as a victory, then managing overstaffing can also be celebrated.

4. **Regularly celebrate the success of all – catch your pupils and staff doing good things.**

    For pupils there came a developing sense of security and value. Pupil successes were fed back; they were shared and celebrated. Positive partnerships with feeder schools and active visits into the community by the management team helped to spread the word that things were changing.

    Soon, the local press began to publish releases about pupils' successes. Our local radio began to use staff expertise for education broadcasts.

    Even publish the speed of the grass growing if it means you feel better about yourselves.

5. **Always reiterate and build on your uniqueness and encourage co-operative enterprise towards a shared vision.**

    Individual staff development was encouraged by joining pilot programmes, raising the levels of both expertise and morale. The introduction of *Investors in People* and the pioneering *Schools Mean Business* brought many people together – parents, pupils and major employees.

    In 1992, the management team and the technology department made a successful bid for technology school status and thereby created a superb learning environment for technology. We were not a one-suit outfit, and our annual musicals, produced and written by staff, were to win us international awards.

    Your vision should be based on your unique identity – not just on where you are on someone else's league table. Have the Popeye mentality – I am what I am!

    All fans of league tables in education should think carefully about where they stand in this debate.

6. **Recognise that real institutional and personal self-esteem means you can handle misfortune when it strikes.**

    The Meadow Well riots, which were occurring just at this time less than a quarter of a mile away from our school, destroyed houses, shops and a youth centre. Yet, it is a fact that the school suffered not even so much as a broken window. An HMI report at the time included the words:

    Visiting Norham was an uplifting experience.

Understandably, this was also the year that the Local Education Authority finally agreed that the school had a future.

Describing a school as a failing school is a failure of the system, not of the school.

Hard-line Interventionists and the promoters of heroic turnarounds should take note of this.

7. **Go on to build excellence into everything you do. Build a reputation, build memories and always consider that yesterday's success can also foster a dangerous complacency.**

In 1992 *The Independent* newspaper commented:

The pupil-centred approach has penetrated all aspects of school life, sometimes with spectacular results.

Above all, build quality into *everything* you do. It should go without saying that our priorities were the quality of teaching and learning. We did not stop there. The quality of planning, management systems, people development, performance assessment, pupil reward systems were also on our radar. We did not stop there! The entrance lobby should ooze quality, the reception should be first class, the toilets should be pristine, the communications with our community exemplary and our school performances as good as the professional theatre. Everything should be quality. Mass inspection advocates must ask themselves if their processes can support this total quality approach.

By 1995, Norham Community Technology College had been identified as one of the top eight technology colleges in the country. In the following year, we would be oversubscribed, with about 20 per cent of our pupils coming from outside our catchment area. Sustainable and continuous improvement, based on installing a Total Quality Management Systems approach, directly involving our local community, was considered central to our work, and it had certainly delivered.

8. **Finally, in the real world of employment mobility, have a good succession plan and ensure that the improvements made are genuinely sustainable.**

It is no surprise to me that, later on in 1998, under the leadership of Margaret Stone OBE, my one time deputy, the school was ranked by the *Observer* newspaper as the eighth-best state school in the country.

This success was to continue: in 1999, Norham was named on the List of Outstanding Schools in the Chief HMI's Report to Parliament. In the same year, it was the first school in the country to be a finalist in the Investors in People National Awards for outstanding practice. Then, in the year 2000, Norham made it into the top 50 specialist schools nationally, measured in terms of the greatest percentage improvement in the proportion of A*–C passes at GCSE. But to be sober for a moment, the above statistics represent other people's criteria for success:

Your personal criteria for success should be that you like yourself and are proud of who you have become.

If you ask me how this dramatic turn-around of a clearly failing school was achieved, I'm cautious. It certainly was not done overnight – *fast* improvement is one thing; *sustainable* improvement is another. Most of our success came from the resilience, commitment and character shown by our staff, students and community. The turning point was in achieving a shared vision of where we wanted to be and an understanding of the barriers to success that would face us.

Yes, we wanted to be world class – but on our own terms and in our own way.

REFLECTIONS

Our leaving 'do', with my secretary, Vera Armstrong.

When I look back, I think I am a little uncomfortable regarding the profession I joined in 1966. Corporal punishment was rife, union disputes were high on the agenda and children with special needs were described as sub-normal and backward.

On the other hand, many wonderful teachers and education leaders were promoting an inclusive, comprehensive education that considered children's needs as paramount. During the period I worked in schools I was proud that we were moving in the right direction. We raised the school-leaving age, focused on the pastoral care of children and tried to respond to the new technological revolution.

Then, along came the 1988 Act. Child-centred education, comprehensive schools and the school leader as a curriculum leader were under attack. We now consider education as a servant of the national economy. Local authorities are shunted aside as a new, centralised, prescribed, subject-focused curriculum, backed by a powerful inspectorate, is introduced. Nonetheless, the Act did try to ensure some curriculum consistency across all schools.

I also faced events I never would dream of encountering, when young people would burn down the area in which they lived. I would also be amazed at children from an area of severe social and economic hardship performing at Buxton Opera House.

I learn so much from South American philosophers, English educationalists and US engineers. I believe I have learned from my own school experience and I am self-confident with regard to my own values, principles and beliefs.

I still have hope that we can change the system, that schools can be transformed and all children can succeed.

Perhaps, in the next stage of my career, I will be able to have a greater influence over the education system; or, will my personal pebble ripple across the education pond and be swallowed up by the enormity of the task?

Looking ahead to Part Three of this book, during the latter part of my life in education, I feel like I am returning to my school days; there is a renewed focus on academic subjects.

I am now about to enter the final part of my life in education. I step out of the school and the classroom and enter the world of strategy, politics and power. I am now able to be a part of designing the system, rather than simply being part of the system. I will learn the biggest lesson of all: there is no hiding place for the designer.

PART THREE

Leading:
policies, planning, politicians

Still going

CHAPTER 49

CROSSING THE GREAT DIVIDE

I become an executive director within a local education authority, which achieves 'Beacon Status' for tackling school failure, with no school in an Ofsted failing category. Since 1966 I have worked in close proximity with children. Every day I am with them, their aspirations and despair stare at me in the face. I now move away from direct engagement with children and their communities.

Learning to lead involves discovering new things we can't do.

They made me the Director because I don't understand how a council works. It would be too risky to give this much power to somebody who does.

In 1996, I was appointed as Director of Education and Chief Education Officer in North Tyneside – one of very few headteachers to take on this role. As a headteacher, I had learned my trade gradually, starting out in the classroom and moving through the ranks. Here I was leaving my own school just at the time when it had developed a national reputation for good practice.

On my first day on the job, an elderly councillor stopped me in the corridor and gave me some more sage advice:

Divn't run before yer can waallk. In your case, bonnie lad – learn to crawl first!

In the Middle Ages, scientists believed the earth was flat. Indeed, those who professed to believe it was round were considered ignorant and stupid. So, the big question I would have to answer during my term of office was this:

Would my zero background in local authority administration be a help to me, or a hindrance?

In a study by the Harvard Business School, the biggest fear of chief executive officers is being found out and being exposed as incompetent. I expect this is a natural reaction for most people when they find themselves promoted into a role that is 'bigger' than anything they have done before. Have no doubt, moving from headship to the post of an executive director in a local authority was extremely daunting.

Laurence J Peter developed the 'Peter Principle' theory, which resonated with many of us to cause yet more anxiety:

The selection of a candidate for a position is based on the candidate's performance in their current role, rather than on abilities relevant to the intended role.

As it was, I had been appointed to my new post largely on the basis that my school was doing well. Nevertheless, operating as a headteacher had provided me with an armoury of useful skills and knowledge. On the other hand, I knew that I had so much to learn. To put it another way, I was promoted to a position in which I might prove to be incompetent. I would have to learn competence in the performance of the job. In common with most aspirants, I had never before waited until I was truly competent before I took up a new job. I reflected that this also applied long ago when I was learning to ride my first bike without stabilisers.

Probably, the first thing incompetent newcomers should do is to surround their new post with the most competent people they can find. I was fortunate because I was ably supported by Councillor Janet Hunter, the Lead Member for Lifelong Learning, who clearly positioned herself as a significant leader. As a 'new boy' to local government, I was heavily dependent on the expertise of individual staff members like Pat Jefferson, Gill Alexander, Peter Parish and Mark Longstaff, all with long experience of and considerable expertise at working within local government. I was also able to make a reasonable contribution from my own experience as a headteacher. Here, I thought, was a model that could work: having politicians, administrators and school leaders all working together.

As a team, we were also united by a common belief that we needed to harness the power of local government and its key partners to support and enable schools to become self-managing and self-directing. In effect, we wanted to forge a 'new relationship with schools'. We also wished to demonstrate that we were a 'learning organisation', an organisation that was firmly determined *to* develop this idea by emphasising leadership as a key dimension of change. The notion of school failure was considered simply unacceptable. Central to our thinking at this point was the concept of a community of learning providers working together to achieve ambitious targets for:

- **raising standards of attainment;**
- **improving attendance;**
- **reducing exclusions; and**
- **raising the attainment of 'looked after' children.**

School representatives sat on new partnership boards, dealing with education, regeneration and social inclusion, health, and crime and community safety, as well as lifelong learning.

Our 'Schools for the Future' strategy was developed in partnership with the full range of social services, adult education, the education business partnership, the Tyne and Wear Health Action Zone and the voluntary sector.

In truth, there was a genuine whole-council approach to supporting school improvement. Other departments in the Council added leverage to improving attainment in our schools in the most disadvantaged areas. They did this by deploying complementary regeneration strategies to improve the surrounding communities. We implemented strategies to identify and remove surplus school places, thereby ensuring schools were financially viable. For example, we tackled reorganisation from a three-tier to a two-tier system in some parts of our borough.

One major development resulted from the fact that, unusually, I came from a headteacher background: this was the more substantial use we made of headteacher secondments. Also, we introduced the concept of School Improvement Partners, using the expertise of both headteachers and local authority officers, by encouraging them to operate jointly to support and challenge schools. The improvement targets were monitored by steering groups, comprising officers, inspectors, school representatives and other key partners relevant to the individual priorities.

Headteachers, inspectors and local authority officers worked together to publish guidance materials on school improvement, producing what we called the *School Improvement Toolkit*. Following a favourable review in the *Times Educational Supplement*, other LEAs began using these materials. Building on this success, the LEA was, in 1998, awarded a licence by Ofsted to run training courses for school managers on school self-review.

As a former headteacher, I was particularly concerned that challenge and support from the local authority should be self-evidently intelligent. Such 'intelligent accountability' essentially depends on the quality of data and information, including contextual information, that we apply to the situation. Critical to this was the establishment of a new data management team in 1998, which produced data outlining the performance of schools relative to other schools in our authority. We then became one of the first LEAs to develop and pilot baseline assessment materials and subsequently to have a baseline assessment scheme accredited by QCA.

As well as being challenged continuously by Ofsted there were also termly reports, which had to be presented to elected members of the Reference Group for Lifelong Learning, who supported and challenged our work. We were also held to account by the Select Committee for Lifelong Learning. Headteachers accepted this level of challenge, because they trusted the basis of the challenge and, more importantly, found that genuine *support* was very much to the fore.

In addition, we undertook annual assessments of schools and LEA performance against national performance indicators. These were used to assist with the early identification of problems and to enable the networking of good practice with our statistical neighbours.

The Council, because of the mechanisms we had installed, became extremely successful in ensuring that schools did not develop serious weaknesses or fall into the Ofsted special measures category. We used strategies that complied with a model of intervention that was proportionate, in effect:

Intervention in inverse proportion to measured success.

Our intervention strategies ranged from consultancy support for school leadership and management to special projects focusing on acknowledged weaknesses, for example, in literacy within particular school clusters.

As a 'learning organisation' that placed leadership at the centre of its work, the Council was determined to ensure that its elected members and officers were well trained and motivated to develop the key policy commitments it made. Inspectors underwent a rigorous training programme fully focused on school improvement and the strategy for vulnerable schools in particular. Officers and Elected Members shared joint leadership training, which ensured that there was a shared understanding of the characteristics of highly successful leaders and their behaviour.

Without a doubt, we were innovative and exerted an influence well beyond our borders. For example, we established a Regional Leadership Centre, which was equipped to offer the latest national and international training programmes to people in our region. The purpose of the Centre was to promote excellence in leadership and management. It accessed a network of local and national expertise to promote training opportunities, drawing on the latest international and national research.

Our Annual Standing Conference was able to attract some of the most significant educationalists from across the UK and abroad, including Canada and the USA. One of the most popular contributors was John Abbott, Canadian author of *The Child is Father of the Man*.

Headteachers were invited to join the Council's Training and Development Team. Key elements in this training provision were Organisational Development and Total Quality Management.

Working closely in concert with a newly established Centre for Advanced Industry, we used the latest technology to network mentoring training and research within schools and other local authorities in our region.

The results were pronounced and gratifying: by 1999 no school in North Tyneside had been found to require 'special measures'. The overall school standards in North Tyneside were high when compared both to its statistical neighbours and nationally.

In the same year, we were awarded Beacon Council Status for our progress in 'tackling school failure'. So, North Tyneside Council had succeeded at this point in transforming education within the area by signing up to a 'New Relationship with Schools'.

The question for all local authorities over the next few years would be how they will go about developing a new relationship with all education providers, including the emerging academies.

CHAPTER 50

PLAYING THE PERCENTAGES

For most of the 1990s, I adhered to the Deming nostrum: '*without data you're just another person with an opinion*'. The danger is that a simple graph or a number may be overvalued, revealing in a flash everything about a school. Of course, data is only really as useful as the context in which it is gathered and presented.

Always turn data into information and information into insight.

Before you tell her your name, ask her what her plans are for using the data.

After my first year as Director of Education, the percentage improvement in the secondary school examination results in the Borough improved dramatically. At a meeting in the Council Chamber, my team and I were praised by the Leader for achieving such success.

My answer was frank.

- First, it was really very little to do with me. The results were largely a product of years of work that had preceded my tenure.

- Second, the variation in results only related to one year, there was no trend and we were unable to clearly identify the causal factors involved.

- Third, the results would probably dip in the following year, due to normal variation – something statisticians like to call 'regression to the mean' – and the type of cohort of children passing through the system.

One of my fellow Directors whispered to me:

Not a good answer. You should have claimed the credit and then start preparing your excuses for the following year.

Then came the killer question from the Chamber:

I've just come back from Paris and all the children can speak French. Why are our French results so bad?

I was just on the point of telling my story about Maurice Chevalier when the Chair of the Education Committee stepped in and saved my bacon.

Let me say right from the outset that our ability to analyse the strengths and weaknesses of a school has been one of the greatest improvements in the last quarter of a century. Also, Ofsted's contribution to our understanding of how well a school is doing has been tremendous.

However, I have concerns. For as long as I can remember parents ask a very simple question when discussing their child's school:

What is this school like?

When I was a young teacher, my answer to this question would usually be focused on the curriculum we offered, pupil behaviour, extra-curricular activities available and, most importantly, *whether the children enjoyed being there*.

In total what we would say was:

This is a really good school: the children are happy and well-behaved, the lessons are really good and we do lots of exciting things.

Today the answer has to be much more forensic: it will detail the percentage of pupils who achieve 5+ GCSE grades A* to C with English and mathematics, and the percentage of lessons that are adjudged 'good'. We will now also have progress indicators to highlight. This means that a secondary school will be judged by the amount of *progress* a child makes.

Fyodor Dostoevsky wrote his classic novel *Crime and Punishment* in 1866. His concern regarding treating people as objects still rings true today:

*A percentage! What splendid words they have; they are so scientific, so consolatory...
Once you've said 'percentage,' there's nothing more to worry about. If we had any other
word ... maybe we might feel more uneasy.*

Nearly 20 years ago some of our friends from Chicago, Illinois in the USA, who worked
as education advisers in their own state, visited us in the UK. I asked them how they
went about advising and supporting schools. Today in the UK education advisers
are trained intensively in the use of data to analyse the strengths and weaknesses
of schools. Thus, a report about the school will specify in incredible detail the key
percentages in matters like teaching, behaviour, attendance records, levels of progress
and the impact of special initiatives, such as the Pupil Premium.

When I met the school improvement specialist from Chicago all those years ago, he
described his work in these terms:

*Well, Les, I pop into the staff room and ask: 'How's it going guys?' They tell me ... then
I have a little think and give them good advice.*

I accept this was more than two decades ago and I understand that today the system
of school support in the USA is also moving progressively towards our more analyt-
ical approach. But this move should not be accepted uncritically. A sign that used to
hang in Einstein's office at Princeton University reminds us to be careful about what
we measure and how we value it:

Not everything that counts can be counted and not everything that can be counted counts.

School inspectors at the more domestic level also rely heavily on data. But, no matter
how hard external inspectors work, we must always remember that a school inspection primarily provides a picture of a school based on measurable data, not *all* data.
Much potential data is simply not there.

The other important thing to remember about the judgements of most external
inspections is that they measure the *here and now* or the *past*. Quite rightly, they don't
attempt to measure what may be.

It was probably not pure chance that the advent of a centralised inspection system
coincided almost exactly with the invention of the Excel spreadsheet and computer
databases. Microsoft released the first version of Excel in 1985 and then exported it
to Windows. Thus, the first version occurred one year before the 1988 Education Act.

It would be really interesting nowadays to imagine an inspection regime without
computers. With the advent of computers, we had become 'pupil quantifiers'. External
inspectors have since developed and sophisticated the art of using data and information to evaluate schools. This then begs the question as to whether they can evaluate
the intangibles like climate, culture and ethos. Ironically, these intangibles are probably the lead indicators for success.

Similarly, this is an issue with school inspection. Of course, it is vitally important
to understand where a school has been and what it is like at present. But for the
majority of parents, there is a need to ask the question about what it will be like
when their own child arrives in a year's time.

A question that we may ask about schools is:

Does the school have the right context for improvement?

Unfortunately, this 'contextual' aspect of schools receives insufficient focus. In business, potential investors are likely to be very interested in future levels of performance. They will insist on having 'lead indicators' to inform their judgements. Of course, in education we can assess lead indicators like staff turnover, recent appointments, leadership team capacity, predicted pupil intake and financial standing. But this approach is not infallible. Take a look at Newcastle United football team's performance now, and ask yourself the question:

Is the context there right for future improvement?

Sorry, perhaps I shouldn't have asked!

The arrival of performance indicators and league tables has without doubt helped to inform and support parents in choosing the right school for their child. However, such data may sometimes lead us to have a more limited perception of the value of the whole child.

The motto chosen by the founders of the Statistical Society in 1834 was:

Aliis exterendum, which means let others thresh it out.

Parents rarely judge their own children by statistical information. They care about all aspects of their child's development and, in the end, they will use common sense when making decisions. In the end, these parents will 'thresh it out'.

CHAPTER 51

SCHOOL DEVELOPMENT PLANNING

Planning is important. If you can picture the future, then you can do something about it now. The School Plan becomes central to school improvement. Unfortunately, the plans sometimes become ends in themselves. We sometimes believe that it is the School Development Plan that motivates teachers rather than leaders.

Planners need to listen to those who are affected by the plans.

Don't you think your development plan needs more detail?

A radio sketch in the 70s featured Blackbeard, the pirate. His ship is under attack and he is desperate to make the right decisions:

Right me' hearties ... we are down to ten men. The mainsail is broken. The ship is on fire. Midshipman Billy has had his leg blown off. Me beard is on fire and, worst of all, we are sinking. What should we do?

There is a pause, and then comes the answer:

We need a plan!

If I'd been on board, I would have shouted, helpfully:

Me hearties. We need a ship improvement plan, with SMART objectives!

In the early 1990s, long before the discovery of system leadership, emotionally intelligent leadership or self-evaluation came 'planning'. Not just ordinary planning; this was planning with knobs on.

The central government in the 1990s had been dramatically increasing the output of legislation and the planning which accompanied it. The 1993 Education Act was possibly the largest piece of legislation in the history of education. At the time, headteachers felt overwhelmed by the amount of legislation we would have to respond to, and by the plans we would have to deliver. I felt a bit like Homer Simpson:

Every time a new idea would enter my brain, another one was pushed out.

However, there was some hope, because in 1994 Sir Ron Dearing produced the first major review of the National Curriculum. He suggested that the National Curriculum had become an unwieldy structure and that the content should be reduced. Moreover, less time should be spent on testing and a fifth of the time should be available for use at the discretion of schools. We also saw the beginning of the new hierarchy of subjects, with art, music, geography and history becoming optional.

Any headteacher optimism was misguided. Dearing did *not* herald a future in which centralised control over the minutiae of what happened within schools would be relaxed. We were confused. Here was a government that had emphasised 'choice and diversity' and 'encouraging the market', while increasingly producing plans that emphasised central direction. As one of my colleagues – more aware than most – said at the time:

They don't really trust the market and they trust headteachers even less.

As a headteacher, I had been attracted by the view that planning was the key to improving results. In my own school, supported by the LEA, we even produced our own book on the subject. It was entitled: *How to Write a School Development Plan*. Eventually, in 1994, this was published by Heinemann and for a time it was one of Heinemann's most popular educational books, selling well abroad, even in Japan.

My senior staff even had the pleasure of appearing at a book signing event in Waterstone's bookshop.

In my second year of being the Director of Education, I became heavily involved in working with the Department for Education and Skills in the development and piloting of Education Development Planning. Our mantra was:

By failing to plan we are planning to fail.

The education planning approach at that time was yet another stage in facilitating management development going right back to the First World War. In the 1880s and 90s, Frederick W Taylor believed it was management's task to:

- **design jobs properly; and**
- **provide incentives to motivate workers to achieve higher productivity.**

Similarly but somewhat earlier in France, Jules Henri Fayol had concluded that management needed five basic administrative functions:

- **planning;**
- **organising;**
- **commanding;**
- **coordinating; and**
- **controlling.**

Meanwhile, in Germany, Max Weber focused his attention on organisational structure, dividing organisations into hierarchies with clear lines of authority and control.

It was clear that even in the 1990s the views of Frederick W Taylor were still influential. The School Development Plan was to be the means by which we would ensure teachers would work hard and raise standards.

In the 1990s, we tended to ignore the views of the Harvard Professor, Elton Mayo, who proposed that managers should become more 'people oriented' and that participation in social groups and 'group pressure', as opposed to organisational structure or demands from management, would improve productivity. The concept of the 'servant-leader', which calls for leaders to place the priorities and needs of their followers before their own or that of the organisation, would not be proposed as a management approach by Robert K Greenleaf until much later.

Before 1998, there had been no systematic attempt at a national level to drive up education standards through central planning. The first major attempts to do so were the National Literacy Strategy, quickly followed by the National Numeracy Strategy. Then along came the Key Stage 3 Strategy – for 11–14 year-olds – and the Early Years Foundation Stage. These developments culminated in the remit of the National Strategies.

The National Strategies in the period up to 2011 involved a host of programmes; for example, consider the following.

- **Early Years Foundation Stage.**
- **Communication, Language and Literacy Programme.**
- **Core subject pedagogy and subject knowledge.**
- **National Challenge Programme support for schools below floor targets.**
- **School Improvement Partner Programme.**
- **Behaviour and Attendance Programme.**

- **Social and Emotional Aspects of Learning Programme.**
- **Inclusion Development Programme.**
- **Achievement for All Programme.**

The National Strategies were delivered by a national team of experts and a regional delivery team that worked with and supported local authorities in providing training and support to education providers. Local authorities, in their turn, were funded to employ some 2000 consultants to help deliver the National Strategies' training locally.

In 1981, John Lennon, in the song 'Beautiful Boy', reflected that:

Life is what happens to you while you're busy making plans.

Have no doubt, we were busy!

In 2011, the Department for Children, Schools and Families – in noting that it had paid major dividends – described the National Strategies as having become:

One of the most ambitious management programmes in education.

So, one has to ask, 'if they were so successful, why did they end?' It was subsequently argued that the National Strategies programme was always intended to be a fixed-term intervention to achieve accelerated improvement in standards, and of course, there was always the cost!

It was then argued that the time was right for the central government to step back from much of the central provision and initiatives and to consolidate resources and decision-making at the school level. This would allow schools to determine their own needs and to commission appropriate support.

The system, government claimed, is now ready to move towards more collaborative practice between teachers within and across schools.

Perhaps we were beginning to apply 'Blackadder Speak', or had we subconsciously absorbed the messages of Blackadder from TV screened during the 1980s and 90s? Baldrick, the stupid servant, famously promoted his 'cunning plans', which he thought up to deal with a pressing problem or crisis. While these were always ridiculed scathingly by Blackadder for their implausibility, these plans were frequently resorted to, when the situation became desperate.

The one saving grace with the Blackadder approach to planning is that at least the plan was travelling *upwards* – indeed from the very bottom – into the organisation. It is, however, still true that the plan was clearly invented by an idiot. Nevertheless, the principle that the 'customer' should be involved in the design and redesign of development plans was now being seen as critical.

The voice of the customer or receiver of the plans is often not heard and this can be a dangerous omission.

In the future, I guess there will be senior politicians arguing that education will need to move away from central planning altogether and leave education to the influences of the 'market'. In the 1990s we were constantly confused about the future. We will almost certainly continue to be confused in the twenty-first century.

CHAPTER 52

THE DEATH OF THE DIRECTOR

I am gradually being drawn into the world of politicians. Increasingly, I am wondering whether the differences between national and local government are not about education at all. Perhaps the real battle is about who runs the country, central or local government. I am awarded the OBE but not allowed to use the title after my name.

Make visible the too-often hidden relationship between education and political power.

When elephants fight, the grass gets trampled.

ncreasingly, as a Chief Education Officer, it began to dawn on me that there were 'forces beyond my understanding' – just as it had for Luke Skywalker!

As my fellow *Star Wars* fans would probably have said, the 1944 Act and, most recently, the 1988 Act were major disturbances in the 'force'. Throughout my time as a CEO I, like many of my fellow CEOs, was buffeted and battered by forces we didn't control. On reflection, I believe I had entered another world. It was a world in which the battle lines, lying between central and local government, were clearly visible. I was, in fact, right in the middle of a war.

As a headteacher, the relationship between central and local government didn't really interest me. I was only interested in the relationship between local government and my school. Many people had warned me not to take the Director's job. Even on the day before I was interviewed for the post, a former Director had contacted me. His advice was blunt:

If you do take this job, do one thing: learn how to be a bricklayer. Then build a bloody big wall between you and the Councillors and make sure they keep out of your territory.

At the time, I didn't really understand the relationship between the executive and the politicians. For some, the lines were very clearly drawn and should not be stepped over. For others, it was different; the executive and politicians were members of the same political party, would perhaps meet socially and probably pre-plan solutions outside business hours.

Just before I took up my post, I had been awarded the OBE for my work as a headteacher. I was then coolly informed that it was not Council policy to use these letters after my name. This brought it forcibly home to me that I was now working within a more politically charged environment. I worried that I had not the least idea how to lay bricks.

The role of Chief Education Officer can trace its history back to the clerks who worked in old School Boards. The 1902 Education Act had introduced a range of new roles with various titles, including Education Officer, Chief Education Officer, Director of Education and so on.

One of the earliest Directors in our region was Spurley Hey. He became the Director of Education in Newcastle in 1911. Directors such as Hey firmly established the key value and influence of the office. He had had an interesting background. At ten years old, he was a part-time worker in Fox's Steelworks and then became a pupil-teacher at Stocksbridge School. As a young man, he gained a scholarship to St John's Diocesan Training College in York. He was clearly a man of many parts, because somewhat later he played for Barnsley Football Club, providing the meagre pittance that helped to fund his part-time BA at London University.

Spurley Hey, with his contemporaries, James Graham of Leeds and Percival Sharp of Sheffield, were nicknamed the 'Three Musketeers' because of their attacks on their 'Cardinal Richelieu', operating as the Board of Education.

The first specific reference in law to the role of the director of education was in the 1944 Education Act, which required each local education authority to appoint a 'fit person' to be its chief education officer, although, up to 1972, any such appointment could be vetoed by the Secretary of State. The role was expected to:

be the principal adviser to the Council as the Local Education Authority, and safely implement all the decisions and policies of the Authority.

When I attended my first meeting with the other chief education officers, a long-serving director questioned my ability to do the job, as I had not taken the administrative route. This was the route he had himself taken, after teaching for a couple of years, and seemed to him to be totally appropriate. Shortly afterwards Sir David Bell, who eventually rose to be Permanent Secretary to the Secretary of State for Education, moved from headship to the post of Director of Education in Newcastle. From then on, more and more headteachers would take on roles as directors of education.

By the time I became a chief education officer in 1996, the power, the authority and the influence of the job had been seriously curtailed. Up to the 1970s many chief education officers, such as Sir Alec Clegg in the old West Riding of Yorkshire, exercised immense influence over policy and were clearly seen as the 'Masters of Education' within their localities.

For several years before my arrival, education committees had been playing an increasingly active role. The political parties were much more disciplined and had clear ideas of what they wanted to do, thereby reducing the ability of chief education officers to influence policy.

While in no way as powerful as the old directors of education, chief education officers still possessed considerable powers. They were information gatekeepers and controlled significant resources necessary to formulate and implement policy. Their power also came from their more cutting-edge understanding of the trends in educational thinking and of the deficiencies in the existing policy. Of course, they would on some occasions lose the initiative and have to produce plans for policies that they, personally, would not have put forward.

Coming from a headteacher background, I was used to my governing body giving me quite a lot of rope regarding policy development. I was acutely aware that the oversight by the political governance of a local authority was much more powerful than that of a local governing body over a headteacher. My freedom to make decisions was much more constrained. Rather, my job appeared to be a facilitating role, creating coalitions, negotiating and reconciling or, as I tended to view it, 'padding about'.

Essentially, I had gained more schools but had less power than before. I also joined the 'Corporate Management Team' and, indeed, corporatism was dominant in the 1990s. At one 'away day' event, the Corporate Directors were asked to position themselves in a room in relation to what they considered to be the corporate centre of the Council:

- **three went into a rugby scrum facing inwards;**
- **one stood by the door; and**
- **I went outside into the garden.**

My rationale was that I felt more concerned with serving the schools than with serving the corporation.

The Thatcherite centralist policies employed to undermine local authorities were at this time still being perpetuated by New Labour. The year-on-year reduction in school funds, combined with the increasing number of initiatives that were being directed from the central government, limited our ability to invest in local education initiatives. Increasingly marginalised as chief education officers and as headteachers, we were the *receivers* rather than the *promoters* of change.

There is a Swahili proverb, which says:

When two elephants fight, the grass gets trampled.

The 'elephants' in my book were central and local government. The 'grass' was the chief education officer and the schools. We were caught in the middle, often finding ourselves in almost impossible situations. When a strengthened HM Inspectorate joined in, coupled with the growth of union activity, the increasing power of governing bodies, the changing relations between LEAs and schools and all the new centralised government initiatives, we felt we were being trampled on by a whole herd of elephants!

Sir Tim Brighouse: the last of the great Chief Education Officers.

Tim Brighouse, perhaps the last of the great chief education officers, led the Birmingham Local Education Authority. He had a strong belief that the relationship between local authorities and central government could be resolved satisfactorily. The solution, he believed, was to develop partnerships between LEAs, leading local professionals and local communities.

Tim Brighouse had left his role in 2004. From April 2006, education and social care services for children in each local authority were brought together under the unified post of Director of Children's Services. This signalled the end of the role of Director of Education. There would be no more 'musketeers'.

CHAPTER 53

A NEAR-DEATH EXPERIENCE

As I become more and more involved in strategy and planning, my memories of what it was like to work 'at the chalkface' are beginning to fade. Then things change radically when my doctor tells me I have cancer. I need an operation and I will undergo 30 weeks of chemotherapy. My focus and priorities change and I am certain about one thing: I do not want my children to remember me as a strategist and planner.

We all need to work out how we want to be remembered.

To be honest, you're healthy. I'm sending you for a colonoscopy because I find all headteachers a little irritating.

Throughout 1998, in my third year of being a chief education officer, I periodically experienced severe pains in my stomach. I went to the hospital at least a couple of times during the 12 months I was suffering from these symptoms. The first time the consultant, after giving me a sonar scan, announced that the stomach pain was probably the result of eating peanuts. On the second occasion, no firm conclusions were reached.

In the meantime, I continued with the task of implementing the reorganisation of the three-tier system and installing our school improvement strategy.

One of the most wonderful things you can do as the Director of Education is to visit schools and talk to the staff and children. And, indeed, I would be invited to numerous school events, musicals and prize-givings. Having said this, I must admit that I was probably heard to say that, if I had to go to one more performance of *Oliver!*, I would shoot myself.

One idea we hit upon within the local authority was to put on an Annual Gala Performance for our schools It was a simple idea, in which each school would save a short extract from a performance each year and then at the year-end we would put them all together into a single show. It was as I watched the Gala Performance that one of my colleagues mentioned that a number of our headteachers had remarked on my grey pallor. It was a portent and the next day was one of those rare times that I was absent from work.

It was only when my doctor visited me at home the next day, when I was lying in bed, that I realised something was seriously wrong. I had always been taught by my parents never to upset doctors and teachers because they were too important. So, when the doctor asked me how I was, I answered:

Not so bad.

Then, just as the doctor was leaving, the pain was so extreme that I swore out loud:

****, that hurts!

My doctor, being unused to such bad language from me, realised that something was really wrong and immediately arranged for an ambulance to take me to hospital. Within a couple of days, I was diagnosed with colon cancer and duly operated upon.

Following the operation, I received 30 sessions of chemotherapy. One slight problem was I had always hated injections. So, I went to see our local dentist, who was also a hypnotherapist. It was almost theatrical and he really did 'put me under' by swinging a fob watch in front of me. I can remember those soothing words, now:

You like needles, you like the smooth way they enter your skin.

My phobia was effectively dealt with and I decided that I would never miss a single session of chemotherapy, no matter how ill I felt during the process.

In order to have a family holiday, my wife and I arranged to go to France immediately after one Thursday session, to return the next week. I told the hypnotherapist about this plan and I remember him saying:

You will have a fabulous time and fabulous it will be.

From that day to this, I have always had the most fabulous holidays. In fact, I am sure that hypnosis is a really cheap way of having great holidays. Go under the influence and a week at Cullercoats will truly be the bee's knees.

Have no doubt, the aggressive chemotherapy I received was awful. I would return from the hospital every Thursday morning, be very ill until Monday morning and then return to the role of Director of Education until Wednesday. Then, the cycle would repeat.

Occasionally, there were low ebbs and I would wonder what people would remember of me if I were to die. Part of me thought this might be a good time to die because most of my friends were still hale and healthy, so I would have a good funeral, surrounded by friendly faces. I even imagined being there 'in spirit' and listening in to all the wonderful things being said about me. Things like:

He never bought rounds.

He was hopeless at football.

His jokes were crap.

However, more seriously, I did think about what my four children would remember about me, not just as a father but also as an educationalist. I taught in the period when the recipe for good teaching was considered to be – 'one-quarter preparation and three-quarters theatre'. Possibly, in today's climate, it is the other way round.

Education had been my life and I wanted them to believe I had made a real contribution to society that was worth remembering. Although I wanted to be remembered as a good headteacher and a good chief education officer, these seemed unimportant at the time. I had come to the conclusion that what I wanted most of all was to be remembered as a good teacher and a good dad. That was all.

So, I composed a letter to my children. Many years later they gave me back the letter. This is what it said:

Letter from a teacher. October 1st 1998:

This week the Prime Minister said that lots of teachers should be sacked. I know you must be wondering if your dad is one of the ones who should have been sacked and if he was a bad teacher.

You know I once loved teaching and I think I was a good teacher.

When you were little, I used to prepare my lessons every night, ready for the next day. I used to get quite excited, when I made what we called 'visual aids'. One of my favourites was a giant Roman soldier. I drew a fifteen-foot-high soldier on large sheets of white paper, which I cadged from the local newspaper. The children spent three weeks sticking old bits of leather, milk bottle tops and cloth onto it. It was great! Everyone came to my classroom, until I took down the soldier. The caretaker said it made it difficult to clean the walls. We were all very sad, when it was put in the bin.

Another great lesson I remember was when I read 'The Borrowers' to 11 year-olds. I used to walk on the tops of the desks, being the 'human bean' who frightened the little people who lived under the floorboards. The pupils would hide beneath the desks and pop up every so often to 'borrow' pens, books, boxes I had left lying on top of the desks. One day, one of Her Majesty's Inspectors came in and told me off for 'harming public property' (the desks)!

I hope you will be pleased that I continued to walk on the desks, after the inspector left the school.

Love Dad

CHAPTER 54

THE BRADFORD INTERVENTION

Following my recovery from cancer, I am requested by the DfE to support Bradford District Council, who subsequently ask me if I would lead their interim management team and support the outsourcing of their education services. To some, the argument seemed simple. 'Some local authorities are not capable of running an education service. The private sector could do it better.' I am now thrust into the front line between central and local control over education.

Those who maintain their core values in times of turbulence and change are able to survive.

It can be rough in the stormy seas of change management. However, real leadership is going down with the ship.

One of my favourite films in 1998 was *Sliding Doors*. Gwyneth Paltrow starred in this romantic comedy, which explored the nature of fate and self-determination. The film describes how an advertising agency worker loses her job and returns home early to find her boyfriend in bed with his ex-partner. Then, apparently in an alternative reality, she arrives home a few minutes too late and remains with her boyfriend, oblivious to his infidelity.

After announcing my resignation from my post as Director of Education, I considered what the future might hold. I established an education consultancy company called Northern Education. While I had thoroughly enjoyed working with wonderful local politicians, LEA officers and headteachers, I decided I wanted a different style of life. Another of my great ideas was to disappear into Northumberland with my family and live in the beautiful coastal village of Alnmouth, and I would write a book.

Meanwhile, my fellow chief education officers across the North East and Cumbria held a little farewell party for me. For this event, the Director-General of the DfE had come 'up North' specially. After the speeches, he boldly announced to everyone that I was to work with the DfE in Bradford. I was caught completely off-guard, as this was the first I had heard about it. Later he apologised and told me that he had understood that I *had* been asked and had accepted.

Thus, another door surprisingly slid open and I decided to walk through it. It had been only four years since I was a headteacher, who didn't quite *get* the politics of education. I was now about to enter the most politically charged atmosphere in education at the time, the relationship between national and local government. This would be fought out in Bradford and my cosy dreams of living in a little seaside village in Northumberland would have to be put on hold.

In the year 2000, a highly critical report on Bradford Local Education Authority by the Office for Standards in Education was published. Nationally, Bradford was ranked 137th out of 150 LEAs in terms of its GCSE results.

Bradford's neighbours at the bottom of this league table were the likes of Manchester, Hull and Middlesbrough, urban areas, all of which shared a similar range of socio-economic problems.

In May that year, I was asked to prepare an action plan for Bradford, which addressed the key concerns within the Ofsted report. Then, in August, Sir Anthony Tippet, a former Vice Admiral, was drafted in to chair the new Education Policy Partnership, and I was appointed by the DfE to work alongside him.

The combination of a senior naval officer and a history teacher was likely to prove an interesting model! At our first meeting, he announced to the members of the newly founded Education Partnership Board that he would 'task me' to construct a plan, to which I responded:

Always ask, never task.

Not another bloody communist, came Sir Anthony's reply.

After that clearing of the air, we got on like a house on fire. Shortly afterwards a cartoon was published in the local *Telegraph and Argus,* depicting the Admiral with Councillor David Ward, the Executive Member for Education and myself as the crew, attempting to steer the ship through Ofsted's stormy waters. A deal was subsequently struck with Bradford Council, which agreed to appoint me to a new post of Assistant Chief Executive, with responsibility for Education.

Somewhat unusually, my salary was paid by the central government. As a result, on arrival in Bradford, I was greeted by the headlines in the Bradford *Telegraph and Argus*:

Steering the good ship Bradford through Ofsted's stormy waters.

NEW SCHOOLS CHIEF FOR FREE.

Perhaps this was a fair description of the situation!

The bombshell decision to remove control of Education Services from Bradford Council was then finally announced by the School Standards Minister. This changed the whole situation for me too, because I was then asked to lead the interim management of the Education Service and chair the procurement process. This process would lead in due course to the outsourcing of Bradford education services to the private sector.

While this period may be remembered for the major challenge it posed for the role and autonomy of local education by central government, it was also a time of significant change across the spectrum. The challenge was not *whether* local authorities should oversee schools but *how* they should do it. How could a local authority do things differently in the future? Many options had been considered:

- change the leadership;

- develop a strategic partnership with a service organisation; or

- outsource the education services.

In the case of Bradford, it was the last of these options that was chosen.

The Minister, Estelle Morris, introduced me to the Bradford Secondary Headteachers' Group. Naturally, in these circumstances, I was extremely nervous; they were a formidable group.

The Chair of the Headteachers' Group asked if I supported the Chief Executive's proposal to allocate an extra £6m to the secondary schools' budget. To put this into perspective, the overall budget for Bradford secondary schools was £6m below the

Chris Woodhead, the Chief HMI, and Estelle Morris, the Minister for School Standards.

national mean. At the same time, the budget Bradford primary schools received was £3m less than the mean.

I indicated that I didn't agree with this unbalanced redistribution of funds and, somewhat rashly, introduced what might be termed the concept of 'equal poverty'. To put it more diplomatically, I suggested that, if the secondary schools would give up some of this extra £6m to the primary schools, while both would remain below the mean, at least there would be fairness. This argument went down 'like a sponge leg in a flood'. I left the meeting feeling embarrassed, particularly as I had been chastised by the Head of Bingley Grammar School for misquoting Thomas More.

I returned to my hotel, wishing I had never taken on the job. The next morning a deputation of headteachers came directly to the hotel, led by the Chair of the Group, Gareth Dawkins. He indicated that they had met following the meeting and had agreed to the rationale for rebalancing the additional monies to benefit the primary schools. This was indeed a significant moment and a significant statement of intent to work in a values-driven environment and to seek a moral consensus.

The Bradford *Telegraph and Argus* had earlier reported my desire to develop a 'new relationship with schools', based on the approach I had previously developed as a director of education. For me, the new approach was more about building relationships that were based on partnership and principles, with the underpinning principle being always putting the child at the centre of what we would do.

So, at last, the tender for outsourced Education Services in Bradford was issued. It was to be the biggest contract ever issued in the UK for Education Services provision. As a result, a number of the major service companies in the UK put their names forward to deliver the service. These included Capita, Tribal, Nord Anglia, Amey and Serco. In the end, Serco won a ten-year contract to deliver Education Services in Bradford.

There was a surprising degree of consensus across all the political parties to do things differently. In Bradford we worked with a Labour Government that was encouraging the outsourcing of education services, collaborating with the Tory Leader of the Council, and enjoying the support of the local Liberal Executive Member for Education. They were all united in their desire to do the best for children. The struggle for power between central and local government was a subliminal reality but was secondary to the focus on children.

There were hiccups, as things progressed, and one or two people across the political spectrum changed their minds and advocated that the outsourcing process should stop and other options should be considered. However, they also suggested that the model of involving headteachers in the management of the Authority was showing signs of making a positive impact and the interim approach currently adopted should continue.

At this time, the DfE suddenly became nervous. They were listening to the rumour that I was about to announce my lack of confidence in the outsourcing strategy and that I was preparing to leave. A DfE deputation duly arrived from London, just as I was having a curry in one of Bradford's wonderful restaurants. I told them that I did have concerns but that I had agreed to do the job and I would see it through. I understood the nature of the line between my executive functions and policy.

In the end, all the key players in Bradford, including the school leaders, felt it was in the best interests of the children to continue the outsourcing process. T S Eliot once said:

Only those who risk going too far can possibly find out how far it is possible to go.

We were about to find out.

CHAPTER 55

A FRESH START: SOMETIMES THERE IS NO EASY FIX

We enter the age of the miraculous solution and the quick fix. This is the age of the Superhead and Fresh Start. Giving someone or an organisation a fresh start seems such a good thing to do. There is something incredibly hopeful about a new beginning. The danger is thinking that a fresh start is easy, a magic bullet, which can address endemic failure overnight. It cannot.

Constantly changing structures and replacing people do not necessarily provide long-term solutions.

Every time the web gets broken, I blame the flies and start again.

At the turn of the century, there was an increasing view that failing schools could be turned around quite easily. A school would be put into the magical 'special measures', providing a programme of intensive reform and inspection, which would put the school back on the road to success – easy, peasy.

The Secretary of State, David Blunkett, who was no shrinking violet, even announced that he would consider closing any school that failed to deliver at least 15 per cent A to C grades for GCSE.

Of course, there were success stories to be found. For example, there was Northcote School in Wolverhampton, the first secondary school ever to be put into special measures. It came out of special measures two years later. The headteacher, Geoff Hampton, was subsequently given a knighthood for engineering this success.

Easy as A, B, C: David Blunkett, Secretary of State for Education, took a strong line on standards in schools.

Unfortunately, quick fixes like this are sometimes unsustainable and by 1999 the Ofsted inspectors were in evidence again at the school. While they found some worthwhile strengths there, they also found a number of significant weaknesses. For example, pointing out that the teaching was 'not good enough' and the quality of sixth form provision was 'poor'.

Even more worrying for many headteachers was the knowledge that putting a school into 'special measures' could make the situation worse. In some cases, more discerning parents simply took their children out of the school and the school then spiralled down into an even deeper chasm.

In the west end of Newcastle, Blakelaw School was based in one of the most disadvantaged areas of the city. The children were described as:

... having low levels of literacy and numeracy, poor communication skills and being steeped in an atmosphere of indifference.

Very few people in the area had sustainable jobs and many of the parents felt they had been let down by the education system.

In 1996, the school was judged by inspectors to be failing and plans were put in place for its closure. However, government education officials then postponed making a final decision. Then, in October 1997, the Local Education Authority submitted plans for the school to be included in the government's new Fresh Start scheme.

This new scheme aimed to revitalise 'failing' inner-city comprehensive schools by appointing so-called Superheads. A firm belief at the time was that every school could be 'turned around' when led by such a paragon. The Fresh Start scheme was based on the idea of 'reconstitution', which had been developed in San Francisco in 1984. Paradoxically, by 1997 – at the point when Blakelaw would be reconstituted – the model had been discredited by the American Federation of Teachers and even by those who had launched the idea!

Over the years I have sat in many meetings when someone announces the adoption of a new great idea from abroad. For example, when I worked with the Warnock Commission, a representative from the USA asked in a conference how many were introducing the American 'Modern Math' approach to mathematics teaching. About half of those in the audience confirmed that they were. He then rather cruelly said:

We tried that too, and it didn't work.

In due course, in September 1998, as part of the Fresh Start programme, Firfield Community School replaced Blakelaw School. And, of course, along with the new name came a new headteacher. The school was provided with a new school uniform, lots of new computers and the building was significantly upgraded.

The inspectors who were monitoring the progress of the new school noted improvements in standards and pupil behaviour, but they also pointed to a number of continuing problems, which would need to be addressed, including standards in numeracy, the inconsistent quality of lessons and pupil attendance.

Equally important for the local authority was the school's failure to overcome its poor reputation and attract more pupils. The need for more pupils was vitally important, as the extra funding, which was part of the Fresh Start programme, was dependent on the school becoming full within three years. The ambitious targets that had been set for pupil numbers had *not* been secured, so the extra cash had not materialised.

A further bombshell occurred on Tuesday 14 March 2000, when the superhead who had been appointed to lead Firfield School resigned from the post. The immediate cause was that *Channel Four News* had reported that the school had been trying to get rid of difficult pupils by persuading parents to claim they were going to educate them at home. Such crises are catching and two other superheads within the UK resigned within a matter of five days.

The night before the Superhead of Firfield School cleared her desk, I had received a phone call from the Director of Education in Newcastle. He asked if I could go into the school and support the deputy headteacher, Russ Wallace, who was being drafted in rather hastily as headteacher.

Sitting together in the recently vacated head's office at Firfield, we agreed co-operatively on a way forward. Russ undertook to do the day-to-day management, while I was deputed to focus on future strategy. Russ had incredible charisma and was able to relate to children, staff and parents in a superb way, so, when another DfE sponsored superhead visited the school to offer support, we declined gracefully. Russ and I both considered that to change the school required a team effort, not the supposed magic of any one individual.

At this time the term 'superhead' was falling into disrepute but this did not mean that this was the end of the matter and this controversial term is still used today. The headteacher market was becoming increasingly like the football manager market, with ever-rising salaries available for those prepared to take the most challenging jobs. Secondary headteachers would be soon commanding salaries of £120,000 or more, often accompanied by considerable performance-related bonuses.

By the year 2001, it was considered that the Firfield Fresh Start experiment had failed and Firfield School and West Denton High Schools were scheduled for closure in August 2002. They were to be replaced by a new 11–18 school. The Director of Education for Newcastle, Phil Turner, described the Fresh Start as a 'brave attempt' but clearly considered that the model was flawed and he had no alternative but to move to closure.

Even when faced with closure, Russ and I decided that we would continue to drive for improvement. Many people talk about the importance of having a powerful vision for a school and we decided that we wanted to demonstrate that we could design a shared and positive vision for how we would *close* the school. We agreed that we wanted the children and the staff to walk away on the final day with their heads held high, feeling proud of what they had achieved.

Russ and I both loved cowboy pictures and decided that we wanted to look like John Wayne in the film *She Wore a Yellow Ribbon*. In this famous film, John Wayne retired from the Cavalry knowing that he had done a good job and that he had made a diffe-rence. We wanted to do the same and in solidarity; the Head of Art painted a mural of John Wayne on the art room wall to remind us of our dream.

In our last year at Firfield School, Ofsted praised the 'significant' progress that had been made and also the fact that the GCSE results had improved. Even at the point of closure we never gave up and Russ, the staff and the children walked into the sunset proud of what they had achieved. The staff also held their heads high enough for five of them to go on to become headteachers in other schools. More importantly, the children left with confidence, looking forward to the future in their new school.

Not everything changes and the concept of a fresh start as a panacea for all problems in schools is still prevalent within some parts of the education community. There is also a naive belief that a simple educational 'fix' will provide a sustainable solution when it is abundantly clear that the problems are so firmly located within the eco-nomic, social and cultural framework schools operate.

A teachers' union leader, commenting on the government's Fresh Start policy, said:

The reality is becoming clear that, even with brilliant heads and staff, these schools do not succeed. The fault lies not with the teachers but with the kind of children that attend these schools.

To be honest, I can never remember any national or local government official ever saying that Fresh Start would provide a quick fix. But I find considerable difficulty with the view that the *fault* lies with the children. Fresh Start could never be a magic bullet; but neither could the headteachers, no matter how good they were.

I continue to believe that it is perfectly possible to create great schools in areas of severe disadvantage. If we do not, then it is our society that is failing, not the school, and certainly not the children.

CHAPTER 56

FURTHER EDUCATION

I enter the world of further education and take up the post of CEO and principal of a further education college. I am faced with the same challenge I received when I moved from headship to become a director of education. What do you know? It is like entering a next-door neighbour's house, which you have never really visited. Much is familiar and reflects my own experience. A lot is new and surprising.

Go beyond our own institutions and learn from other sectors.

The worlds of local government, national politics and the private sector were very different and often alien to a former school-based history teacher. They were as far removed from my early personal experience as the moon from the earth. And then, the world of further education (FE) seemed to exist in another galaxy. On top of this, the landscape of FE colleges had itself significantly changed in the decade before my direct involvement.

In the early 1990s, the Conservative Government was highly critical of the existing arrangements in place for training a skilled workforce. They also attacked the failings of the Manpower Services Commission's Skills Training Agency. The government took the view that a key means of addressing these failings was to focus on employment issues at a more local level. This change would involve the creation of a hundred local employer-led quangos, which were to be called Training and Enterprise Councils, thereafter referred to as TECs. At the same time, a Further Education Funding Council, under the chairmanship of Sir Robert Gunn, was established along with a new funding and quality audit regime.

By 1992, all the colleges were to become corporate bodies with distinct legal identities and direct responsibilities for their own financial and business administration. FE colleges would, then, once they were outside local authority administrative and funding arrangements, compete with each other for students, as the funding would then follow the student – now to be referred to as the 'customer'. The idea behind this was that this 'quasi market' would weed out poor-quality, inefficient provision. To put it another way, the customers would vote with their feet and good colleges would grow, while poorer colleges would be driven out of business. These weak institutions would be forced into mergers, be taken over or even face closure, overall resulting in a much leaner FE sector.

Tyne Met College.

Within a matter of a couple of weeks after returning to the North East from involvement in the radical solutions in Bradford, I was asked if I would be interested in applying for the role of Chief Executive and principal of an FE college. Having a cautious disposition, I immediately consulted my team of advisers in God's Departure Lounge.

My gadgee-like friends' response sounded like this:

Further education is a world away from what you are used to. An FE college is a really complex organisation ... it's part college, part business.

They were exactly right, an FE college was a new type of organisation for me. So, I decided to apply.

Before long, in 2002, I took up the post of Chief Executive and principal of North Tyneside Further Education College.

Having worked primarily in schools and local authorities, this was a totally new ball game for me. At my first meeting with the staff, I gave them a great deal of confidence by owning up to the fact that:

I cannot even spell FE.

While the running of an FE college had many similarities when compared to running a school, a local authority or a private business, there were also many distinctive aspects. For me, at the time, the unique character of FE resided in a combination of characteristics:

- its 'corporate governance';

- its 'business partnership orientation';

- its overtly 'proactive nature'; and

- its strong belief in 'educational inclusion'.

It was clear to me that this was a hard balancing act to achieve!

Within a decade of my facing these elements at the College, I would see them replicated with the emergence of multi-academy trusts.

Overall, my entry to the FE sector provided me with a tremendous privilege and an unparalleled learning opportunity. Because of it:

- **I had the honour of working with some of the most creative and progressive educationalists and governors you could ever wish to meet;**

- **my new colleagues possessed a certainty that their job was to be absolutely inclusive and would provide effective 'second chances' for young people;**

- **the College did things I had never expected. The emphasis was placed on students as 'customers', coupled with the sophisticated feedback mechanisms that were developed;**

- the organisation's ability to work collaboratively with local business was impressive; and

- the breadth of the curriculum offered was incredible, ranging from higher degrees in law to qualifications in the performing arts and in engineering.

... and I could go on adding to this list.

There was, nevertheless, a problem. While the College had been described as 'satisfactory' by Ofsted, one of its faculties had been failed and our academic sixth form component required significant development. First, we addressed Ofsted's concerns regarding the faculty and it proved to be a problem that could be sorted out rapidly, within a period of three months.

The academic sixth form issue was more complicated. At this juncture, our neighbouring sixth form college had just been put into special measures by Ofsted. As we were to some extent in the same boat, we agreed to work with the sixth form college to address our individual and our joint concerns. Jointly, we established a new Governing Committee to identify and explore the opportunities for collaboration. It soon became clear that, rather than a temporary fix, a merger would offer the best way forward. The two institutions were so different that this route would be a major challenge. One institution placed its main emphasis on vocational education and inclusion, while the other stressed academic excellence. On the other hand, perhaps this was a perfect marriage? We do know that opposites attract!

After a fraught gestation period, in March 2005 the two colleges merged to become Tyne Metropolitan College, providing broad-ranging programmes of education for over 15,000 students, served by 500 staff and having a budget of £21 million. In an instant, the College became the third-largest employer in the whole of North Tyneside.

We tried to be radical in our structure by creating four distinctive faculties:

- a centre for professional care and education;

- a centre for business and technology;

- a centre for creative and leisure studies; and

- a sixth form academy.

Remember, this was more than a decade before the Education Act that eventually allowed *all* sixth form colleges to become academies.

Another innovation we undertook was the introduction of the International Baccalaureate. Again, this step was well in advance of the English Baccalaureate becoming government policy. However, the most radical aspect of how we worked during the amalgamation was to reject the obsessive focus on the traditional targets for improvement – like student success outcomes – and to set our sights firmly on targets relating to *quality* and *organisational development*.

At the time we set out on these changes, our staff were the lowest paid in the region. Our new rationale was to suggest that, if we increased the pay of our staff, we would be more likely to retain and attract those of a high calibre and would thereby be more likely to increase student numbers in order to defray the costs. The result, we believed, would be the achievement of an operational surplus. This was a very big risk to take, but supported by a very able team, including the vice-principal and the finance and HR directors, we agreed to take this way forward. The eureka moment was justified when student numbers duly increased and we achieved an operational surplus of £400,000.

Our Quality Improvement Strategy was combined with an Organisational Change Programme that resulted in the introduction of a number of 'new-style' targets, which focused on:

- reducing bureaucracy;

- increasing responsibility;

- improving the standards of our processes and outputs;

- enhancing the clarity of our direction of travel and our systems;

- emphasising the rewards, which would accompany success;

- celebrating success; and

- reinforcing the notion of team commitment.

All our targets were introduced for the Senior Leadership Team, the middle management and the whole organisation as a whole; each year we measured whether we had achieved them. What we found was that as the organisational climate improved, so too did the outputs we achieved. The College success rates moved from bottom quartile, nationally, to top quartile within four years.

There is an often-quoted mantra from the Department of Education that:

standards will decline during an amalgamation.

The argument backing this judgement is that, at a time of organisational turbulence and change, the focus on teaching and learning simply goes out of the window. At Tyne Metropolitan College we demonstrated that this inevitability was mistaken. The DfE and the Learning and Skills Council (LSC) both recognised this when they described this amalgamation as 'exemplary'.

Following this turbulent experience, we moved on to the formal opening of the amalgamated college in the second week of July 2005.

Tony Blair opening Tyne Metropolitan College.

Tony Blair, the then Prime Minister, agreed to perform the opening ceremony. Then, one week before the proposed ceremony, at 8.50am on 7 July, three bombs exploded simultaneously in London, leaving 52 people dead and over 700 injured. This was the worst bombing in London since the Second World War.

The next day, I left a message at Downing Street, simply saying we would absolutely understand if the Prime Minister would not be able to come. Then, at 8.00am on Monday morning, Downing Street rang to say that Mr Blair would not let us down. He arrived, spot on time and spent most of the morning talking to our students and staff.

I will always be grateful to him for this act of courtesy.

Sometime later, Mark Knopfler agreed to open a new facility within the College. As he put it, he would have *given his right arm to come to Tyne Met College*. Quite a compliment from one of the world's greatest guitarists, but I knew what he meant.

As early as 1989 Kenneth Baker, Secretary of State for Education, had announced that he would address the 'Cinderella image' of FE by investing in colleges so that they would enjoy equal status alongside the school and university sectors.

Further education deserves greater attention and greater understanding across the board. It's been a long time coming.

CHAPTER 57

FUTURE-PROOFING OUR SCHOOLS

The 'Building Schools for the Future' programme spreads rapidly. When new shopping malls and football stadia were built in the 90s, I began to wonder whether we loved shopping and football more than our children. I am now excited, having played football on schoolyards that had a 30-degree slope, checked smokers in outside toilets, used a bucket to catch rain during lessons and worked in schools designed by architects supported by consultant burglars.

The quality of the physical environment should reflect our love and regard for young people.

I say, this plan looks unusual. Yes, Minister, it's a toilet with a school outside.

One of the greatest challenges for education is to prepare children for a future that is difficult, and perhaps even impossible, to predict. As Nils Bohr said:

Prediction is very difficult, particularly if it is about the future.

It is, therefore, quite a task to invest heavily in new school buildings based on what we *think* young people will need decades from now. And, indeed, it is a critical part of 'future-proofing' to ensure that our school buildings are, and will be, fit for purpose. This involves:

- **preventing decay over time;**
- **strengthening on a continuous basis;**
- **extending the life of demonstrably good provision; and**
- **planning ahead in a perceptive way.**

Thinking laterally, I often wonder whether the education we offer children is really designed to fit the buildings, rather than the other way round.

The schools I attended as a child and worked in during the 1960s and 1970s had outside toilets. As a child, I was used to going to the 'outside lavvy' in my own home. It was sometimes quite a scary experience. I would have to leave the warmth of the house and walk out into the cold and dark. The only light available was often a candle and, in deepest winter, a paraffin lamp, which was lit in order to stop the pipes from freezing. In those days, if I had been asked to predict the future, I would have said that outside 'netties' were here to stay. My grandfather would have agreed, as he was disgusted by the thought of having toilets *inside* a house. One of his proudest possessions was the potty he kept under the bed. It was decorated with flowers and a little inscription which read:

Waste not, want not.

I never did get the import of this inscription.

Of course, our views of what constitutes acceptable school accommodation has changed over the years. However, I became increasingly frustrated with the state of school buildings, particularly when I witnessed what was happening in the private sector. At one point In 1995, I wrote a letter to Sir John Hall, a powerful north-eastern entrepreneur, declaring that two particular developments in the North East – in which he was the key developer – namely the Metro Shopping Centre and the new Newcastle United Football Stadium, led me to conclude that as a society we now cared more about shopping and football than we did about our children. I never got a reply, probably because there was no good justification to be had – and no profit in it.

Headteachers were given control of their budgets in the 1990s. As you might expect, the first thing I did was to improve the toilets. I had a phrase I frequently used at the time:

Bogs before brains.

This may sound very basic but, of course, it was backed by a time-honoured educational rationale. Maslow, a famous psychologist in the 1940s, presented us with his famous triangular 'hierarchy of needs'. He considered that all people have 'basic needs', which must be fulfilled before the 'higher-order' needs, such as love, belonging and learning, can be successfully addressed. Put simply, hungry children don't usually make successful students.

Simply allowing teachers to influence the design of schools directly does not necessarily produce good outcomes. Norham Community High School, where I had been headteacher, had been built in the 1970s and was generally in pretty good condition, with very spacious classrooms. But there were also some major flaws. In particular, the corridors were only one and a half metres wide, meaning that break-times were as uncomfortable as the Newcastle A1 by-pass at 5.00pm. In addition, the classrooms had extremely limited storage cupboards. When I talked to architects who had been involved in the design of the building about these problems, they explained that the big classrooms and narrow corridors were a product of the consultation process with teachers. The teachers at the time had, fairly predictably, expressed more interest in what their classrooms would look like, rather than what they considered to be more marginal issues, like the traffic circulation around the school.

My school had been described as the 'School of the Future' by the *Yorkshire Post*. What the paper didn't report was the ironic fact that, while my technology provision would be 'state of the art', my corridors still continued to be rabbit burrows, inadequately protected by a leaking roof.

Around the year 2000, Building Schools for the Future (BSF), a major investment programme in secondary school buildings, made its appearance. It was certainly an encouraging sign that the idea of predicting the future of education and then designing schools accordingly was still central to our thinking.

This principle of significantly upgrading our schools for the new millennium met with general support from across the political spectrum. To me, it represented one of the most ambitious and visionary education projects of the last half-century. It was ambitious in several ways: in terms of cost, speed of implementation and scope. The intention was that *all* secondary schools would eventually be transformed.

The involvement of headteachers and governors working closely in collaboration with architects did lead to some highly creative and innovative building solutions. However, there were also a few schools where the designs were simply a form of madness. I remember one school – it won an international award for architectural design – which looked undeniably spectacular but, when I visited it, I found the teachers complaining that they could not show off children's work on the classroom walls because they had all been designed to slope at 45 degrees.

The BSF programme spread rapidly. During the year 2005–06, 14 local authorities took part but, by the end of 2009, a total of 96 local authorities had joined the programme. It has always been interesting and rather puzzling to me that primary schools were not brought in right from the start. Indeed, it was not until 2007 that the Primary Capital Programme was introduced, but this expanded rapidly and involved 675 building projects in England over the next three years.

The BSF programme was applauded for its aims and its aspirational qualities. Nevertheless, there were, at the time, reasonable concerns about the overall cost-effectiveness of the programme. It is probably sensible that today the school building and maintenance programme is being developed within more realistic financial limits.

We have moved a long way from the type of school buildings that I attended as a child. Now, whenever I visit the schools and colleges within the North East, I am gob-smacked by some of the wonderful facilities our children have access to. Education provides our pupils with access to the future. Designing schools to reflect the future needs of students continues to be a necessity and a constant challenge.

There are still schools that are not fit for purpose and we still have a long way to go in improving this environment for education. But I continue to stand by the principle that the quality of the learning environment should reflect the importance we place on children's learning. That must be a given.

CHAPTER 58

DEVELOPING A REGIONAL VOICE: SCHOOLS NORTH EAST

Right from my early days as a teacher I have advocated for a regional, as well as a national, curriculum. I am asked to review the regional skills strategy for the North East and realise that schools have never previously been engaged with this sort of strategy. At the time there is no regional representative voice for schools. I instigate the establishment of Schools North East, which will continue to be a powerful advocate for schools within our region.

Leaders realise that, because something hasn't been done before, it doesn't mean that it shouldn't be done.

Sorry, no questions.

Every so often the blindingly obvious will hit you in the face. As a headteacher, I always thought I spoke on behalf of the teachers in my school. However, and certainly in my early years of headship, headteacher views were rarely sought. The DfE would work primarily through the directors of education.

But things were beginning to change and increasingly during the 1990s headteacher opinions would be asked for. Even so, when I became a director of education in 1996, I was quite disappointed by the stance taken by some of my fellow directors of local authority services. Nationally, the directors of education continued to see themselves as the 'voice of schools'.

Schools North East launch.

In 2017 Schools North East celebrated its tenth anniversary and its professional conferences were very popular and often involved hundreds of delegates. The organisation attracted highly influential speakers, including the Secretary of State and Her Majesty's Chief Inspector. At one Schools North East conference, which was hosting more than 450 delegates, Ofsted's Chief Inspector stressed the urgency of the need for schools and employers to work together. With this sort of influential backing, it was clear that this was an organisation run by headteachers which was rapidly becoming the voice of schools across the whole North East region.

The thinking behind Schools North East had started in 2007, when I was asked by the Regional Development Agency, One NorthEast, to review the Regional Education and Skills Strategy. There was a clear assumption in this invitation that I would consult with further education colleges, local authorities, independent training providers and universities. I noted that schools were simply not on the One NorthEast radar.

Indeed, the Regional Development Agencies had traditionally engaged with:

● **the Association of Colleges – representing further education establishments;**

● **the Universities 4 the North East – being the representative body for the universities within the region; and**

● **the Association of Learning Providers – which represented independent training providers.**

In our region, One NorthEast and the Learning Skills Council had further established direct links with representative organisations including:

● **the CBI;**

● **the Chambers of Commerce; and**

● **the TUC.**

However, the astounding fact was that there had, at this point, never been a mechanism to engage with a group representing all the *schools* across the region. Quite obviously, there was a schism between the operations and services offered by school-linked networks and the official awareness of the economic and social aspirations of the region. Thus, schools, education and other agents of regeneration, although focusing on similar issues, were rarely invited to contribute positively to the common good through opportunities for joint working.

Essentially schools were detached and disengaged from the regional economic agenda at a strategic level. In fact, the school sector had no direct links with any planning organisations directly related to the Regional Economic Strategy.

Things needed to change and the key drivers for change at the time were forward thinkers in Government Office NE, the schools, the FE colleges and other independent education and skills providers. There was a fair wind for a change and for moving things forward because of the importance and the proximity at our local level of the 14–19 Agenda. For example, One NorthEast and the LSC both wanted to establish a Regional Commission for 14–19 Education with representation from schools, as well as further education. At this point, I was approached to facilitate the establishment of this Commission.

The first problem was there was no existing mechanism for ensuring representation of, and feedback from or to, the schools' sector. While FE colleges and independent providers had representative organisations that were directly involved with the regional skills agenda, the schools had no such representative body.

I asked if my remit could be broadened to include identifying ways in which education could engage with the regional economic strategy and to seek mechanisms by which schools within the region might be more effectively involved.

Chris Zarraga: CEO, Schools North East.

In undertaking the agreed brief, we surveyed 300 schools, organised 10 seminars and held an overarching conference involving schools, regional agencies and regional experts in education and skills. The notion of developing a network of schools that would engage with moves to create a regional education and skills strategy received overwhelming support. Feedback suggested that the proposed new school and education networks linking with the regional economic strategy were considered both 'essential' and 'ground-breaking'.

At the time all this was going on, schools were increasingly becoming 'self-managing' and it was felt they would welcome recognition and support as employers active in a business sector, seeking to drive forward business efficiency and operational effectiveness.

The CBI and the Chambers of Commerce increasingly wanted to engage directly with schools and opportunities already being provided by Business Link were being enthusiastically taken up by schools.

There was great support from all parties for improved coherence and co-ordination within the region. While significant resources were being directed to business development and business start-ups in the North East region, schools were unable to benefit directly from the expertise within this area. Equally, while Aim Higher, another education initiative, and Aspire, an employer-led initiative, both focused on the aspirations of young people, they had tended to work separately.

All the parties we consulted unequivocally supported stronger strategic leadership and a collective voice for the school sector. The economic and skills development agencies, including One NorthEast, recognised the critical role that schools would play in addressing the economic and social needs of the North East region. A key question during the process was:

Are we talking about all our schools?

We decided that the strategy should seek to be fully inclusive and involve the increasing number of independent schools, such as private schools, academies and trust schools in our region. In 2007, this was considered quite a radical step.

We sounded out our proposals with all the secondary, primary and special schools in the region, including the independent schools. In the event, support for the establishment of such a network of schools in our region was extremely high. The consensus was to establish the network as a charitable trust and to call it 'Schools North East'. Subsequently, the proposal was met with a resounding 'yes' from all quarters. The near-universal sentiment from all education and training sectors as well as employers was:

This should have happened before now.

Those involved in the schools and businesses seeking to establish the project considered this to be a highly significant opportunity for education leadership development within the North East region. We believed that, if we could harness the power of the school sector to focus on developing a dynamic economy, a healthy environment and a distinctive North East culture, we would have completed the link between economic development and the individual needs of children and young people.

In addition, the wider support from national and regional leaders was phenomenal. For example, James Ramsbotham, Chief Executive of the North East Chambers of Commerce, recognised that:

There was no mechanism for communicating with schools – this will really help – heads are remarkably in the dark with regard to regional matters.

Kevin Rowan, Regional Director of the TUC, commented that:

There is an obvious logic to what you are doing – why haven't we done it before?

Steve Munby, the Chief Executive for the National College for School Leadership, simply said:

It is a great idea.

Lord David Puttnam, a tremendous advocate for Schools North East.

I was particularly delighted when Lord David Puttnam, the famous film producer who won an Academy Award for *Chariots of Fire,* agreed to be the patron of Schools North East.

Since 2007 Schools North East has become an important feature of the North East educational landscape, ably led by wonderful leaders, including Beccy Earnshaw, David Pearmain, John Hardy and Chris Zarraga. However, there still remains a significant challenge for all those involved. More than ever, those who care about the success of the North East and its economy will need the support of schools within the region working collaboratively with other education and skill providers and employers.

It is still a case of work in progress and we cannot transform the North East without a powerful coalition between those who provide education, skills and employment within the region.

The challenge for Schools North East and all other regional leaders is to understand that real transformation can only be achieved by breaking into the parallel, but sometimes seemingly hermetically sealed, universes that we occupy.

CHAPTER 59

THE YOUNG PEOPLE'S LEARNING AGENCY

I am now about to take on the type of role that would normally be held by captains of industry. The Secretary of State appoints me to be Chair of the Young People's Learning Agency (YPLA). It is an opportunity to apply the Gestalt principle and bring together the disparate parts of the education system and see if we can achieve a consensus. The YPLA is then required to oversee academies, which goes down like a lead balloon with nearly everyone.

Build consensus and a shared vision at the beginning of a change programme in order to achieve success at the end.

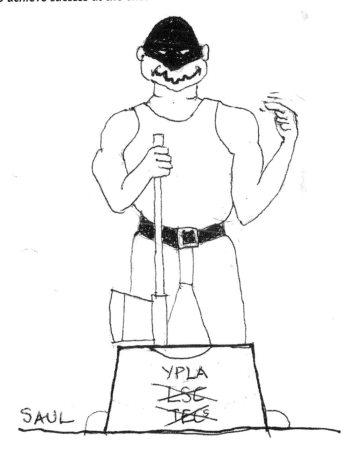

Next!

Early in 2009, I was again sitting in God's Departure Lounge. One of our local group of gadgees suggested I should put myself forward for the post of Chair of a new national strategy and commissioning agency, which would be called the Young People's Learning Agency (YPLA). This new body, together with the Skills Funding Agency (SFA), would jointly undertake to succeed the Learning and Skills Council (LSC).

The LSC had been established in April 2001, replacing the 72 Training and Enterprise Councils and the Further Education Funding Council for England. With a budget of over £12 billion, the LSC was described at the time as:

Britain's largest quango.

This monster quango was now to be replaced. Already, a full year before the abolition of the LSC, it had been announced that the funding responsibilities for 16–19-year-old learners were to be transferred to the YPLA. In parallel, the new SFA was in its turn to distribute funding to adult learners.

My first reaction to the suggestion that I might get involved was a resounding 'no'. Surely, I thought, this sort of role would best suit someone from the commercial sector. It was certainly the case that all the previous chairs had been well-known business people.

For example, the LSC had had two Chairs since its formation in 2001.

- **The founding Chair was Bryan Sanderson, a former Managing Director of BP and subsequently Chairman of BUPA, the Standard Chartered Bank and Northern Rock.**

- **The serving Chair was Chris Banks, former Managing Director of Coca-Cola Great Britain.**

When stepping down, Bryan Sanderson had made it quite clear that he had felt a lack of support from the Association of Colleges. It didn't get easier and during Chris Banks' final year the handling of the college building programme by LSC had been severely criticised.

The job was looking increasingly like a 'poisoned chalice'. So, after a couple more pints I decided to apply.

In due course, in June 2009, I was appointed by the Secretary of State, Ed Balls, to the position of Chair of the Young People's Learning Agency Committee, operating within the Learning and Skills National Council.

It was a distinctly unusual step to appoint a chair of a national education board who had direct experience of school headship. My background as principal of an FE college and director within a local authority were, I guess, key considerations that were brought into the final adjudication. As usual, I thought, I was rising to my natural level of incompetence. Whatever my misgivings, following a meeting with the Secretary of State, I accepted the role and walked out into the bright light of Westminster, slightly dazed, wondering and worrying again about what I had let myself in for.

In the interim I was placed on the LSC as Chair of the YPLA Committee by the Secretary of State, joining a Board that was on the point of being disbanded. I suddenly knew what it felt like to be a cuckoo in the nest!

So it was that in July 2009 I attended my first LSC meeting, which was understandably rather despondent. The group had known since March that it was to be abolished and that funding responsibilities for 16–19-year-old learners would be transferred to the YPLA. Just before I took up my role, there was a major upset regarding the LSC management of the FE college building programme when the Council was informed that the July Public Accounts Committee had described the LSC's handling of its college building programme as an example of:

catastrophic mismanagement.

This was a difficult moment for me, occurring just as I had been appointed Chair Designate of the YPLA. This was especially so, as my immediate task was to work with the outgoing Chair of the LSC, while, at the same time, taking the lead in establishing the YPLA and ensuring that it would be open for business by April 2010.

My first task was to recommend the appointment of the Chief Executive, Peter Lauener, and to establish the membership of the Board of the YPLA. Peter turned out to be a brilliant Chief Executive and the ideal person for the role, which proved to be a key factor in the success of the YPLA Board. It soon became clear that the Chief Executive and the YPLA leadership valued good governance and saw the development of a strong Board as critical for their work.

What we didn't know at the time was that Ian Wright MP, a highly intelligent and capable government minister, with whom we had worked very closely, would soon have to be replaced, following the 2010 General Election.

To lead the establishment of the successor agency within this turbulent climate was a major challenge. This was especially so because Peter Lauener, the Chief Executive Designate of the YPLA, and I all understood that the self-esteem of colleagues within the LSC was likely to be a critical factor in our ability to create the YPLA. We made every effort to recognise the considerable strengths and contribution demonstrated by the previous regime. The politicians we worked with, particularly the Minister, Ian Wright, recognised that the normal and near-obligatory model of 'trashing the old to validate the new' was absolutely the wrong thing to do in this case. As a result, from the outset, the YPLA would include many staff from the LSC and began to operate with a great deal of goodwill and cooperation from the outgoing organisation.

Eventually, on 1 April 2010, the YPLA formally replaced the LSC, which had been, in its heyday, the UK's largest non-departmental public body or quango. Many of the LSC's statutory powers and duties that were previously within its remit were transferred to the SFA and to local authorities across England.

As one of his final acts as Minister of State for Schools, Jim Knight announced that the YPLA would also have responsibility for the 203 Academies that were operational at the time. This action was not universally welcomed and the Shadow Schools Minister noted that the role was clearly an 'add-on'. Going further, the Liberal Democrat Education Spokesman said bluntly that the government should have allowed local government to oversee the academies. The reaction from the founding academy sponsors was angry, to say the least. They were clearly against this latest move and said that new funding arrangements managed by the YPLA would lead to state-funded independent schools becoming, as they put it:

lapdogs of the government.

One academy chief executive said he was concerned that the interests of academies would be lost when funding and day-to-day control were passed to the YPLA:

We believe the YPLA exists to ensure compliance. That will lead to Academies becoming the lapdog of the YPLA and losing the very freedoms that enable them to improve.

The Managing Director of the academy groups regretted the expansion of the academies programme, suggesting that:

You have to keep it sparse, if you want to keep the original message.

Clearly, the growth of more academies was viewed with concern by many parties. The Independent Academies Association told MPs about its doubts:

If the Tories put pressure on every school to become an academy, it doesn't fit in with its original ethos.

You can be sure that when Peter Lauener, the Minister, Vernon Coker, and I met up with the early sponsors, the meeting proved to be pretty stormy.

One of the Chief Executives present at the meeting looked me straight in the eye and said that he was used to having a direct line to Lord Adonis and the Secretary of State, so why on earth should he report to me?

At the other end of the political spectrum, the Local Government Association was also very much opposed to the establishment of the YPLA.

Baroness Shireen Ritchie, who, by the way, happened to be the stepmother of the film director Guy Ritchie, was Chair of the Local Government Association's Family and Children's Services Committee at the time. While, throughout, she was always very courteous and charming, she also cogently expressed her opposition to the proposal.

I soon reached the conclusion that the one thing that seemed to unite the whole of the education community was their opposition to the basic concept of the YPLA.

Lord Adonis with Secretary of State Ed Balls
How could I compete with an Adonis?

Understandably, given this context, the FE sector itself was also very wary. FE colleges had frequently expressed their concern that school sixth forms received more favourable treatment with regard to students' funding. The other independent providers of post-16 education also considered that their voice did not receive the attention it deserved. Then, chuntering at the heels of the educational establishment, the private sector, represented by the CBI, the Chambers of Commerce and the Institute of Directors, continually articulated their view that the education sector was:

turning out young people without the necessary skills and aptitudes for work.

Peter Lauener and I, in our gloomier moments, almost decided to adopt the Millwall supporters' chant:

No one likes us, but we don't care.

But, of course, we *did* care. Moreover, I had accepted the position because of my personal experience of schools, local government, FE and the private sector, all of which had helped me to understand that many of the concerns raised by various interest groups were rational and deserved recognition.

One month after the YPLA started its work, the Coalition Government came into power.

The new Secretary of State for Education, Michael Gove, announced the bonfire of the vanities; many of those 'arm's length' bodies, the distrusted quangos, bit the dust.

It was very clear that the clock was ticking and the YPLA, which had replaced the LSC, which had replaced the TECs, was now to be replaced. We would spend two years awaiting the axe.

CHAPTER 60

CANCER CARE AND CAPABILITY

To get cancer once is bad; to get cancer twice is just plain careless. This time, as Chair of the YPLA, now to be under the direction of another Secretary of State, I decide to 'carry on as normal'. Cancer also makes me reflect on the relationship between caring for children and being capable of helping them. I also pee on the Secretary of State's carpet.

We all want to be confident, capable and caring, exactly what we want for our children.

The Peter Principle now applies to you. You have risen to your own level of incontinence.

In May 2010, just after the election, I was walking by my doctor's surgery. For some reason, a whim perhaps, I decided to ask for a test for prostate cancer. I had no particular symptoms of the disease but I felt I should follow the advice of the medical advertisements and my wife, and check myself out.

A week later I was informed that I had prostate cancer. I had some track record in this regard, as ten years earlier I had been told I had colon cancer, so I knew what might be involved. It transpired that what I had was an aggressive form of prostate cancer. I was given two choices, either hormone therapy or an operation. I plumped for the latter and thus faced having my prostate removed. For months I had to wear a cunning apparatus, which directed my urine into a bag that was strapped to my leg. I then had access to a neat little tap, which I could open in order to empty the bag.

While sitting in the Ministerial Briefing Room with the new Secretary of State, Michael Gove, I felt my shoe becoming a little bit squelchy. We had just been discussing my Geordie accent. In doing so, Michael Gove had been speaking with a strong Scottish accent, mentioning that he had been brought up in Aberdeen. I then realised with some horror that I had neglected to properly close the tap on the apparatus strapped to my leg. I suggested that my colleague talk about a particular topic as a distraction, while I, subtly, bent beneath the table and successfully adjusted the tap. I wish other problems were as easily solved!

At the time, I was engaged in chairing an organisation called Coping with Cancer North East. I remember that, when I asked our Chief Executive, Judith Woodruff, how much stress we should put on caring for those in need, compared to the emphasis we put on skills and expertise, her answer was immediate and unequivocal:

Care is number one.

My response, having been the subject of numerous hospital operations was:

I care about care and I also care how good the surgeons are.

It is a common experience that we often question the motivations and expertise of politicians, teachers and doctors, particularly when they are involved in industrial disputes. Self-righteously we say, 'how can they really care about the children, if they put their professional self-interest first?'

Often it goes further than this and I hear people question whether teaching still qualifies as a vocation. Indeed, it is true that teaching has become, like many other professions, subject to external bureaucratic control by people who are more concerned about achieving statistical targets than caring for those they serve.

I have always believed care for children should be the *essential prerequisite* of anyone deciding to be a teacher, or an education director or, indeed, a Secretary of State for Education.

This may be the biggest single challenge in our new educational world:

The centrality of care within our profession.

But can *care* for the individual child, particularly for those who find success hard to come by, realistically survive in a world driven by competition and market forces?

It is certainly a fact of professional life that increasingly school leaders are judged by their technical expertise – expertise in data management, financial management and planning being particularly highly valued. Yet, conversely we would always want teachers to put their care of children first, before everything else.

Equally, in other professional contexts like medicine, we would want those who operate in our hospitals to care about the patients on the tables in front of them. Nevertheless, when I look at those who have responsibility for the lives of other people, such as surgeons, the emphasis I would place on technical expertise is also very pronounced. Somewhat regrettably, a booklet produced by the Royal College of Surgeons entitled *So You Want to be a Surgeon* does not once mention the need to care about people or suggest that the potential surgeon should have a concern about the well-being of patients. Perhaps the Hippocratic Oath is all that is required?

When the Royal College seeks to ascertain whether someone is cut out to be a surgeon, they say the following is required:

- **specialist knowledge for accurate diagnosis of a patient's condition;**

- **good communication skills – for speaking to your medical team, your patients and their families; for listening to, and understanding, the concerns of a wide range of people and earning their trust;**

- **extensive experience of pre-operative and post-operative care; and**

- **a bright, eager mind, manual dexterity and the physical skills for performing an operation.**

On both occasions I had cancer it was sorted by cutting out bits of me during surgery.

Following the operations, I was often asked what the surgeon was like and to say if he or she was 'good'. This is a difficult question to respond to and, certainly, I couldn't describe their bedside manner on the evidence of such a slight acquaintance. It is also difficult to judge technical expertise when you are flat out, unconscious and in an uncritical state. I guess that, like most people, I judged their expertise by their results.

It is an unavoidable quandary when a hospital or school trust is faced with making judgements, which are based on the survival rate of patients or the success rate of students – what do we, as observers, want their response to be?

One of the challenges for all those working in schools is where we, as individuals, sit on the continuum of professional behaviour. At one end of the spectrum, we may have too little care for the children, while, at the other extreme, we may have too much emotional involvement with them. If doctors, teachers and also politicians take a cold, objective and uncaring stance for their clients, they may even avoid risking their reputations by taking on high-risk challenges. Conversely, if they are driven by their emotional concern for the well-being of the individual, they may take on extra responsibility without having the expertise or capacity to deal with it.

I have often considered that care, like revenge, can best be delivered in a cold climate. But take a moment to imagine a surgeon who cares so much for the well-being of the patient that the hand holding the scalpel is shaking during the operation – or, perhaps, that the anxiety generated is clearly affecting the decisions being made. To keep a sense of balance, now think about the surgeon who doesn't care one jot whether the patient lives or dies.

In the last resort, when you are about to have major surgery, capability is all. Yes, I do hope the surgeon cares about me and is confident in doing the job. But, put simply, I want surgeons to be demonstrably good at their job.

When I am asked why I have been involved in education for so long, I rarely say it is because I care about children. Please don't misunderstand this, I *do* care about children because they are human beings. But you must ask yourself whether pupils will be happy with my caring side and personal confidence if, at the same time, I was not being a capable teacher and they learned very little. So, there is always a balance to be struck between having:

- **professional knowledge and understanding;**

- **professional skills and abilities; and**

- **professional levels of personal commitment.**

As a headteacher, one of the strap-lines I used for describing our school ethos was:

Caring, confident and capable.

I would argue that, for my own children, I would want them to be all three of these: concerned about other people; positive in their outlook; and expert in what they do.

These elements function rather like a three-legged stool. If any one leg is missing, or even if one leg is too short, we will do a disservice to the child. As leaders, obliged to accomplish great things, we must first show our children that we truly care about them and then demonstrate our knowledge, skills and abilities by helping them to advance.

The problem is that we can demonstrate our care for children in so many different ways.

Nevertheless, the serious challenge I would present to any government minister would be:

Are you driven by care for children, or care for the economy or care for your personal political ideology?

If the economy and political ideology are too dominant, at the expense of everything else, then I would seriously worry about our children's personal and social development.

However, ministers who care or are driven by a passionate commitment to what is best for children cannot of itself be sufficient. They need also to heed the advice of those with professional knowledge and understanding. There's no doubt that good ministers will always do just that.

CHAPTER 61

PUTTING THE 'FUN' INTO FUNDING

The one thing that is constant in education in the UK is change. Over a period of eight years I am Chair of the Learning Skills Council, Young People's Committee, Chair of the Young People's Learning Agency (YPLA) and Chair of the Education Funding Agency Advisory Group. The latter group's annual budget is eventually bigger than the gross domestic product of Saudi Arabia.

When we manage change successfully, we create a context in which organisations and people can develop and thrive.

The minister says the successful headteachers are those who can manage small change.

Charles Darwin revealingly once said:

It is not the strongest or the most intelligent who will survive, but those who can best manage change.

To fear change is to fear the opportunities offered by new possibilities. The self-esteem of those involved in change is therefore critical. So here was I, slap bang in the middle of a complex story of government changes, restructures, re-brandings and reorganisations.

The 2010 General Election resulted in the first hung parliament in the UK for 36 years. For what seemed a particularly frantic period, a series of negotiations took place that led to the formation of the first Coalition Government since the Second World War.

I was very proud that the membership of the YPLA Agency Board reflected a sufficiently wide constituency, including the Local Government Association, the private sector, the 'third sector', the academies and other schools. As the Chair of the YPLA, I wasn't at all sure at the time how things would pan out under a new Conservative government.

The YPLA Board reflecting my view that all sectors of education should have a voice.

What followed was a kind of Bonfire Night, which took the form of a 'bonfire of the quangos'. Because, in October 2010, the government announced plans to curb public spending through the abolition of a large number of quasi-autonomous non-governmental organisations – not so fondly known as 'quangos'. Over 30 were simply abolished without much ceremony, including luminous bodies like:

- British Shipbuilders;

- The Royal Commission on Environmental Pollution; and

- The Legal Services Ombudsman.

Some were teasingly placed in the 'to be abolished with reservations' group. This group included many bodies associated with our work in education:

- The British Education Communications and Technology Agency;

- The General Teaching Council for England;

- The Qualifications and Curriculum Development Agency; and

- The School Food Trust.

The YPLA was placed in the 'quangos under review' group, in which we were joined by the following, among others:

- The National College for Leadership of Schools;

- Children's Services Partnership for Schools;

- The Training and Development Agency;

- The Office of the Children's Commissioner; and

- The Children and Family Court Advisory and Support Service.

It was during this review period that I first met Michael Gove. In Portcullis House, opposite the House of Commons, I sat waiting for him in the café. He immediately walked over and offered to buy me a coffee. My impression was very favourable and he was absolutely charming and attentive, as he carefully probed me with regard to the operation of the YPLA.

Secretary of State for Education, Michael Gove: charming, attentive and a man with an axe.

Despite these personal omens, on 26 January 2011, Gove duly introduced the Education Bill into the House of Commons and, by 14 November, it had become law. It transpired that the YPLA would cease to exist on 31 March 2012.

Some of the statutory responsibilities of the YPLA reverted to the Secretary of State for Education, while many of its functions were transferred to the newly created Education Funding Agency (EFA). This was an executive agency, which would be sited within the Department of Education itself.

It had almost become a tradition that, whenever an agency like the YPLA closed under these circumstances, a new Chief Executive and Chair would be appointed. This had happened earlier with the demise of the Further Education Funding Council, the Training and Enterprise Council and the LSC. Now, of course, it was the turn of the YPLA. However, learning from our personal experience of the transition from the LSC to the YPLA, Peter Lauener and I considered that achieving a smooth transition to the new organisation would work best if it directly involved members of the outgoing organisation.

Michael Gove accepted our point of view and then wrote to the two of us, suggesting that we lead the transition from the YPLA to the EFA. At the same time, we were asked to prepare the ground for absorbing into the EFA, yet another quango, Partnerships for Schools. I must give some credit to Michael Gove for supporting the idea that the Executive and the Board should take leadership responsibility for transferring to the EFA. This meant that the Board was able to be both positive and proactive in supporting a significant change in direction and could proceed to work with the DfE and Partnerships for Schools to ensure a smooth transition.

The last Board meeting of the YPLA was attended by Lord Jonathan Hill, the Under-Secretary of State. The final act was to pass a resolution commending all YPLA staff for their outstanding contribution to the organisation and for the support they had given to the establishment of the EFA. The achievements of our staff were indeed immense, especially given the challenge of the changing remit and the transition programme and we all felt privileged to have been part of it. Moreover, we felt proud that we had helped to engineer the establishment of the successor organisation.

Given the varied constituencies on the Board, the keyword during our period at the YPLA was 'consensus'. We found that consensus was more likely to be achieved when we applied some basic principles to complex and contentious issues. One issue that comes to mind for us at the time was the fair distribution of post-16 funding. The principles we used to support consensus-building and maintain our constancy of purpose were these:

- **making the student central to our deliberations;**

- **valuing all our providers equally;**

- **governing policy with integrity; and**

- **building trust by seeking to understand and empathise with the perspectives of the other parties involved.**

I do believe that, within the two short years of the life of the YPLA, we created a structure that is still recognised as one of the most effective National Education Boards and certainly one well able to adapt to change. Moreover, it lives on in the sense that the new EFA Advisory Group included members from the YPLA Board, thereby ensuring continuity.

During this whole period, the predominant feature was the ever-present and fundamental nature of change. We navigated through a successful reorganisation, saw a significant number of staff being reallocated to academy roles, witnessed a boost to our central data and systems capacity and provided more resources in the field of financial assurance expertise. The ability of the YPLA staff to focus on organisational improvement was remarkable. The fact is that a central component of our self-esteem came from the belief that we were good at responding to and embracing change.

The EFA was to be a very different organisation. It was an executive agency created to carry out ministerial orders or policy. In this, it was unlike the YPLA, which had been more self-determining and enjoyed a greater independence. My role as Chair had been much more in an advisory capacity and I also had a membership of the SFA Advisory Board.

Peter Lauener became Chief Executive of both the YPLA and the SFA. The time I stepped down from the role as Chair of the Advisory Group, the EFA's annual budget had grown to £56.8 billion and it supported all state-provided education for the 8 million children aged 3 to 16, and the 1.6 million young people aged 16 to 19.

In addition, it was responsible for funding the educational support for those with the highest needs and for funding and monitoring the academies, university technical colleges, studio schools, and free schools, as well as overseeing the building maintenance programmes for schools and sixth form colleges. In addition, from 2016 onwards, the SFA and the EFA Advisory Board had been working closely together preparing the ground for a possible merger.

I was lucky to have had the opportunity to observe at first hand the constant changes that major national funding education agencies have had to undergo. My conclusion is that:

Simply focusing on results will not lead to change; focusing on change will get results.

Change management requires the full range of high-level technical skills provided by those working within human resources, financial and legal services. It all needs leaders who can create a climate in which there continues to be a positive response to change.

CHAPTER 62

DOWNHILLS

It is always a great sadness to see local and national government fighting with parents and other community representatives over the future of the education of the children in their care. I agree to chair an 'Interim Executive Board' for a primary school in North London and Downhills Primary School becomes a test case regarding the power of local governing bodies and the power of the Secretary of State. For me, it is a test case on how people should behave when in front of children.

The interests of children are paramount.

When I look back over my time in education there is a common theme during my career. The fact is I tend to take on jobs that are incredibly challenging – and a bit risky. I also try to adhere to the principles and values which I hold most dear. I have certainly worked hard to build bridges between all those who have a stake in the education of our children. The only question I have asked myself throughout has been:

Will these children be better off through my involvement?

The Downhills Primary School experience challenged me as a professional but, more importantly, it challenged my values.

In March 2012, the Secretary of State, Michael Gove, decided to issue an Academy Order, stating that Downhills Primary School in Haringey should be converted into an academy. It would be sponsored by the Harris Federation and Haringey Council would cease to maintain the school. The Secretary of State reconstituted the Downhills governing body as an interim executive board. He then asked if I would chair the new board and lead the consultation process on the Secretary of State's order.

Downhills Primary School.

Downhills was to become nationally prominent, to some even notorious, as a major test of the relationship between the Secretary of State and parental choice, local communities, central and local government and those for and against the process of academisation.

As usual, when faced with a new challenge, my first reaction was to say 'no'. My own view was that an invitation is always better than forced intervention and that would be my preferred way of operating. Nevertheless, I also admit that there are occasions when imposed solutions provide the only way forward, so, in the end, I set out on yet another un-trodden path. Fortunately Dominic Herrington, the present national Schools Commissioner, provided me with tremendous support throughout this difficult period, always professional and most of all considerate. Before I started, I made my own philosophy clear:

The Board must operate transparently and in keeping with the Nolan principles of public life. We should seek to be highly consultative and carefully test all the alternatives on offer. Most important of all, the best interests of the children would be our central concern throughout.

Downhills Primary was a school with a long history of under-performance. Following its Ofsted inspection in January 2012 the school had been judged to require special measures because it was failing to give its pupils an acceptable standard of education.

The school was at the centre of an extremely vociferous national and local campaign against the imposition of academy status and against the proposed provider, the Harris Federation, in particular. The 'Save Downhills' campaign included public demonstrations, picket lines, numerous letters to the press, very active blogs, petitions and a specially constructed website. In addition, the school's internet email had also been used to promote the campaign, and the teaching staff had undertaken a one-day strike. It was within this context that the Interim Executive Board was asked to work.

On my first visit to the school, I was faced by a group of parents who were waiting outside the school gate. The other members of the Interim Executive Board had already 'run the gauntlet' and were inside the school; some had suffered a lot of abuse from parents as they entered the grounds.

I walked towards the group of parents and activists. I was using a stick, as I was still recovering from an operation. I decided to sit down on the wall outside the school and talk to them. Their evident sympathy for my plight somewhat tempered their anger about what was happening to the school. Also, because I was sitting down and they were surrounding me, I felt we could have a real conversation, rather than a stand-up argument. They explained their point of view in a very pleasant and agreeable way and I was able to explain my own position, promising that, in doing so, I would chair the Board in a principled way.

The Board and I thought it was critically important that the consultation process was beyond reproach. Accordingly, we proposed to widen the scope of the consultation and include the option that Downhills might remain a local authority school, as well as the option to become an academy or to become an academy within the Harris Federation.

Partly due to the high degree of scrutiny we were under, we carried out one of the most rigorous consultation exercises ever undertaken over the conversion to academy status. We held 18 meetings, answered 258 individual questions and responded to 29 letters and emails. There were three separate parent drop-in sessions and special meetings for Turkish and Somali parents. We engaged translation and interpretation services to ensure that all minority groups were fully involved and able to participate. We also commissioned the organisation *Populus* to run an independent poll, so that we could hear the voices of as many parents as possible. This was because many parents seemed reluctant to go to the meetings. We engaged with the wider community, too, and consulted the local MP and the neighbouring children's centre.

The consultation process began on Friday 20 April 2012 and concluded on Friday 1 June 2012. In the final analysis: A total of 94 per cent of respondents – 220 in all – stated that they did not want Downhills to become an academy and that they were in support of Downhills School continuing as a local authority school. Populus sampled over 100 parents and carers of children who went to Downhills Primary School and their survey found that 80 per cent of these individuals supported the school remaining under the control of Haringey Local Authority.

I also interviewed local government officials and elected members, as well as going to the House of Commons to meet the local MP, David Lammy. David had himself attended Downhills School before being awarded an Inner London Education Authority choral scholarship to sing at Peterborough Cathedral and attend The King's School in Peterborough.

When constructing the Interim Executive Board's concluding report for the Secretary of State, we returned to the core principle that the best interests of the present and future children within Downhills Primary School were to be the paramount consideration. We decided not to provide a recommendation to the Secretary of State. However, in the concluding part of our report, we simply outlined the situation and the alternative ways forward. We clearly stated that:

The overwhelming view of the parents was that they did not wish the school to become an academy.

We reported that there was a general consensus that radical structural solutions were important at Downhills School if it were to deliver and sustain rapid improvement. We also expressed some confidence that the Harris Federation would be able to deliver the solutions that were important for the school.

We also stated that we would not recommend any further period of consultation, as we believed there was a need for whoever was to lead the school to be absolutely and rapidly focused on the improvements required. A further period of instability and lack of clarity with regard to leadership and governance would, we felt, not be in the best interests of the children.

At 3.00pm I emailed our report to the Secretary of State and within two hours the decision was made. Downhills School was, with immediate effect, to convert to become an academy, sponsored by the Harris Federation. While the staff, the parents and the local authority all considered the process had been fair and transparent, the parents disagreed with the Secretary of State's response and conclusion and sought a judicial review. The High Court judge duly delivered the verdict, saying that:

Given the school's 'egregious' past performance, the decision was rational.

The voice of parents and the local community and the best interests of children were all central considerations when arriving at the decision to convert the school to an academy. Such concerns are at the heart of all education decision-making. But, in the end, the best interests of children must always be paramount.

The new academy opened in September 2012, sponsored by the Harris Federation. By 2014, the Ofsted Report was describing the school as:

Good across all areas, with outstanding leadership and management and that pupils' progress has improved rapidly since the academy opened in 2012.

Have the children benefitted from the changes that were introduced?

Absolutely, yes!

Should they have to suffer the sight of those who are responsible for them fighting in plain view?

Absolutely not!

CHAPTER 63

NORTHERN EDUCATION

I establish the Northern Education Multi-Academy Trust. There is one simple challenge. Can we create an organisation that reflects my belief that all children have enormous potential and it is our job to remove the barriers which get in the way? Then, there is a wonderful moment. We take over a school that covers the area in which I was born, where my former primary and secondary schools stood.

True leaders don't create more followers, they create more leaders.

Is being a Trustee a bit like what I did in Durham prison?

Was it an accident that I end up establishing a Trust that will eventually operate in my home area, with all the memories of my childhood education?

I have always been fascinated by chaos theory. When playing snooker, the smallest difference in the speed and direction of the cue ball will cause the pack of reds to scatter in wildly different directions every time.

When the YPLA was given the remit to oversee academies within England, I was encouraged to sponsor an academy and eventually a multi-academy trust.

The Board of Northern Education deciding to sponsor an academy. Chaired by Estelle Morris with Brian Oglethorpe, Les Walton, Kevin McAleese, Diane Greaves and Ian Kershaw.

Establishing the Northern Education Trust was the result of a series of seemingly random events: chaos theory in practice!

I have already described the chain of events that can be summarised as follows.

1. Leave headship to take up the role of CEO in North Tyneside.

2. Leave my role as CEO in North Tyneside, following cancer.

3. Create Northern Education (Ltd).

4. Approached by the Director-General of the DfE to support Bradford.

5. Appointed CEO of North Tyneside FE College, eventually becoming Tyne Metropolitan College.

6. Go to the pub where am I am persuaded to apply for the role of Chair of the Young People's Learning Agency (YPLA).

7. Appointed by Secretary of State, Ed Balls, as Chair of the YPLA, because of my unique background in schools, local authorities and further education.

8. Jim Knight, the Minister of State for Schools, then announces the YPLA will have responsibility for the 203 academies that are operating at the time.

9. Lesley Longstone, the Director-General of the DfE, suggests it would be a good idea for me to sponsor an academy, as I am to be Chair of the organisation that oversees all the academies in England.

10. At the same time, my company, Northern Education, has a long-standing partnership with Bolton.

11. The local authority then announces that they would welcome Northern Education sponsoring a school in one of the most deprived areas of Bolton.

If any of these links in the chain had not been forged, I wonder whether the Northern Education Trust (NET) would have been formed.

Although the decision to establish NET appeared to be the result of random incidents, chaos theory shows that, in reality, there is an underlying order that is difficult to see. The underlying order was the direction that education had been taking under New Labour, the Coalition and Conservative governments. This was a growing centralisation of education oversight and increasing school self-management. I was simply going with the flow, while at the same time retaining my core principles and values.

During this period, the main political mantra was: 'become an academy and be free from local authority control', a forerunner of the Brexit mantra 'take back control'.

In 2014, Dominic Cummings, who was the special adviser to Michael Gove, telephoned me from London, requesting that we could meet up in Durham. It was clear to me from our conversation that his focus was much more on the reduction of local authority control than greater freedom for schools. Later, I began to understand it was also about significantly re-engineering the role of the civil service.

Right from the start, the NET Board tried to hold the 'middle ground' between central direction and school self-management. We wanted an emphasis on child-centred education and a focus on outcomes. Our vision and values are described as:

Outcomes focused, child-centred.

We laid down certain conditions. We would:

- be an advocate for the needs of the severely educationally disadvantaged children within the northern region;

- primarily take on schools that were in severe difficulty in areas of deprivation and with a history of endemic failure;

- refuse to blame children if they struggle to succeed;

- work in partnership with local government and never be 'forced' on to an unwilling school or local authority;

- introduce new thinking and challenge old orthodoxies;

- believe child-centred education is compatible with a focus on academic subjects and performance improvement;

- create a curriculum that would encourage the joy of learning while enabling children to succeed;

- stimulate, excite and inspire children;

- value personal and social education, the extended curriculum and creativity;

- build positive relationships with parents and the community;

- build constructive relationships with all staff and their representative organisations; and

- never place external inspection as the main focus of the organisation.

Following our sponsorship of a secondary school in Bolton, we were then asked to take on more schools. In 2012, we formed the NET. It has now grown to 21 schools (11 primary and 10 secondary), with a turnover of almost £85 million.

As Chair of the Trust, I asked, 'Are the majority of children in our schools better off than before we were involved?'

There are various ways we can answer this. While we never saw an Ofsted grade as a key objective, it is useful to compare the Ofsted judgements on our schools when we first took them over with their subsequent judgements. In the beginning, eight were in special measures and three had serious weaknesses. Only three schools were good or outstanding. At time of writing, none of our schools is inadequate; 16 are now good or outstanding. Results and destinations for students are better. This is a truly remarkable achievement and one I have no doubt will continue.

More importantly, we consider the views of our students, parents and staff more informative than any Ofsted grade. An independent survey of the attitudes of our 11,800 pupils, their parents/carers and our 2000 plus staff produced extremely satisfactory results with high overall satisfaction scores by parents and staff at primary and secondary academies. Most pleasing of all was that the values of the Trust were strongly endorsed (80 per cent of pupils said Yes to 'Is each other's welfare everyone's first concern?').

But, of course, it has also highlighted areas where we need to do more.

What do we believe in and why do we do it?

We chose this hard path because our trustees share a fundamental belief that, if we place children, their welfare and achievements at the centre of everything we do, then personal reputation is secondary. We were always driven by the thought: 'What is in the best interests of the pupil?' which has led to us taking on a larger proportion of schools that have been failing for many years than many other trusts. We did this when some providers had pulled out and others had refused.

Children in these schools deserve much better than quick fixes and the Trust makes every effort to embrace them within the supportive NET family. All children and staff have the capacity to change and, where possible, that capacity should be built from within.

I have now stepped down from the Trust. Will the NET continue to improve the lives of our children? Of course it will. It is now in the very good hands of an outstanding CEO and Chair, Rob Tarn and Mark Sanders OBE, respectively.

The Trust's vision and values reflect the values and principles I have focused on for so many years.

The Northern Education Trust values and principles

1. We care passionately about the education and welfare of young people.

2. We believe that all young people, irrespective of background or ability, will be successful in our Trust.

3. We are not and will never be selective. We believe that local schools are for all children.

4. We are always inclusive. Our mechanisms to support the most vulnerable child to succeed and overcome barriers to learning are a key aspect of our work.

5. Our approach to education recognises that outcomes are important and also allows children to gain experiences and values which prepare them fully for life in modern Britain. This includes workplace skills and appropriate advice for future progression.

6. We have high expectations of behaviour.

7. We adopt the local authority admissions protocol and work closely with them.

8. We would always wish to act in such a way that has a positive effect on a neighbouring school or community. We care passionately about children in all schools, not just our own.

9. That all employees act with integrity and embrace the value that 'we are the Trust'.

10. We work regionally and nationally to develop approaches to MAT improvement that influence the wider school-led system.

What would have happened, if I had not got cancer, become the CEO of an FE college or gone to the pub on that night? In an alternative reality, would an organisation such as the NET exist, albeit with a different name and different people, but essentially doing the same thing? My answer is 'yes'. The underlying direction of increasing centralisation and school self-management is embedded within the education system. However, that organisation may have had very different values.

So, where are we now? The COVID-19 pandemic in 2020–21 provided the ultimate challenge to the education system, which includes multi-academy trust models and local authorities co-existing in the same education universe. Good and resilient trusts and local authorities have stood up to the challenge well.

Strong trusts, such as NET, have demonstrated proactive creativity that has been truly astounding. On the other hand, good local authorities, with a strategic understanding of the locality and region, combined with the ability to coordinate a local response, have been a revelation to many. Of course, some multi-academy trusts and local authorities that lack capacity or strong leadership have not fared so well.

So, what of the future? In our present 'Covid Chaos' perhaps a new order is evolving, one in which there is a recognition there needs to be a balance between central direction and local decision-making. Perhaps this rebalanced system will lead to new and thriving partnerships of self-managing school trusts and local government.

As Bob Woof, the former Blaydon MP, used to say: *'the future is yet to come.'*

CHAPTER 64

REBALANCING THE SYSTEM

So, what is next? As we move deeper into the second decade of the twenty-first century I feel the education system is increasingly out of kilter. There is too much emphasis on compliance and inspection and not enough on support and development. When I step down from the ESFA, I have a conversation with the Minister at the time. We both agree that there is a need to quality assure and develop the quality of advice and support that schools receive. Following further consultation with respected colleagues, we decide to establish the Association of Education Advisers (AoEA), which is independent of national and local government.

The best of us who wish to continuously improve the lives of children and young people invite external and high-quality support and challenge.

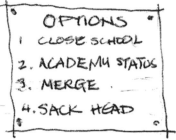

Good grief. I need some advice.

believe the realisation or fulfilment of everyone's talents and potential is a need in everyone. This has been a central theme throughout my whole life in education. This is not only true for our children but also for all our staff who work in schools and colleges. External support and challenge, which is independent and focused on the needs of children and schools, should be welcomed by those who wish to improve. Those who support schools should be there to help remove the barriers to the natural desire to improve and develop the education of our children. Based on these key beliefs, supported by a team of highly knowledgeable and skilled colleagues, we decided to establish the Association of Education Advisers (AoEA) in 2017.

The vision of AoEA is that every school, college and education provider has access to high-quality support, advice and challenge, which is independent and focused on improving outcomes for children, schools and their communities.

Our mission is to provide an accredited quality standard, to offer continuous professional development and to create a community for those who advise and support schools, colleges and other education providers. Our belief is that all children, teachers and leaders want to improve and to promote a culture in which support and challenge are welcomed and dependence on external compliance and regulation is reduced.

In keeping with one of the key principles of this book, in order to understand what we should do in the future, we must look to the past and work out how we got here.

Ever since local authorities were established, schools have been receiving visits from 'officers of the Authority'. Some of this number would be there to provide a link with the Authority, others to inspect the school on behalf of the Authority and the remainder to provide advice across the subject and organisational spectrum.

Once, I worked with a headteacher who felt under extreme pressure. The difficulty was that he'd been receiving reports which indicated his school's results were going to be really bad by the end of the year. Having care for his health and well-being, I asked if he'd slept OK:

Like a baby, he said, I wake up crying every half an hour.

The role of an adviser can be very challenging, particularly if you are working with headteachers and governors who are going through a bad patch.

Such experienced education advisers have always played a critical and honourable part within the education system. Over the years, they have been deployed using a range of different role descriptions, being termed: School Improvement Partners, or National Challenge Advisers or National Leaders in Education. Nowadays, there are numerous specialist advisers, covering different types of schools and offering different subject specialisms, including governance, change management, finance and people development.

An education adviser can work in numerous ways with schools but, primarily, they choose to support the school's ability to plan, review and implement emerging education strategies.

During the 1970s and 1980s, local authorities employed a significant number of advisers, particularly subject advisers. They were mainly former heads of department, who had decided to take a different career path from the traditional route from deputy headship and thence to headteacher by choosing to work for the local authority more directly.

Headteachers were also routinely allocated a 'school adviser', who was specifically linked with the school and primarily worked directly with them.

As a history teacher, I placed considerable value on the opportunity to talk to the local authority subject adviser, using them as a sounding board for ideas and developments. The interaction was very straightforward: the subject advisers would bring with them the latest thinking and information about subject-specific requirements. In addition, they would also run training programmes, focusing on the knowledge and skills that subject departments required.

This system worked reasonably well until the early 1990s when local management of schools began and Ofsted was introduced. The relationship with advisers began to change significantly and headteachers began to suggest that former heads of department who had little or no experience of running a school might not, in the new era, be able to properly support and challenge them.

When I became a director of education, the local authority began increasingly to involve headteachers to work as advisers. I subsequently introduced this model to Bradford, where we called them School Improvement Partners. In Bradford, I began by selecting a team of outstanding headteachers to work in a very challenging context. These inspirational headteachers included Jayne Bingham, Dianna Drake, Francoise Leake, David Kershaw CBE, Kevin McAleese CBE and Tony Thorne.

Once I had appointed this new advisory team, I held a 'getting to know each other' session. As part of this, I decided to ask each headteacher to say one thing about themselves that other people didn't know.

Kevin McAleese then topped the table for surprises by saying that he had had the distinction of his ship having been boarded by pirates on the China seas when he was serving in the Merchant Navy. By contrast, my announcement, that I had plugged in Jerry Lee Lewis's piano at a gig, didn't seem too impressive. The DfE then considered spreading this advisory model across the whole of the UK and asked Newcastle Local Authority and Northern Education to lead one of the national pilots.

The model that we put forward in our pilot required the advisers to be 'relatively independent' of the local authority and the school, and thereby to be in a position to challenge and support both in turn. I remember attending a meeting at the DfE where Sir John Dunford vigorously argued for the independence of school improvement partners from local authorities, while the representative of the local authorities, equally enthusiastically, mooted the idea that they would work directly to the local authority.

In the end, the government decided that the school improvement partners would be funded by the DfE and commissioned by the local authorities. Even so, some local authorities did support the Newcastle model notion of the relative autonomy of school improvement partners.

Nevertheless, the DfE Guidelines in 2004 clearly stated that the School Improvement Partners were required to:

respect the autonomy of the school.

Despite this, most School Improvement Partners nationally were seen as officers of the local authority. As a result, in 2006, the National College for School Leadership started to identify serving headteachers 'who had achieved excellent results in their schools'. They were to be called National Leaders in Education. This was clearly a significant step towards maintaining advisory independence from the local authorities. Of course, this model was funded by the national government and could never be seen as truly independent.

Later, in 2008, the Secretary of State, Ed Balls, launched the £400m National Challenge programme, which was to target the 638 lowest-performing schools nationally. At the same time, 70 schools would become academies by September 2010. The central government control over school advisers was clearly being strengthened. National Challenge Advisers, a key component of the National Challenge programme, were then appointed to work with the targeted schools.

The direction radically changed in 2010, when the new Coalition Government announced that the statutory requirement for local authorities to appoint School Improvement Partners was to be removed and the funding withdrawn. At the same time, the DfE closed down the National Challenge programme.

Schools continue to receive advice from the Office of the Schools Commissioner or from the Local Authority or the advisers they commission themselves. Yet, these advisers do not have to conform to any national standard for education advisers working within schools. There is no national quality assurance or accreditation of advisers beyond the work of Ofsted.

In 2016, in discussing the issue of school advisers with Lord Nash, the Under-Secretary of State for Education, I suggested that this was a significant gap in the system. There already exists a qualification for school leaders and a quality standard for Ofsted inspectors. Also, schools are obliged to use accredited accountants with regard to their financial affairs. Yet, there exists this yawning gap in the lack of any accreditation for those who are tasked with advising schools.

In 2017, we launched the AoEA. The concept received a great deal of support nationally. This development was inspired by the simple belief that those who advise, either on behalf of national and local government, trusts, federations or individual schools, should be accredited, developed and trained with the same rigour as our school leaders and inspectors. Essentially, the new body has established national quality standards, which are independent of government, designed for education specialists who can both support and challenge schools.

If we are to develop a world-class school system, then the advice schools are offered must be of the highest quality, rigorously validated, independent and primarily designed to serve the needs of our children and our schools.

CHAPTER 65

THE ART OF LEAVING

I am now heavily involved in raising the quality of support and advice that our schools receive. The AoEA is developing well. I am also termed 'old and vulnerable' by a pandemic-focused government. I have attended many leaving do's. Some people have left in anger, some in despair, others in relief, and others in triumph. If ever I do leave God's Departure Lounge, I will go with a sense of hope and expectation that we will eventually design the world-class education system that all our children deserve.

When we truly care about something, we hope that, when we leave the thing we love, everything will be OK.

Has anyone seen my successful career in education?

For my fan, the one who has read this book, there has been a constant theme: the desire to provide stability for children, encouraging them to enjoy the present and remember the past, while, at the same time, looking towards the future with hope and optimism.

When I decided to put this book together, I initially decided to write about every year of my life. And that is more or less what I have done: I have described my childhood, my schooling, my student years, my teaching, the time when I became a headteacher and then a director of education and concluding with my most recent adventures on the national scene. I have tried to introduce some humour into my writing, while at the same time making some modestly concealed serious points.

To adapt Bob Monkhouse's words:

When I started this book, everyone laughed at my ambition to write humorously – no one is laughing now!

Now, at the time of writing, I am in my late 70s. My first chapter was about my thoughts as a foetus, three months before my birth. The final chapters present a retrospective view of my time in education. So, this current chapter is about me considering my future. Those who know me well will tell you I have announced my intended retirement every year since I contracted cancer in 1999. Since then, I have observed the retirements of: my personal doctor, my surgeons, my contemporary politicians and, of course, many close colleagues.

There are several things I have discovered during this life passage. First, I have learned that, if you love your work, then you never really retire, you just go on doing it for free. Second, I have to admit that we all *do* change and so I now sport white hair and have a wrinkly face. Third, I have concluded conversely that we don't really change very much at all. Finally, I know two particular things for certain: that the secret of youth is learning; and that doing nothing is rarely a waste of time.

It is to my chagrin that the responsibilities I have progressively undertaken seem to be pushing me towards maturity and wisdom, ascribed qualities I have fought against all my life. To put it another way, I want to live for a long time yet and I just don't simply want to become aged.

However, while I have outgrown ambition, desire for power and a love for the top table, that does not mean I am without modest ambitions. These are the sort of ambitions that are untrammelled by the trappings of power and status. Wealth also means less and less to me. In the words of Samuel Johnson:

It is better to live a rich life than to die rich.

One of the best parts of getting old is that you don't have to laugh at anyone else's jokes. It is no longer necessary in order to gain preferment. Certainly, the basic truth remains that:

Educationalists can never retire and will only stop learning when they stop living.

Over the years, I have attended so many retirement parties that they merge into a melancholy mist. Bob Newhart, the American stand-up comedian, once described a retirement party in his 1960 album, the *Button-Down Mind of Bob Newhart*. This performance is still one of the best-selling comedy albums in history.

Newhart recounts how an accountant, during his retirement speech, tells everyone that he had to:

Get half-stoned every morning to get down to this crummy job. You put in 50 years and they give you this crummy watch – working out at 28 cents a year.

He then announces that:

If it hadn't been for the money I've taken out of petty cash, I wouldn't have got by.

He then confirms the rumours that he intends going off with Miss Wilson, the cashier, who has just embezzled $200,000 from the company. She, it appears, is currently down in Mexico, while he is still:

Up here with this crummy watch.

He completes his speech by announcing that he had some tapes of activities at office parties that he would sell for $1500 each:

... though the June picnic may run at $1575.

I have already indicated that I've been to memorable leaving do's – Jack, the caretaker, and Bob, the former prisoner of war, come to mind. However, I particularly remember one I attended in a school in Newcastle, where the headteacher pronounced that he could not have done any more for his school, except for one thing:

Getting the children to learn and the teachers to teach.

Enough said, I think.

My most memorable retirement party of all time was Charlie Smith's. Charlie was a senior teacher, highly respected across Gateshead. At work, Charlie was the professional's professional. I learned so much from him, including the biggest lesson of all – that, when out of school, you could be yourself but in school, you were always playing the part of the teacher, with all the professional standards that went with the job. When, on occasion, he joined us in the pub, he was a truly funny man but, back at work the next day, he would transform himself into a dedicated and serious professional.

As a young 30 year-old teacher, I felt very honoured to organise his retirement party. Because of the esteem in which he was held, the Director of Education, the local Member of Parliament and numerous other dignitaries turned up. Charlie only asked one thing of me:

Leave me a gap of 15 minutes after the Director's speech.

When the Director finished, I waited. Charlie, one of the quietest and most dignified men I had ever met, then winked at me. In that instant, Bubbles turned up. She wore a costume made of balloons with a python draped around her neck. After asking the local MP to pop her balloons, she draped the python around the neck of the headteacher and danced off into the sunset.

Bloody hell, Charlie, I whispered, you could have told me ... it's all right for you. I have to come to work tomorrow.

Charlie, wise as ever, whispered:

Getting older doesn't mean you are getting old.

EPILOGUE

We're keeping you on life support until you have paid off your student loans.

So what have I learned?

The main thing leaders need to learn is that they need to keep on learning.

That is it.

That is all.

So, what do I want?

I don't really want much. But, for the future of education, I want ten things and – as in all the best 'management speak' – all ten things begin with the same letter.

1. **Constancy of purpose** maintained by those who are responsible for education in a constantly changing environment.

2. **Consensus** on education policy, shared by the various political parties.

3. **Clarity** on the direction education will take and on how the education system should operate.

4. **Consistency** as to what we expect from our schools and colleges.

5. **Cohesiveness** within a system involving all stakeholders devoted to improving the life chances of young people.

6. **Continuous learning** now and forever.

7. **Child-centredness** in everything we do for children.

8. **Caring for children** so that they do the right things.

9. **Capable** children so they can succeed now and in the future.

10. **Confident children** who go forward with hope.

My grandchildren deserve this – as do all children.

APPENDIX 1: NATIONAL FIGURES

APPENDIX 2: EDUCATIONALISTS AND INFLUENCERS

APPENDIX 3: LEGISLATION AND REPORTS

APPENDIX 4: BOOKS REFERENCED

APPENDIX 5: NORTHERN HEROES

APPENDIX 6: POPULAR CULTURE

INDEX

Our titles are available in a range of electronic formats. To order, or for details of our bulk discounts, please go to our website www.criticalpublishing.com or contact our distributor, Ingram Publisher Services (IPS UK), 10 Thornbury Road, Plymouth PL6 7PP, telephone 01752 202301 or email IPSUK.orders@ingramcontent.com.